Teaching Mathematics Using ICT

Teaching Mathematics Using ICT

THIRD EDITION

Adrian Oldknow, Ron Taylor and Linda Tetlow

continuum

To our friend and inspiration:
Warwick Evans

Continuum International Publishing Group

The Tower Building	80 Maiden Lane
11 York Road	Suite 704
London SE1 7NX	New York 10038

www.continummbooks.com

First published 2000
Second edition published 2003
This edition published 2010

British Library Cataloguing-in-Publication Data

A catalogue record for this book is available from the British Library.

ISBN 9781441156884

Designed and typeset by Ben Cracknell Studios
Printed and bound in Great Britain by MPG Books Group Ltd

Contents

Acknowledgements

The authors would like to express their thanks to the following companies and organizations which have provided invaluable help with access to hardware, software and other resources:

Badsey Publications, Becta, Bowland Trust, CabriLog, Chartwell-Yorke, Crocodile Clips, DCSF, Freudenthal Institute, HP, IDS, Intel, London Grid for Learning, Microsoft Corporation, MathsNet, Modellus, NRich, Open Source Physics, QCDA, Quintic, Research Machines plc, Scala/Art Resource NY, Sciencescope, SMARTBoard, Steljes, TDA, Teachers TV, Texas Instruments, Vernier, XLogger and Yenka.

Also to staff and students (present and past) from the following schools for their cooperation:

Charterhouse School, Godalming; Henry Beaufort School, Winchester; Henry Cort School, Fareham; Hounsdown School, Totton; The Petersfield School, Petersfield; City of Portsmouth Girls' School; The Mountbatten School, Romsey; Regents Park School, Southampton; Tanbridge House School, Horsham; Wildern School, Hedge End.

And to the following colleagues: Afzal Ahmed, Alison Clarke-Wilson, Carol Knights, University of Chichester, and also to the following individuals: Jose-Paulo Vianna and Grant Tetlow, for their help and advice.

List of abbreviations and glossary

AGF	Approximate Gradient Function
ASA	angle, side, angle – a condition for congruent triangles
AT	Attainment target, see MA 1,2,3,4
ATM	Association of Teachers of Mathematics
avi	Audio video interleave. A multimedia container format introduced by Microsoft for video files
Becta	British Educational Communications and Technology Agency (formerly NCET)
BERR	Department for Business, Enterprise and Regulatory Reform
BETT	British Education and Training Technology, an annual trade fair held in Olympia, London
BIS	Department for Business Innovation and Skills
bmp	file format used to store bitmap digital images
CAD	computer-aided design
CADCAM	computer-aided design and computer-aided manufacturing
CAS	computer algebra system
CBL	Calculator Based Laboratory
CBR	Calculator Based Ranger
CD-ROM	compact disc containing read-only files
CPD	continuing professional development
CSV	comma separated variable

Curriculum Dimensions	Seven cross-curricular themes
	   Identity and cultural diversity
	   Healthy lifestyles
	   Community participation
	   Enterprise
	   Global dimension and sustainable development
	   Technology and the media
	   Creativity and critical thinking

D&T	design and technology

DCSF	Department for Children, Schools and Families, formerly the DES
DES	See DCSF
DfES	Department for Education and Skills
DHS	data-handling and modelling software
DGS	dynamic geometry software
DIN	Deutsches Institut für Normung
DIUS	Department for Innovation, Universities and Skills, now part of BIS
GC	graphing calculator
GIF	graphics interchange format, a bitmap format used for simple, usually graphic, images
GPS	global positioning system
GPS	graph-plotting software
GSP	Geometer's sketchpad
GSP	geo-stationary positioning
hz	hertz
ICT	Information and Communication Technology
ILS	integrated learning system
IT	Information Technology
IFS	Iterated Function System
ITT	initial teacher training
IWB	interactive whiteboard
JPEG or jpg	Commonly used method of compression for digital photographic images. The Joint Photographic Experts Group standard
KMV	A file type containing geographical data which can be used to plot journeys in software such as Google Earth
KS1	Key stage 1: 5–7 years
KS2	Key stage 2: 7–11 years
KS3	Key stage 3: 11–14 years
KS4	Key stage 4: 14–16 years
KS5	Key stage 5: 16–19 years
LAN	Local Area Network
LCD	liquid crystal display
LED	light emitting diode
MA	Mathematical Association
MA1	Attainment target 1 Using and Applying mathematics
MA2	AT 2 Number and Algebra
MA3	AT 3 Geometry and Measures
MA4	AT 4 Statistics
MB	megabyte, a measure of file size equal to 1 million bytes or characters
Mb	megabit, 1 million bits. One byte equals 8 bits (binary digits). Download speeds are given in mbps or megabits per second.
NANAMIC	National Association for Numeracy and Mathematics in Colleges
NCET	See Becta
NCETM	The National Centre for Excellence in the Teaching of Mathematics

NCTM	The National Council of Teachers of Mathematics (USA)
NLVM	The National Library of Virtual Manipulatives at Utah State University
OCR	optical character recognition
OFSTED	The Office for Standards in Education, Children's Services and Skills
OHP	overhead projector
OHT	overhead transparency
OS	operating system, e.g. Linux, Windows XP, Vista, Windows 7
PC	personal computer
PCMCIA	personal computer memory card international association. These cards are used for computer memory storage expansion
pdf	portable document format – a file format developed by Adobe Systems

PLTS	Personal learning and thinking skills
	    Independent enquirers
	    Creative thinkers
	    Independent learners
	    Team workers
	    Self-managers
	    Effective participants

QCA	See QCDA
QCDA	The Qualifications and Curriculum Development Agency, formerly QCA
RAM	random access memory
RHS	right-angle, hypotenuse, side – a condition for congruent triangles
ROM	read only memory
SSAT	Specialist Schools and Academies Trust
SSS	side, side, side – a condition for congruent triangles
STEM	science, technology, engineering and mathematics
swf	small web format. A file format used particularly for animated vector graphics. Associated with Shockwave, Flash, Macromedia and Adobe
TCT	Technology Colleges Trust
TDA	Training and Development Agency for schools, formerly the Teacher Training Agency (TTA)
tiff	tagged image file format: a file format for storing images, particularly for image manipulation operations and OCR
TIMSS	Trends in International Mathematics and Science Study, an international assessment of mathematics and science education
TIN	TI-Nspire™ a hand-held device and software ICT suite for mathematics and science – TI-Nspire™ is a trademark of Texas Instruments Inc.
TTA	See TDA
UMPC	ultra-mobile PC
URL	uniform resource locator – web address
USB	Universal Serial Bar
VDU	visual display unit
VGA	video graphics array: VGA connectors are used to connect PCs to data projectors, external monitors, etc.
VLE	virtual learning environment
WPSS	Wireless Dynamic Sensor System

Introduction

This book is a revised and updated version of the second edition entitled *Teaching Mathematics using ICT* published in 2003. We have taken the opportunity to bring both the educational context, and the references to resources up to date. We have also made some changes to the structure. While the mathematics curriculum has changed little in the intervening period, the changes in technology have been dramatic – consistent with 'Moore's law' about the performance doubling every two years, with similar changes in accessibility and price as well.

The relationships between mathematics, teaching and computers are long-standing and complex. The actual practice of mathematics has changed its nature considerably because of the availability of powerful computers, both in the workplace and on researchers' desks. But those very computers themselves are only powerful because of the variety of clever mathematical applications on which their operation relies. These include coding, data-compression, fractals, cryptography and computational geometry. Experiments in the applications of computer technology to teaching have been widespread over the last 30 years or so. The advent of fast and widespread communications such as e-mail, the internet and video-conferencing are radically changing our access to data and information. The fierce competition and the size of the market for computer-based consumer products has ensured that prices have fallen to a point where it is now quite normal (in some areas of some countries, at least) for students' bedrooms to be better equipped than their school classrooms. So it is not surprising that many countries are now taking stock of their educational response to this 'Information Age'.

We shall need to emphasize here, and throughout the book, that mathematics is rather different from many subjects in its relationship to ICT-supported pedagogy. We take the view that at least one major rationale for including the compulsory study of mathematics in the secondary school is that it is widely applied in the world outside school – and that this implies that students will need to be able to use ICT tools both to solve mathematical problems and to communicate their results to others. Many of the techniques associated with school mathematics were developed to solve important problems at times when tools such as electronic calculators and computers were not available. The very existence of these computational tools is now having a profound effect on the way mathematics is being developed and applied in the world outside education. New skills of modelling, estimating, validating, hypothesizing and finding information are becoming more important than many traditional ones, such as accuracy of recall. Formal changes in education necessarily take longer to bring about than changes in practice in industry or commerce. An important issue for mathematics teachers is to ensure that their students are well prepared for their future lives and careers by gaining necessary skills, whether or not the curriculum and examination system explicitly encourage them.

The widespread presence of Information and Communication Technology (ICT) in the mathematics classroom will not necessarily have any impact in bringing into question the current relevance of any particularly long-standing aspect of the mathematics curriculum. To take an extreme example, we could imagine some very effective multimedia software that provides a self-learning guide to using obsolete tools such as a slide-rule, or a table of logarithms, for multiplication. The point here is that the use of the technology as a teaching aid will not, by itself, bring into question whether the content and skills being taught are actually relevant at all in our current technological society. Indeed, those responsible for the development of mathematics curricula may be unaware of the obsolescence, or significantly diminished importance, of some of its content. There are also aspects of content, such as matrices and complex numbers at advanced level, which are increasingly important in other subjects such as geography or engineering. These may have been ruled out of current curricula on the grounds of difficulty in teaching and learning proficiency of basic techniques. However, ICT tools can obviate the need for proficiency with such techniques: many models of graphing calculators can, for example, manipulate both matrix and complex expressions. So ICT can enable students to concentrate on more interesting and important aspects of content.

Despite the inertia of the formal curriculum, mathematics teachers need to be able to examine more critically the basis on which the knowledge, understanding and skills of the curriculum are founded. A less obvious issue, but one which is arguably at least as important, is that citizens in a technological society need to have an informed view of just what computers can, and cannot, do. All too often we hear phrases such as 'the computer won't let us do that', as if it was an animate (and stubborn) object. An increasing number of subjects, such as geography, chemistry and economics, make use of computer simulations. We know, and our students need to know, that these are not infallible but just someone's mathematical model of a situation that needs to be treated with a healthy amount of scepticism! So modelling and validation are now important aspects of mathematics that students should experience during their secondary school education.

Of course, most teachers do not have a great deal of control over the curriculum they teach. So they need to be able to apply ICT in ways that enhance the teaching and learning of the current established curriculum while also seeking to bring out some of the important relationships between mathematics and computer technology referred to above. The role of ICT in the teaching and learning process is not just confined to uses such as an 'electronic blackboard' to assist in a teacher's exposition, or for 'hands-on' use by students working at a task, important as both those applications are. The technology may aid the teacher in the preparation for a lesson, e.g. in gathering data, or preparing materials. It may also have a role to play in the assessment of students' learning. So this is truly a book aimed to support the full *integration* of ICT into secondary school mathematics teaching. While we have seen a recent period of attention to so-called 'gifted and talented' students, we share the same view as the majority of UK mathematics educators, that such students should not be accelerated into taking more and more qualifications, but offered enrichment opportunities to help them develop their talents across a broader front. ICT is an ideal enabler of such approaches to individualized learning, as well as providing the means to keep groups of students with common needs and interests in touch with each other. Similarly we are well aware that while a large amount of so-called 'special needs' resources has been generated in mathematics, much of this really consists of window-dressing of drill-and-practice in arithmetic skills. Again ICT enables students with particular difficulties to access resources which enable them to engage with interesting mathematics without many of the communication problems faced with using printed and non-multimedia materials.

We are acutely aware of widespread differences in the resourcing of mathematics departments. We have at times stared in wonder at demonstrations of fancy uses of the latest state-of-the-art technology and have come away with the frustration of knowing that such equipment would be out of our reach for the foreseeable future.

So we have taken great care to be as realistic as possible about the kinds of resources that our readers may be able to get their hands on. We have tried to concentrate on generic ideas which can be realized using a variety of different forms of ICT including, wherever possible, cheaper hand-held devices such as graphing calculators and personal computers. We have been fortunate to be able to work with a number of partners to try to ensure that as many examples of resources as possible can be found on the internet, and on the supporting website for this book. We have also tried to make this book as accessible and relevant as possible to mathematics teachers from different countries and cultures.

Our book draws upon our own experiences and beliefs, which we hope would apply to any country's mathematics curriculum.

We conclude with an introduction to the structure of the book.

Chapter 1 is there to whet your appetite for using ICT to enliven mathematics teaching and learning.

Chapters 2 and **3** are for you to work at privately! They are there to help you get a feel not just for the hardware, software and other ICT tools, but also to get some experience in using them to tackle some interesting bits of mathematics. Very often in working on courses with teachers we use the maxim: 'Start from the mathematics.' Of course you'll want to be thinking also about the role of such tools in teaching as well. By the end of the first three chapters you should be in a strong position to know:

- *what* ICT there is to use.

Chapter 4 builds on the practical experience from Chapters 1, 2 and 3 in developing a more analytical structure for the planning, implementation and evaluation of ICT use in teaching and learning. It draws upon many examples and case-studies of teachers innovating with a wide range of ICT. We ask you to review your progress and to draw up an action plan for your future continuing professional development (CPD) in the use of ICT in your teaching. By the end of this chapter you should be in a strong position to know:

- *how* to select and plan for its effective pedagogic use.

In **Chapter 5** we break the curriculum down into bite-size chunks and look for ways in which ICT tools can support teaching and learning of specific pieces of mathematics content, such as number or algebra. However, there are many dangers in creating false divisions between parts of mathematics, and in treating mathematics apart from other subjects – so we also try to inject examples of more synthetic, and cross-subject, approaches. By the end of this chapter you should be in a strong position to know:

- *which* aspects of school mathematics are amenable to its use.

Chapter 6 looks outwards to what others have said, and researched, about the links between mathematics, ICT and education. The range of references in this chapter should be particularly helpful if you intend to undertake any academic work, such as an MA module, as part of your CPD. It is intended to help you answer the additional question:

- *why* should we aim to integrate ICT into mathematics teaching?

Chapter 7 attempts to take a peek into the future, and to look at how ICT, mathematics and mathematical pedagogy may develop in the next generation. At least this should raise the question:

- *where* is it going?

Even if does not actually provide any very reliable answers.
Supporting information can be found on the accompanying website.

A note of warning! The pace of change in ICT developments is very fast, so while we have taken considerable care to ensure that the material is up to date at the time of writing, it may well be that some of the websites to which we refer will change their content or even disappear. Similarly, versions of software which we have used for illustrations may develop and not appear exactly in the form we show. This is the inevitable price of change, but we hope it will not detract too much from the worth of the book. We are aware that different readers will have different experiences and different needs. So you may well want to skip sections on aspects with which you are familiar, or leave sections for later which you think less relevant to your current needs.

✎ *We have tried to give you plenty of opportunities for practical work to complement the text and we highlight these in this way.*

 We also raise pedagogical questions and we highlight these in this way.

We also appreciate the helpful advice we have received from reviewers and others, which we have tried to incorporate into this revised edition. In revising the book we have taken care not just to rush into the latest technology, but have carefully considered the contribution which tried and tested tools, such as graphing calculators, can continue to make. We have certainly had a great deal of challenge, fun and sense of reward in putting this book together. We very much hope that you have a fair share of each in reading through, and working at, the book. We wish you all the best in your future attempts to apply educational ICT in bringing the subject of mathematics to life for your students.

Adrian Oldknow, Ron Taylor and Linda Tetlow
January 2010

Chapter 1

Why bother using ICT?

Anyone who has had experience of trying to encourage others to make use of ICT in their teaching is bound to have at some stage been asked the question 'Why bother?' Here we have chosen an example which we hope will stimulate thinking about when and how ICT can really open up the mathematical potential of an activity.

1.1 CHAINS OF REASONING: HOW LONG IS A PIECE OF STRING?

Here we use as an example a picture of a hanging chain as a starting-point for some mathematics.

What sort of questions would you ask about this hanging chain?

What sort of mathematics might be involved? Geometry, algebra, handling data?

 What shape is a chain hanging under its own weight? How could you find out more about this? What is the sag for a given length of chain?

 What measurements do you need to find in order to get started on these problems? Are there any clues in the picture?

Where in the real world is this a problem to be solved? Who might have need of this information?

What would you expect learners of different ages to get from this activity?

What practical resources and experience would help learners get the most from this activity?

How would the use of ICT by you and by your students enhance the learning experience?

1.2 WHAT SORT OF MATHEMATICS MIGHT BE INVOLVED, AND HOW CAN ICT HELP?

Here are some possibilities firstly for the mathematics and secondly for the technology. For some of these the use of ICT can help to clarify the mathematical processes and concepts and enable linking different areas of mathematics. For others the use of ICT can make more complex areas of mathematics and real-life applications accessible to younger students and hopefully excite their interest for further advanced study. We hope that these ideas may help to persuade you to bother including the use of ICT in your teaching of mathematics.

Mathematical possibilities

Algebra – What function might be a good approximation to this curve? What about a quadratic? What software would help you to find out more?

Geometry – How close is this to an arc of a circle? How could you find the centre and radius – what constructions would you need to do? How can you work out the length of the chain? How could software help?

Handling data – If you could find the coordinates of a number of points on the curve, how could data-handling software help you to fit a curve to this?

More advanced work – How could you use the search facilities available on the internet to find out more about possible functions that might fit the curve of the hanging chain? What other functions could you try? Is it possible to find the length of the chain? Can you find real life applications for this?

How ICT might help to tackle the problem.

Here are some possible ways in which ICT could help to tackle and extend the problem. Only brief details are included here. More detailed information on how to use the various pieces of software is given in Chapters 3 and 5, but there are also specific details for the example in this chapter on the website.

1.2(a) Using dynamic geometry software to fit a circle to the image of the chain

Any dynamic geometry software such as Cabri Geometry 2 Plus or The Geometers' Sketchpad could be used to do this as they all now have the facility to import background images. There are more examples and information about these in chapters 3 and 5. GeoGebra has been used in the illustrations for this example. More detailed instructions, instructions for doing this in other software and possible solutions to some of the questions asked are on the website.

* First the axes were moved to a suitable position and then set to equal scales.
* Then the image of the chain was inserted as background and dragged to a suitable position.
* Then a 'point' tool was used to mark points along the chain and the colour changed to make them more visible.

✎ What constructions would you need to do in order to find the centre of a circle which might go through these points? Try investigating the construction menus for ideas.

---

* The centre of the circle was found by suitable constructions
* Then a circle was drawn with this centre to go through as many points as possible.

✎ How good a fit is the circle? What if the image was enlarged to real-life size?

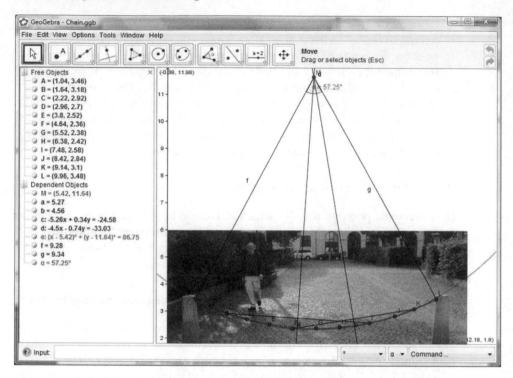

Finding the centre of the circle using GeoGebra

✎ *What further information would you need to be able to estimate the length of the chain?*

- The angle-measuring tool can be used to find the angle subtended by the arc representing the chain at the centre of the circle. It is also possible to measure the radius of the circle. The real-life radius could be estimated if we have some known measurements to compare with say, for example, that the highest point of the chain is 80 cm from the ground.

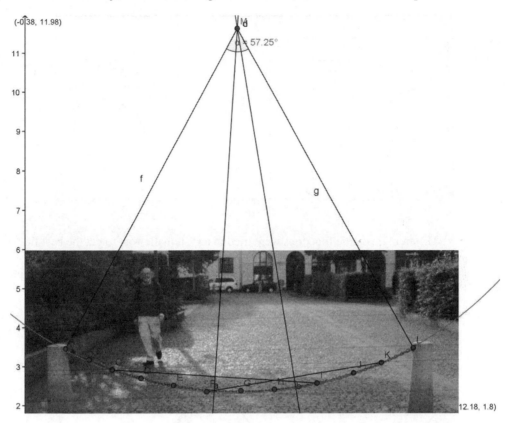

Finding the angle subtended by the chain at the centre of the circle using GeoGebra

1.2(b) Fitting a quadratic function to the image of the chain

Some graphing software such as Autograph has the facility to import background images, but if this or dynamic geometry software (DGS) is used to obtain the coordinates for points on an image of the chain then these coordinates can be entered into graphing calculators for class use. TI-Nspire™ software has been used for screen-shots here but much of the procedure could be done on other graphing calculators.

- The coordinates were entered into a list/spreadsheet page.
- A scatterplot was created on a graphing page.
- A quadratic function was chosen and inserted in a first attempt to fit the data.

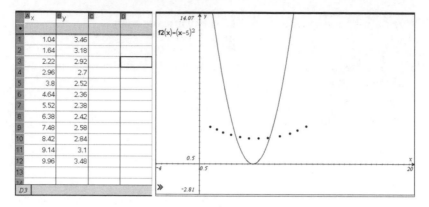

- Different quadratic functions were tried in a systematic way to get the best fit.

Note: A particularly interesting feature of TI-Nspire™ is the ablity to grab the graph of certain functions and to drag them to fit the points. Note also the form that the function displayed takes.

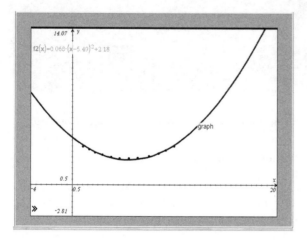

 What would your students learn from the process of trial and improvement needed to fit the graph if they didn't have the facility to grab and drag it? How would the learning experience be changed with this facility?

1.2(c) Using data-handling features to fit a quadratic function

- If the coordinates of points on the chain are entered into a list/spreadsheet then it is possible to use the statistical analysis features to fit a quadratic or 2nd order regression curve to them.

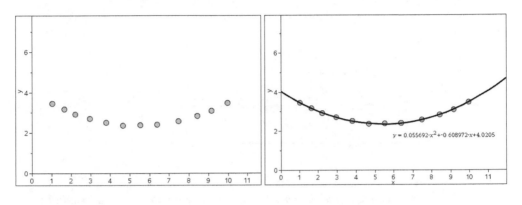

> ✎ *How do the results from the two methods of fitting a curve compare? Would using the measurements of the full-size, real-life chain make a difference? Would any other regression functions be possible?*

1.2(d) Further research on hanging chains

> ✎ *What more can you find out about hanging chains and functions to model them, for example using internet research? What applications does this have in the real world?*

What would your students gain from undertaking this type of research?

> ✎ *The image overleaf was created using trial and improvement with a particular mathematical function appropriate to a hanging chain. Can you recreate this image or find other similar functions? The function for this image is given on the website.*

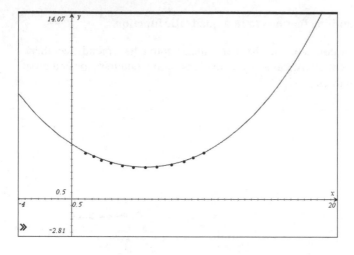

How can you find the length of the chain from the graph of a suitable function? How would the software or graphing calculators help to make this problem more accessible to a wider range of learners?

At what point when approaching the activity does the ICT become really powerful and enable you to tackle this question in a way that would otherwise not be possible?

1.3 GETTING STARTED USING ICT IN MATHEMATICS TEACHING

As you work through this book we hope you will find out more about the types of ICT tools which could be used to answer some of the questions posed earlier in this chapter, and how these tools can be used to enhance mathematics teaching and learning. We hope that the examples we have shown will whet your appetite and help you to get started with thinking about this. We hope also that it will get you thinking about other problems that you might use to capture students' interest and engage them in the learning process for which ICT could be an effective tool.

Depending on your confidence and experience you might choose to take one of the following routes:

adopt – use our prepared files on the website with 'get you going' sheets
adapt – use your own photographs to generate discussion
create – create your own problem which uses a similar type of approach and software.

We hope that whichever approach you take you will reflect on the impact on the students' learning with the different approaches.

If this is new to you then you might want to try it with a small group first. There are other ways in which you might like to dip your toe in when using ICT tools for the first time. Later in the book, in Chapter 4, you will meet examples where teachers have used certain ICT tools for the first time with their classes.

How does this type of activity meet the requirements of the mathematics curriculum?

We hope that by thinking about or tackling the 'Chain' activity yourself you have already encountered a range of potential mathematical content and can see why the use of ICT in the mathematics classroom might be of positive benefit. The mathematical key concepts, processes and content that arise during the activity will depend on the age and mathematical background of your learners and the approaches that you choose to use. The National Curriculum for mathematics for 11–16 year olds in England includes not only content but also key concepts and processes, and curriculum opportunities. These are some examples which might be addressed by activities of this type.

From 'Curriculum opportunities'

- become familiar with a range of resources, including ICT, so that they can select appropriately. This includes using practical resources and ICT, such as spreadsheets, dynamic geometry, graphing software and calculators, to develop mathematical ideas.

From 'Key concepts'

- selecting appropriate mathematical tools and methods, including ICT
- posing questions and developing convincing arguments
- understanding that mathematics is used as a tool in a wide range of contexts
- recognizing the limitations and scope of a model or representation.

From 'Key processes'

- select mathematical information, methods, tools and models to use. (ICT tools can be used for mathematical applications, including iteration and algorithms)
- visualize and work with dynamic images
- explore the effects of varying values and look for invariance and covariance
- take account of feedback and learn from mistakes
- identify a range of techniques that could be used to tackle a problem
- appreciating that more than one approach may be necessary
- make accurate mathematical diagrams, graphs and constructions on paper and on screen
- look at data to find patterns and exceptions.

> **Important note:**
> The emphasis throughout is on the *students* choosing and using appropriate ICT. In order to be able to choose appropriately, pupils must know that such tools exist and how they can be used. Further details of the 'Pupil's entitlement to ICT in mathematics' can be found in section 3.1 of Chapter 3 and on the website.

In addition, the American association, The National Council of Teachers of Mathematics (NCTM), recommends the following as desired characteristics of a college algebra programme, which should

- be real-world based
- use modelling
- emphasize communication skills
- utilize small group projects
- incorporate appropriate technologies
- focus on hands-on student-centred activities rather than be all lecture.

We hope that as you work through this book and become more familiar with the potential resources for teaching mathematics using ICT that you will continue to reflect on its potential impact on both teaching and learning.

Chapter 2

What hardware is out there?

2.1 INTRODUCTION

This, and the next, chapter is for you to work at privately! They should help you get a feel not only for the available hardware, software and other ICT tools, but also to get some experience in using them to tackle some interesting bits of mathematics. Very often in working on courses with teachers we use the maxim: 'Start from the mathematics!'

Of course you will want to be thinking also about the role of such tools in teaching as well. By the end of this chapter you should be in a strong position to know *what* ICT hardware there is to use.

Nowadays we tend to think of computers as a few boxes on (or under) the desk or a thin box on the knee of the person opposite in the train. This reflects the move from the 1960s onwards to concentrate on personal computer use. Then companies purchased desktop PCs (personal computers) to improve the productivity of their employees, and now households purchase similar hardware for the entertainment (and/or education) of family members. But when you purchase a PC or laptop you are buying far more than the combination of silicon chips, circuit boards, video displays, etc. which make up the hardware elements of the system. Like a body without a nervous system, a PC cannot be used without the system's computer programs (the system software – called the operating system), which make it responsive to hardware elements such as the keyboard and the mouse, and allows it to communicate with peripheral hardware such as disks, CD-ROMs, printers and monitors. But again, like a body without a brain, the PC is relatively useless without computer programs to help us carry out the tasks we would like to use it for (the applications software). So for the purposes of this chapter we will include hardware and system software in the next section, and applications software in the subsequent section.

Returning to our company employee using a PC at her/his desk, the application software is likely to include familiar names for items, such as a word-processor, a spreadsheet, a database and support for sending and receiving messages (e-mail). This kind of software is often now called **generic** software (and given a name such as an *office suite*). By 'generic' we really mean multipurpose. Such software can also play an important part in helping teachers to carry out their job more effectively, e.g. by better record-keeping. The household PC is likely to have software for playing games, for getting information from a CD-ROM (such as an encyclopaedia) and for connecting to the internet. Each of these may well have educational applications, but they are aimed at the individual user and may not easily relate to the actual curriculum in schools.

So we can already distinguish two classes of applications software: those that can make the individual learner and teacher more efficient, and those that can contribute to individuals' learning. In the context of the school, though, we need to consider a third context, that of helping the teacher to teach a class more effectively. This will require consideration both of the available specialist and pedagogical software in a given subject such as mathematics, and also the kinds of hardware that are available, and appropriate, for use when teaching a whole class or a group of students.

Thus the aim of this chapter is to ensure that, as far as possible, you are aware of the current range of hardware to support teachers and learners inside and outside the classroom so that you can make informed choices when planning your use of ICT. We have tried to do this in as non-technical a manner as possible, making few assumptions about your previous experience. We hope that you will not feel patronized by this, and will skip over any sections with which you are already quite familiar.

The Teacher Training Agency (now the TDA) publication *The Use of Information and Communications Technology in Subject Teaching: identification of training needs: secondary mathematics* sets out the expected outcomes of ICT training for secondary school mathematics teachers. These were provided in the form of nine points to do with 'effective teaching and assessment methods – section A', and a further nine points to do with 'teachers' knowledge and understanding of, and competence with, information and communication technology – section B'. This chapter is particularly concerned with supporting you in achieving the aim B13: 'Teachers should know those features of ICT which can be used, separately or together, to support teaching and learning.'

Increasingly in English education the term IT (Information Technology) has been replaced by the acronym ICT (Information and Communication Technology). In either case it is to emphasize that computers are just one – albeit very important – element in the range of electronic devices that is revolutionizing our society. For example, a recent directive from the English ministry of education to schools explaining how a source of funding could be used to support ICT was worded as follows: 'Schools may purchase ICT equipment (this may include class sets of portable computing devices; whole class teaching aids such as projection equipment; digital cameras, scanners and digitizers and other equipment which can be used to help create educational resources).' We will now take a closer look at what these, and other, items of equipment can do – with the caveat that nowadays it is sometimes difficult to separate hardware and software – for example, interactive whiteboards are usually supported by a range of software tools which make them easy to use.

2.2 STAND-ALONE AND LAPTOP PCs

Of course, systems vary, but the central element of a PC usually consists of a rather drab box, with the on/off button, one or two slots for disks, and a couple of small lights on the front. On the back is a variety of sockets for connection to the other components. Inside the box is the microprocessor which sends out instructions to the other parts of the PC at a frequency measured in hertz (hz) – which is the rate of one cycle per second. Current PCs usually have 'clock rates' measured in gigahertz, which means over one billion clock-ticks per second! Instructions, and unchanging data, needed by the microprocessor is stored in read only memory (ROM). This is memory which does not change, and is not volatile – that is to say that when you switch the machine off it does not become forgotten. The changing bits of data are stored in random access memory (RAM), which now usually comes in multiples of 512 megabytes (MB). A byte is a measure of information that depends on how the PC stores information – but it can hold the equivalent of between one and four printing characters, like a letter or a digit. So a modern PC with 2GB RAM can hold the equivalent of about eight million printed pages in its 'memory'. RAM is volatile, and its contents are lost when the PC is switched off.

The other key element of the central box is usually hidden within it. This is the hard disk or hard drive, which is non-volatile, and which can hold a massive amount of data, but which cannot be retrieved quite as quickly as from RAM. The capacity of hard disks is measured in gigabytes (GB), which are a billion bytes. Again a modern PC may have about a hundred times as much hard-disk space as RAM, and one use of the hard disk is to extend the available RAM by creating what is known as 'virtual memory'. Most systems allow you to copy the contents of RAM onto the hard drive when you close down the computer (the 'hibernate' or 'suspend' mode) so that you can restart from where you left off. As we shall see later, there may actually be more than one hard disk, but the principal one is also usually referred to as the 'C: drive'. The hard drive of a PC will come with software already installed on it. The essential software is called an operating system (OS). There will usually be other software, especially generic software such as a word-processor, already installed. Software included within the price of a PC is referred to as 'bundled software'.

The main sockets at the back are for the connection of the power supply, the monitor, the printer and the mouse. The keyboard is more or less that of the old-fashioned typewriter, using the familiar QWERTY system. As well as the usual shift-key and shift-lock, for moving between lower- and upper-case symbols, there are special keys called 'Ctrl' (for Control) and 'Alt' (for Alternate). In manuals you will sometimes see shorthand being used where, e.g. Ctrl-C (or ^C) means 'While holding down the Control key press the C key, and then release both.' Similarly Alt-C means using both the Alt and C keys. Most keyboards contain some light bulbs (actually light emitting diodes – LEDs) to show whether any of the keyboard locks (shift, alphabetic, numeric) are currently selected. There is also an additional row of usually 12 keys, called function keys, denoted by symbols such as F7, which have special meanings in different circumstances.

The PC's external display unit is called a 'monitor', although sometimes the older phrase 'visual display unit' (VDU) is used. Nowadays these are almost always colour displays, with a resolution considerably finer than that of a conventional domestic

TV. The size of monitor is usually given in inches – so that a 15 in. monitor will have a maximum diagonal distance from corner to corner of the box of 15 in.; with a rather smaller diagonal distance across the actual display. The 'aspect ratio' is the ratio between the horizontal and vertical measurements of the screen, usually 4:3 or 16:9 – so a 15 in. monitor has a display a bit less than 12 in. wide and 9 in. high. The 'resolution' of the screen is measured in so-called 'pixels' – the smallest picture drawing elements (like atoms). A typical monitor or laptop display may have 1,240 pixels horizontally and 1,024 vertically.

Of course a high-resolution picture in many colour tones will require a large amount of RAM to store it, and this needs to be accessed very quickly. Hence the importance of having a large amount of fast video RAM. The screen may be divided into a number of regions, called 'windows'. The screen will usually show a small movable image (an icon) which looks like an arrow-head. This 'pointer' can be moved around the screen using the 'mouse'. A mouse may have a small ball on its underside that is usually dragged in contact with a 'mouse mat' or it may be an optical version which shines a light downwards. The connection to the PC may be via a cable, or the mouse may be able to send wireless signals to a receiver connected to the PC. (There are also wireless keyboards that work in a similar way.) On the top it may have one, two or three buttons and/or perhaps a wheel. When you have moved the mouse pointer over a part of the display you are interested in, there are three key techniques available. The first is to make just a single click on the left-hand button, which normally highlights the image under the cursor. The second is to hold the left-hand button down while dragging the mouse across its mat, which normally drags the image across the screen. The third is to click the left-hand button twice in rapid succession. This double-click normally causes an action to take place linked with the icon.

Now we return to the slots in the PC's main box. One or more of these is usually for use with a CD or DVD drive diskette. There will usually be two or more slots for connecting USB (Universal Serial Bus) devices such as memory sticks, external modems, scanners and digital cameras. Very often there will also be slots to read the 'flash' XD and SD memory cards associated with digital cameras and other recording devices. We have now dealt with most of the components that are usually to be found on any PC. Returning to the other sockets on the main PC box there is usually a 'parallel port' for attaching a printer cable, audio sockets for attaching speakers and microphones (or a combined headset), and connectors for telephones and network cables.

Most manuals assume everything works perfectly. However, from time to time, you may find your PC failing to respond, or behaving in an unfamiliar way. There is a combination of keys which will usually retrieve the situation: press the Ctrl, Alt and Del (Delete) buttons simultaneously (Ctrl+Alt+Del). Often this will enable the PC to start up from the beginning. This is known as a 're-boot'. You will normally 'close down' your computer by clicking on the 'Start' icon at the bottom left-hand corner of the screen. Now we have established the common ground for most PCs we will take a look at a number of variants now available.

2.3 NETWORKED PCs

Each PC on a network is called a 'workstation' or 'terminal'. Normally it is an ordinary PC with some extra hardware and cabling to allow it to connect to a network. Thus it could be used as a stand-alone PC when not connected. Sometimes (usually with older systems) the terminals do not have any external disk drives, and (rarely) they may not even have an internal hard drive. At the heart of each network is one, (or maybe several), more powerful computer(s) called a 'file-server'. This will have access to a variety of large central storage devices on which the Network Manager will have installed all the software. Often there will be more than one network. For example, there may be one or more networks within a school – called Local Area Networks (LANs), but also the school offices may be connected to a network linking a group of local schools and a central office. Nearly all UK schools now have their own website offering a 'front-window' for the school to those connecting via the internet. Most schools also have a VLE (virtual learning environment) consisting of a large file of information about the school, staff and students, together with copies of syllabuses, curriculum, work-sheets, resources, data-sets and software which staff, students and parents can access from home or in school.

2.4 ULTRA-MOBILE PERSONAL COMPUTERS (UMPCs)

The sale of laptops exceeded that of desktop PCs for the first time in 2007. There has been an increasing demand for smaller, faster, cheaper and powerful personal computing devices. In many ways these are the merger between the very popular commercial 'game/play stations' for entertainment with the conventional laptop computer. With the more recent advent of the so-called 'e-book' computer, and the far-reaching Apple iPhone technology we are now seeing a range of very high-specification UMPCs being developed. Initially, in order to keep prices low, many of these were based on the Linux operating system, but now with the widespread availability of the Windows XP operating system, most are Windows based.

   Modern laptops have clear, flat, colour displays inside their lids. There is a newer generation of laptops called 'tablet PCs' which have a screen that responds to a special pointing device called a 'stylus' which obviates the need for a mouse – they may have a keyboard attached or they may use a 'pop-up' keyboard display on the screen from which characters are selected with the stylus. These usually have systems either to recognize handwriting with the stylus or from speech entered through a built-in microphone, or both. Laptops usually have an alternative to a mouse attached to the keypad – which might be a touch-sensitive pad, or a 'tracker ball'. They can be powered by mains electricity, or by special rechargeable batteries. These batteries currently will power the laptop usually for between two and five hours. When using batteries it is very important to follow the makers' instructions about keeping them in good condition. A nice feature of working with a laptop is that usually the operating system offers a 'suspend mode' where the computer can be 'sent to sleep' at any point and will 'wake up' ready to go from the same place in an application. While there is less room to add additional hardware than on a PC, there are usually one or two small slots to take 'PCMCIA' (personal computer memory card international association) cards, e.g. for connecting to mobile phones or modems. Some laptops do not contain built-in diskette or CD-ROM drives to reduce weight, but can be connected to an external drive, or to a 'host' PC. Nearly all laptops have sockets for connection to external PC monitors. Some laptops also have video sockets for connection to the video input of a TV monitor.

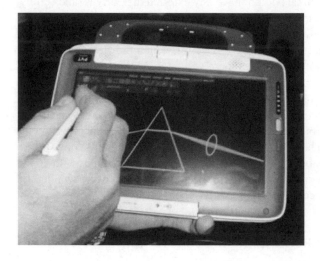

2.5 GRAPHING CALCULATORS

Of particular importance for mathematics, and for numerate subjects such as geography and science, graphing calculators are a blend of calculator and computer technology. Their keyboards normally resemble a calculator keypad where each key may have, say, three different functions. For example, on the TI-84 Plus, the MATH key can be used to obtain a menu of mathematical operation, but in combination with the 'ALPHA' key it will produce the letter 'A' and in combination with the '2nd' key it will produce a TEST menu of symbols such as '>'. The display screen is usually a monochrome LCD with a limited resolution of around 120 by 90 pixels. Graphing calculators (GCs) are powered by ordinary batteries but also have a hearing-aid style battery as back-up. Values, data and programs stored in RAM (typically 32kb or more) are thus retained even when the GC is switched off. Modern GCs may also contain large amounts of 'flash-ROM', which can be used to store applications software, archive data, etc. (effectively the GC's hard-disk drive).

The built-in software will carry out all the normal mathematical, scientific, statistical and financial calculations. In addition the software enables a wide variety of graphs to be drawn and analysed. Some versions will also perform symbolic manipulation. Instead of a mouse, four cursor keys are used to move around the screen. Nearly all models have the capacity to exchange data with similar GCs, with PCs, and with compatible products such as data-loggers. Nearly all models have teachers' versions with large LCD display screens for use with an overhead projector (OHP). Some versions will also connect to a video device, such as a TV or data projector. The new TI-Nspire™ hand-held device is in a category of its own –

showing physical resemblance to a graphing calculator but with the built-in software of a complete suite of mathematical programs.

A wireless classroom network, called TI-Navigator™ has also been developed to allow students in a class to use their hand-held units to connect to a teacher's laptop and large display to enable collaborative work.

2.6 WHOLE-CLASS DISPLAYS

If you are working with a whole class, whether or not they themselves all have access to ICT tools, you may well want to be able to draw everyone's attention to the same display. Just as there are a number of ways of deploying ICT tools in the classroom, so there is a range of means of providing whole-class displays.

- *Large colour monitors*: modern flat-screen digital TVs usually now have a connector for use with a PC.
- *Data projectors*: these connect directly to the VGA output of a PC and contain a high-powered bulb that throws a colour image onto a screen or wall. They can be permanently mounted, or there are portable versions. Prices, size and power consumption have come down fast, and currently they cost about the same as a PC. They accept a variety of input sources such as PC, audio and video.
- *Interactive whiteboards*: their prices have fallen drastically and they are now common in schools, even in mathematics classrooms! The computer's output is displayed via a data projector onto the surface of the board. The whiteboard is 'intelligent' in that you can interact with projected application software by tapping directly onto portions of the board corresponding to buttons, icons, etc., for the software. Currently they cost around the same as a top-of-the-range PC. The main types are **analog**, which responds to touch and does not need special

pens, and **digital** which is used with special styluses. The accompanying
software provides tools to let you write notes and save them, like an 'electronic
flip-chart', to annotate projected displays and to call up useful backgrounds
such as graph paper or music staves. They are often used in conjunction with
other devices such as tablets or voting systems.

- *OHP displays with graphing calculators*: as mentioned above, the output from
most models of GCs, and associated data-capture devices, can be displayed via
OHP, TV or data projector.

2.7 DATA-CAPTURE DEVICES

- *Motion-detectors*: these emit ultrasound signals which are reflected by the
nearest object. By timing the gap between sending and receiving a signal, the
detector can calculate the distance to the nearest object. Estate agents now use
similar devices to measure dimensions of rooms in houses. Sending out signals
at frequent intervals, the detector can track the movement of an object by
storing data on time and distance. Such data can be captured remotely (such as
with students on a running track) and later transferred to a computer or graphing
calculator for analysis and display. For example, the TI Calculator Based
Ranger (CBR) costs about the same as a graphing calculator and has a range of
between 0.5m and 6m.
- *Sensors*: the motion-detector is a special kind of sensor: for measuring distance.
There is a wide range of sensors designed mainly for scientific experiments,
which can measure, e.g., temperature, light intensity, voltage, sound intensity,
force, pressure, acceleration, acidity, heart-rate, amounts of CO_2, etc. Such
sensors (or probes) are usually used in conjunction with a box, called an
'interface', which allows them to be set up by, and to download data to,
computers and graphing calculators. For example, the TI Calculator Based
Laboratory (CBL) costs about twice as much as a graphing calculator and has
probes for temperature, light intensity and voltage. Recently a number of
sensors have been become available for GPS (global positioning system) at
relatively low cost. These allow the path of an object to be tracked in space, and
also for captured data to be labelled not only with the time it was captured but
also its position. We can also expect a new range of wireless sensors. Game
stations have sensing device for movement based either on accelerometers or
stereo cameras, and we can expect these to have a greater impact as well.
- *Digital cameras*: these are common in high street stores. They are cameras
designed for single images, like a conventional camera, and which store them
usually on an internal flash-ROM or diskette. These images can be downloaded
to a PC where they can be edited, saved in one of the conventional formats for
exchanging pictures (such as JPEG) and/or inserted into documents. Most
modern cameras also have a video mode to capture short video-clips, usually of
modest resolution (320 by 240 or 640 by 480). Increasingly both mobile phones
and lightweight laptops have built-in digital and video cameras. There are also
digital video cameras, like a conventional camcorder, which also have large
amounts of local storage. They can transfer data to PCs that can be edited to

produce, say, video-clips in a standard format (such as avi). A small, cheap, lower-quality, digital camera, called a 'webcam', can be used to transmit pictures of the PC operator, or of a class, to a remote destination. Together with fast two-way communication with audio this forms the basis of 'video-conferencing'. These can also be used to share documents, display objects, etc. A more expensive arrangement of high-quality camera and lighting is called a *visualizer* and provides another means to share work. The latest generation of digital cameras, such as the Casio Exilim range, includes the ability to take extremely high speed video at a quality normally associated with professional television playback.

- *Scanners*: these are devices to produce digital images of source objects, such as text, photographs, handwritten documents, etc. The technology is that used in fax machines, and so the sheer volume of sales has led to a rapid fall in prices. The accompanying software often includes tools to enable typed text to be scanned and turned into meaningful text, rather than just a graphic image. This process is called optical character recognition (OCR). Some can also be 'taught' to recognize, and convert, handwriting. It is also possible to use some fax machines as scanners.

2.8 PRINTERS

These have improved dramatically in recent years, and prices have also fallen. The best quality is usually obtained with a laser printer, and colour versions are still expensive. Colour inkjet printers are now very common and can print with a quality comparable with that of a laser printer (but usually more slowly). Ribbon-based (dot matrix) printers, which were the most common ones ten years ago, are now virtually obsolete.

Consumables (laser toner, inkjet cartridges, coated paper, etc.) can be quite expensive. Special kinds of paper, e.g. for photographs, overhead transparencies (OHTs), labels, etc. are available, but can also be quite expensive.

2.9 THE EDUCATIONAL CONTEXT

Now we have considered the main forms of ICT hardware we can attempt to place them in an educational context. This will of course depend upon the extent to which a school already has ICT resources and what it sees as its main purpose. We will consider five separate contexts:

1. A teacher using ICT to help plan, prepare and manage teaching
2. Individual students using ICT outside normal lessons
3. A group of students using ICT within a lesson
4. A teacher providing ICT access for a whole class
5. ICT provision for whole-class teaching.

Finally we will see how each of these was embedded within a major government-funded project called MathsAlive.

A teacher using ICT to help plan, prepare and manage teaching

In order to plan, prepare and manage your teaching you will need to have access to a PC or laptop. This might be a workstation on a school network, possibly in a computer lab, open-access area, library or staff work room. It could be a laptop or stand-alone PC you use in the mathematics office, or at home. You will need to have access to the sorts of application software and hardware for mathematics education relevant to the part of the curriculum in which you plan to work (e.g. graph-plotter, spreadsheet, graphing calculator, data-logger, etc.), other forms of resources (reference books, textbooks, task-sheets, instruments, etc.). You may need to be able to access the internet to retrieve other resources and/or information.

You will need suitable generic software to enable you to prepare your lesson-plans, task-sheets, assessment records, evaluations, etc. You may need to be able to scan in information from other sources, such as a book. You will also need to be able to produce printed output either in place, using a connected printer, or by saving your work so that you can obtain hard copy using another work station, etc.

Individual students using ICT outside normal lessons

You may want to plan that students follow up work, write up reports, prepare for new work, etc. You will need to consider what kinds of access they may have outside the lesson, either in school, at a public library or centre or at home. Thus you will need to know what facilities exist within school, such as open-access areas, use of school networks outside teaching times, availability within the school library, etc., and what software is available. You can also ask students to tell you what access they have to computers locally or within their own homes. You will then need to consider what sorts of software they may have already, and how they may obtain access from other sources. It may be that hand-held technology, such as graphing calculators or TI-Nspire™, would be an alternative. Again you will need to know which students have access to such technology. It may be that the school has provision to lend graphing calculators to students to take off-site. In order to install software on a computer most operating systems now require you to have access as an *administrator*. This can be awkward when schools lend or lease laptops to students, but increasingly software is also becoming available for remote access via a web-browser, avoiding the need to install it.

A group of students using ICT within a lesson

You may be able to arrange access to just one or two PCs in your classroom – perhaps workstations to a network, or PCs on trolleys, or laptops – or maybe you have access to just a few graphing calculators. One way to deploy them is to use them with a sub-group of students. This may be because, say, different groups are working at different aspects of a topic, or that you plan to give each group ICT access in turn. This will of course require planning so that different groups of students have different resources to support their work.

A teacher providing ICT access for a whole class

If the school has one or more computer suites, it may be possible to book a computer room for one or more lessons – in which case students will usually have access to a workstation (perhaps shared) for the whole lesson – but this is not always desirable in the context of mathematics. If the school is well equipped it may be that one or more of the mathematics classrooms have several workstations. Alternatively it may be that there are sufficient laptops available (or other suitable portable devices such as graphing calculators) to share between the class. In an ideal world each student would have access to any ICT tool they might require when the occasion arises and at their normal workspace – and this is not far over the horizon!

ICT provision for whole-class teaching

An important form of organization you need to consider is the use of a single PC, laptop or graphing calculator together with a whole-class display such as data projector, interactive whiteboard (IWB), large monitor/TV or OHP. In planning the activities it is important to ensure that the display will be readable – for example, with geometry software, lines will need to be displayed in thicknesses and colours that all can see, similarly with spreadsheets the fonts and sizes for data in cells will need to be chosen carefully. Ideally the ICT should be a resource for both students and teacher to use to share ideas – and so you will need to think about how access will be available. This might be through students coming up to the front to use the keyboard and/or mouse attached to a PC, or you could have a wireless 'slate', keyboard and/or mouse that could be passed around. If you have a tablet PC this could also be passed around. With an IWB, students need to be able to reach the board!

In 2000/1 the UK government supported a project to use a high level of ICT in delivering the Year 7 (ages 11–12) mathematics curriculum in 20 pilot classes. The project was called 'MathsAlive™'. It was managed by Research Machines, with materials written by an author team from the then University College Chichester and teacher support provided through the Mathematical Association. Hardware, software and supporting materials were chosen to support all five of the above contexts.

1. Each teacher received a laptop, printer and internet connection so that they could download lesson-plans and associated resources outside normal teaching time. They also had access to a website from which they could receive help, as well as communicating with fellow teachers. Many of the resources were in the form of Word documents from which lesson-plans, student materials, task-sheets, assessment tasks, revision notes, etc., could be printed. Of course teachers could also adapt these as required.
2. Students with access to a PC, either at home or in school after lessons, could access a website containing a number of resources, such as a popular software game, 'Sub Patrol'. They could also communicate with their teacher, and each other, by e-mail.
3. Each room was equipped with three PCs so that small groups could have hands-on access to ICT during lesson times, but this required planning so that the other students had alternative tasks to do away from the PCs. Each class

was also equipped with a set of graphing calculators for use in pairs or individually.

4. As far as possible, lessons were planned to take place in the normal mathematics classroom. The exception to this was in the case of providing hands-on access for all students to dynamic geometry software, which did entail moving to an ICT suite. Otherwise class access to ICT was via the set of graphing calculators, which were perfectly adequate for the number, algebra and data-handling activities.

5. Each room had a wall-mounted interactive whiteboard (an analog one, which was touch-sensitive and did not require a special pen), together with a ceiling-mounted data projector and PC with printer, network and internet connections. There was a also an OHP together with a graphing calculator, a data-logger (CBR) and an LCD pad. Most lessons started with pre-prepared plenary activities using the IWB, and many included activities involving the whole class in interacting with it.

Chapter 3

What software is out there?

3.1 INTRODUCTION

This chapter is for you to work at privately! It is here to help you get a feel not only for the available software and other ICT tools, but also to get some experience in using them to tackle some interesting bits of mathematics! Of course you will want to be thinking about the role of such tools in teaching as well. By the end of this chapter you should be in a strong position to know *what* ICT there is to use.

Because there are so many types of software currently available it is useful to consider how any piece of software addresses three particularly important sets of questions for mathematics teachers:

- *Pedagogical*: can it be used to help teach content, to develop concepts, to increase knowledge, to improve understanding, to practise and reinforce skills?
- *Mathematical*: can it be used to compute results, to produce tables, to draw graphs, to solve problems, to manipulate expressions, to compute statistics?
- *Organizational*: can it help me to produce materials more efficiently, to keep records, to manage time, to communicate with others, to find resources?

In 2002 the Mathematical Association produced a guide for the then Teacher Training Agency entitled *ICT and Mathematics: a guide to learning and teaching mathematics 11–19*. This was then updated in 2004 as part of the DfES *KS3 ICT Offer to Schools*. The guide was written to support the CPD of serving mathematics teachers, and the preparation of teachers in training. This report contained a contents list which has been used as a basis for the content of this chapter. Of course the available titles, and their features, change constantly so we can only reflect the current position.

3.4   General purpose software: word-processors, add-ins, spreadsheets
3.5   Graphing calculators
3.6   Mathematical tools: dynamic geometry 2D and 3D, graph-plotters, CAS (computer algebra system), data-handling and modelling
3.7   Data capture: data-logging and video analysis
3.8   Multimedia tools: whiteboard tools, screen capture, design tools, satellite imaging, learning platforms, video-conferencing and online classrooms
3.9   Internet resources and CD-ROMs: data sources and data-handling activities; mathematical software, support and activities; interactive and online activities; classroom activities and pedagogical support
3.10 Overview

We shall give more information about useful websites for mathematics towards the end of this section. This will include those which provide access to sources of free, trial or demonstration software. Some types of software related to mathematics testing are outside the scope of this section. These include integrated learning system (ILS), item-banks of examination questions and revision tests for public examinations.

The student's entitlement

The report by Ofsted (2008) *Mathematics – Understanding the Score* comments that:

> Several years ago, inspection evidence showed that most students had some opportunities to use ICT as a tool to solve or explore mathematical problems. This is no longer the case; mathematics makes a relatively limited contribution to developing pupils' ICT skills. Moreover, despite technological advances, the potential of ICT to enhance the learning of mathematics is too rarely realized.

There are considered to be six major opportunities for learners to benefit from the use of ICT in mathematics:

- learning from feedback
- observing patterns
- seeing connections
- developing visual imagery
- exploring data
- 'teaching' the computer.

For example: students trying to reproduce a particular shaped graph when walking in front of a motion-detector are 'exploring real-time data' and 'learning from feedback' to improve the shape of their graph. Students devising a simple Logo program to draw a shape or inputting formulas into a spreadsheet are 'teaching the computer'. Students using 3D dynamic geometry or 3D software applets to look at plans and elevations could be 'developing visual imagery'.

You might like to bear these six opportunities in mind when working through this chapter. There is a document on the website which gives further details and examples about the student's entitlement to ICT in secondary mathematics.

 How do the different types of software mentioned in the sections of this chapter provide learners with the opportunities listed above?

3.2 'SMALL PROGRAMS', MANIPULATIVES AND APPLETS

These are programs aimed at specific, highly focused, curriculum content. They come in a variety of forms. Perhaps the most frequently used examples are in the form of games or challenges where the interaction by an individual, or a group of students, with the computer, involves them in practising and applying some particular mathematical skill or knowledge. There are many advantages of using ICT in such a context.

Here are just a few:

- the computer responds to students in a non-judgemental way
- it can motivate and hold attention through the use of moving images, sounds, etc.
- students can respond in their own time
- students can refine their strategies as the result of feedback
- the teacher is freed from having to check answers
- students and the teacher can cooperate together in working at problems posed by the computer.

In previous editions of this book we included programs developed by, for example, ATM and SMILE. There is now a wide variety of applets available on the internet so we have included some examples of these here as an illustration. These activities have been chosen because they provide examples of the advantages of using ICT mentioned above and reflect a range of curriculum content. The examples chosen are from a variety of sources. Further details about the websites mentioned here together with other useful websites are given in section 3.9 of this chapter.

3.2(a) Games

Games can be motivating and challenging. They can be used to practise and reinforce skills and concepts in a non-routine way. In these two examples the use of a computer allows students to develop strategies and refine them as the result of feedback. The teacher is freed from having to check answers, allowing more time for questioning and promoting discussion.

'Treasure hunt' from Bowland Maths `http://www.bowlandmaths.org.uk/`
   Bowland Maths consists of a collection of case-studies, each supporting three to

five lessons. To help develop the styles of teaching required, the Bowland Maths materials include five professional development modules which cover the pedagogical challenges in working with students to tackle non-routine unstructured problem-solving. Included with the professional development materials are a number of short computer programs. Treasure Hunt is in the section 'Fostering and managing collaborative discussion'. Learners are encouraged to discuss and develop suitable strategies for finding treasure in a 100 × 100 grid using as few moves as possible.

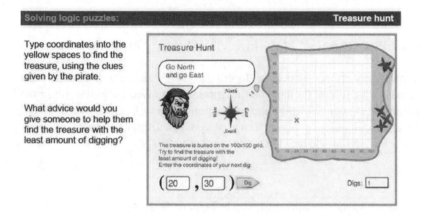

Another example of a game from the Bowland Maths professional development materials, 'Multiplication grids', is described in Chapter 5.

'Diamond collector' from the NRICH website `http://nrich.maths.org/public/index.php`

NRICH is the main website of the Millennium Mathematics Project at Cambridge University. The site publishes a monthly issue of free mathematical enrichment material – problems, puzzles, games, investigations and articles.

In the context of a game, this problem invites students to identify straight lines and state their equations. Students can compete against each other or against the computer either individually or collaboratively.

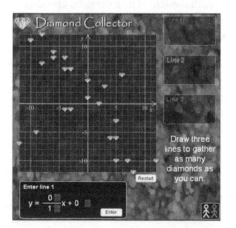

Many students can identify some of the lines easily (e.g. horizontal), but there is incentive to learn about 'harder' lines. The website gives teaching notes, suggestions and strategies such as different levels of difficulty. It also suggests some key questions to stimulate discussion.

3.2(b) Simulations

Simulations can generate large amounts of data which would otherwise be difficult or time-consuming to gather. They can facilitate posing and testing hypotheses. Two examples are:

Top Coach from the NRICH website. Here you can try combinations of different training regimes for your rowing crew and test your hypothesis about which regime gives the best performance.

The website suggests a possible task:

> This team needs a new coach, and you have all been shortlisted for interview. You're going to need to design the best possible training regime. At the interview you will need to present the training regime that you would recommend for this crew. You will need to justify your recommendation with a summary of time-trial results and the results from half a dozen races. This evidence will need to be clearly presented in a handout to be given to the interviewers.

Top Coach

Problem | Teachers' Notes | Hint | Solution | Printable page |

Stage: 3 Challenge Level: ★ ★

Carry out some time trials and gather some data to help you decide on the best training regime for your rowing crew.

Analyse your data and present your findings in a way that provides convincing evidence that you have identified the optimum training regime.

Full Screen Version

gr8		Circuit Training	0	circuits/week	Skip animation
Can you find your eight's optimal training regime?	Running	0	miles/day	Time trial
	Rowing	0	hours/day	Race

Coin-tossing from the National Library of Virtual Manipulatives (NLVM) `http://nlvm.usu.edu/`
This simulation allows you to explore probability concepts by simulating repeated coin-tossing. The process is very fast, so large numbers of tosses are possible for better comparison of theoretical and experimental results.

There are several options. One option allows you to alter the bias of a coin by changing the probability of obtaining a head. Another allows you to keep tossing until you achieve a particular result such as eight heads in a row.

3.2(c) Three dimensions

3D manipulatives enable students to manipulate an object in space to help visualization.

The DALEST project (Developing an Active Learning Environment for the Learning of Stereometry) aims at enhancing middle-school students' 3D geometry understanding and spatial visualization skills by utilizing dynamic visualization images. Partners in the project are the Universities of Cyprus, Southampton, Lisbon, Sofia and Athens, together with N.K.M. Netmasters and Cyprus Mathematics Teachers' Association. The project is co-funded by the European Union under the Socrates Program, MINERVA.

In a paper presented at the Congress of the European Society for Research in Mathematics Education (CERME), Larnaca, Cyprus, 22–26 February 2007 by, C. Christou et al. (2007), entitled 'Developing student spatial ability with 3D software applications' four applications are described. 'Cubix Editor', 'Potter's wheel', 'Stuffed toys' and 'Origami nets'. The applications are available from Elica at `http://www.elica.net/site/index.html`. Three examples from the DALEST project are shown below.

Cubix Editor
In this application students can add and delete cubes by left or right clicking the mouse and can rotate the image to change the viewing angle to view the object created from several directions and thus match it to plans and elevations, by holding and dragging the right mouse button.

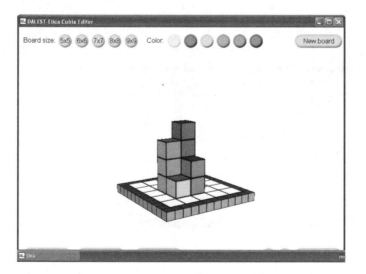

Stuffed toys

In this application students are given different nets of cubes presented in a 3D view. These can be rotated and viewed from different viewing angles. Upon completion, students can open a new window which presents 11 possible nets and then select the net they think corresponds to the 3D net presented earlier

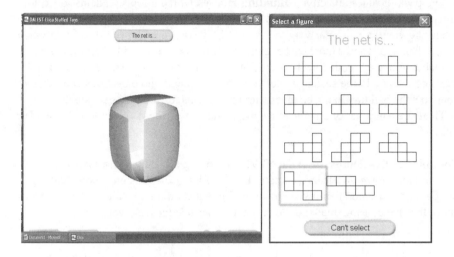

Potter's wheel

When a simple 2D object is rotated in 3D around a vertical axis it can generate a variety of 3D rotational objects. This application provides a design tool where users can experiment with rotating five simple 2D objects, varying their position and orientation relative to the axis to generate different 3D shapes.

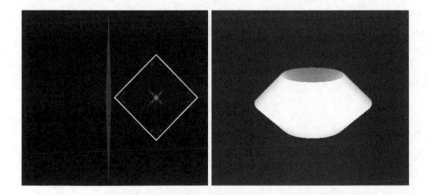

Building Houses with Side View, from the Wisweb website
The Standards unit pack *Improving Learning in Mathematics* is a multi-media resource where learners are encouraged to become more independent and reflective about their mathematics (`http://www.ncetm.org.uk/Default.aspx? page=13&module=res&mode=100&resid=1442`).

The pack includes an activity **Building Houses** which allows students to explore connections between 3D models and their plans and elevations, using the mouse to rotate the view in a similar way to the DALEST software Cubix Editor mentioned above. This applet and a more challenging one Building Houses with Side View are also available from the Freudenthal Institutes' Wiswebsite at `http://www.fi.uu.nl/ wisweb/en/`. In the second applet you are given plans and elevations and asked to construct the building to match these, aiming to use as few bricks as possible.

There are a number of other useful applets on this website if you follow the 'applet' link.

Platonic Solids – Duals, from the NLVM site `http://nlvm.usu.edu/`
This applet allows you to manipulate the five Platonic solids and their duals. The images can be rotated to aid visualization. Students could make and test conjectures about the shape of the dual and the number of faces, edges and vertices.

✎   *What can you find out about Platonic solids and their duals?*

3.2(d) Data capture

There are applications that allow you to capture data. Here are two examples.

Mouse Plotter, from the NRich website
This interactive environment monitors the motion of your mouse and produces a displacement-time graph.

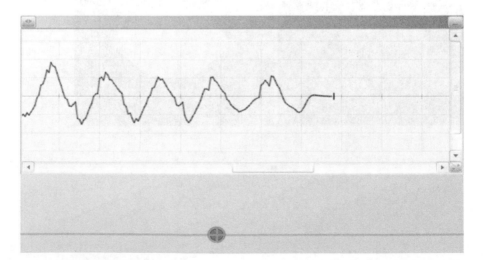

Students can experiment with the interactivity and challenge themselves to draw different shaped graphs. Some graphs to replicate are given in the notes on the website.

✎ *What would you expect the graph to look like if you try to move the mouse in a circle?*

Reaction-timers

There are ways of collecting data on reaction times in the classroom, for example by dropping and catching a ruler and measuring the distance fallen. Using a computer can not only produce results faster but can give much more accurate timings and more interesting data. Hypotheses can be proposed and tested relating to, for example, 'use of preferred versus non preferred hand', 'time of day', etc.

The **NRICH website** has a reaction-timer `http://nrich.maths.org/public/viewer.php?obj_id=6044`. Users need to click on the screen when they see the image appear. There are options for varying the shape and colour to be spotted and the facility to copy the results into an Excel™ spreadsheet. The NRICH page also has some useful questions and teacher's notes.

Here is a reaction timer. It will enable you to collect data on the time it takes you to respond to an image on your computer.

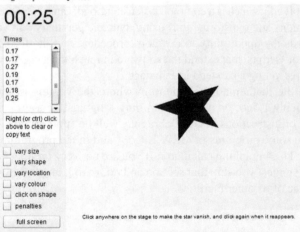

Sheep Dash!, from the BBC

In their science section the BBC website has a page on sheep. Sheep Dash! tests how fast your reactions are by requiring you to click the mouse when you see a sheep break for freedom (`http://www.bbc.co.uk/science/humanbody/ sleep/sheep/reaction_version5.swf`).

Data from the BBC site would need to be manually collected, but it does have the advantage that timings are given to one thousandth of a second.

 An internet search for 'Reaction-timers' produces a number of results. Which would you choose to use in the classroom and how would you use them?

3.3 PROGRAMMING LANGUAGES

The capacity of modern computers, including graphing calculators, is now such that many of the applications that previously required teachers to write blocks of code in a programming language can now be performed within the command structure of suitable software. For example, the simulation of the sums of scores from a number of rolls of two dice, which might have been carried out by a short Basic program, can now be easily carried out using the data lists on a graphing calculator, as you will see later. Similarly the creation of a regular polygon, which is a common task using Logo, can be performed by a number of constructions and transformations using dynamic geometry software. Such software also affords the opportunity to develop 'procedures' in the forms of 'macros', 'custom tools' or 'scripts' that extend the software in much the same way as we will now use procedures in Logo to extend its language.

There are aspects of the mathematics curriculum where the writing of short programs by students using Logo, or the programming language of a graphing calculator or a sequence of instructions in GeoGebra may well be appropriate.

Here we will illustrate some programs in MSW Logo™ and in the programming language of the TI-83 or TI-84 graphing calculator. If you are not very familiar with graphing calculators we suggest you skip that section and return to it later when you have had some experience of its other facilities.

3.3(a) Logo

✎ *Can you write a procedure in Logo that will draw a row of hexagons?*

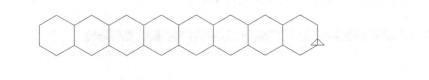

When you start MSW Logo™ the screen shows two windows. The bottom part, known as the Commander, is where you enter instructions. Most Logo commands can be abbreviated, and they can be strung together using spaces to separate them. As a first step to constructing a row of hexagons, with the cursor in the bottom line of the Commander enter the string:

CS FD 100 RT 90 FD 50

and press the Enter key. Your commands are transferred into the 'history' area of the Commander. If there are no errors then you should see the graphic image change on the MSW Logo™ screen window. The triangular arrowhead shows the current position and heading of the cursor and it is known as the 'screen turtle', or just 'turtle', from the earlier use of Logo with floor robots called 'turtles'.

There were just four commands:

CS   Clear Screen
FD 100 Forward 100 units
RT 90   Right Turn 90 degrees
FD 50   Forward 50 units

The power of Logo is in the 'extensibility' of the language, which means you teach it new words, by defining procedures. To illustrate this, type EDIT "HEX in the command line. This opens up another window: the Editor window. Put the cursor before the 'end' statement and press Enter. Then type the line: REPEAT 6 [FD 50 RT 60]. Open the File menu and select the first option: Save & Exit. This has defined the new word HEX which uses a REPEAT loop.

```
Editor                                              _ □ ✕
File  Edit  Search  Set  Test!  Help
to HEX
REPEAT 6 [FD 50 RT 60]|
end
```

This draws six sides by going forward 50 units and then turning right through an (external) angle of 60 degrees. Enter: CS HEX in the command line to draw a hexagon.

```
to HEX
REPEAT 6 [FD 50 RT 60]
end
```

The mathematical challenge is to find where to position the cursor after drawing one hexagon so that the next one joins on cleanly. We can define another procedure using:

EDIT "SLIDE

```
to SLIDE
PU RT 90 FD 100*COS (30) LT
90 PD
end
```

Here we use the commands PU and PD for PenUp and PenDown, so that we do not leave a trace across the last hexagon. We have also used some trigonometry to calculate the required displacement. You can test the program by keying, e.g., CS HEX SLIDE HEX.

Finally we shall put the ideas together by using EDIT "HEXBAND" and entering the program to draw eight hexagons side by side. First, though, we have to clear the screen and move the cursor to the left-hand side of the screen.

```
to HEXBAND
CS PU LT 90 FD 350
RT 90 PD
REPEAT 8 [HEX SLIDE]
end
```

✎ *Can you now define a procedure, maybe called HEXTILE, which puts say four HEXBANDS cleanly above each other?*

Logo for numbers and words

Although Logo is usually used for graphical output, it can be used to print numbers, words, etc. like other programming languages. The procedure ITER illustrates the point

ITER

This little program is using an iteration to find successive approximations to the golden ratio ϕ, which is a solution to the equation: $\phi = 1 + \dfrac{1}{\phi}$

(Note that "x means 'the variable named x', while :x means 'the value stored in the variable named x'. PR is the shorthand for Print.)

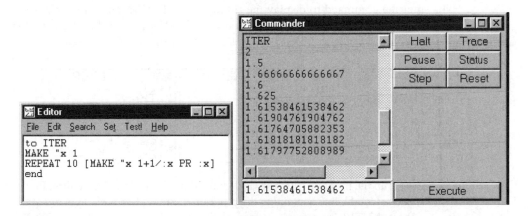

3.3(b) Programming graphing calculators

Below we give more details about the use of graphing calculators using the Texas Instruments TI-83 as an example. Each of our examples can be tackled on most GCs without using any programming at all. But here we give a brief idea of the similarities and differences between a GC programming language and others such as Logo.

First we will enter and run the ITER program. Press the 'PRGM' key to see a menu of the programs already stored on the calculator. If it is a new one there will be no names! Move the cursor right twice to highlight 'NEW' and press 'ENTER'. You are now in the program editor where you first type the name of your program. Just press the keys corresponding to the letters in green above them, e.g. 'x^2' gives 'I', '4' gives 'T', 'SIN' gives 'E' and 'x' gives 'R'. Press 'ENTER' again to start writing the program.

```
EXEC EDIT NEW       PROGRAM
 1 Create New        Name=ITER
```

The first line is entered using the following four keys: '1', 'STO→', 'X,T,θ,*n*' and 'ENTER'. This stores the value 1 into the variable X. In order to enter the next instruction, for the counted loop, press the 'PRGM' key and select item 4 from the 'CTL' menu. When you press 'ENTER' this pastes the phrase 'For(' on the next line. Use 'ALPHA' and 'LOG' to get the letter 'N' and then complete the line 'For (N,1,10)' before pressing 'ENTER'.

If you want to indent the body of the FOR-loop to help clarify the loop structure you can include extra colons using 'ALPHA' and '•'. Hence enter the line '1+1/ X→X' and press 'ENTER'.

To enter the command to display the result, press 'PRGM' and cursor right to select 'I/O' (for Input and Output), and choose item 3: 'Disp'. For the command to 'End' the counted loop use 'PRGM' and select item 7 from the 'CTL' menu.

```
PROGRAM:ITER        CTL I/O EXEC       CTL I/O EXEC
:1→X                1:Input            1:If
:For(N,1,10)        2:Prompt           2:Then
::1+1/X→X           3 Disp             3:Else
::Disp X            4:DispGraph        4 For(
:End                5:DispTable        5:While
:■                  6:Output(          6:Repeat
                    7↓getKey           7↓End
```

In order to run the program, first use '2nd' and 'MODE' to 'QUIT' the editor. Press 'PRGM' and select the line containing the program name 'ITER' which you want to execute. Press 'ENTER' to paste the name into the normal screen, and then 'ENTER' again to run it.

If you want to change the program then press 'PRGM', cursor right over 'EDIT' and down to select the name of the program to edit.

Now there is so much software built in to the TI-83 that there are much more convenient ways, say, of performing an iteration, plotting a hexagon, or of drawing a graph of a function like f(*x*) = 1 + 1/*x*.

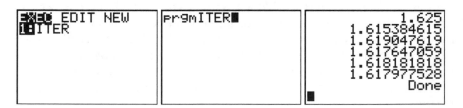

```
EXEC EDIT NEW       prgmITER■                      1.625
 1 ITER                                        1.615384615
                                               1.619047619
                                               1.617647059
                                               1.618181818
                                               1.617977528
                                               ■                Done
```

However, in order to give a feeling for the range of programming commands we will show a possible version of the HEX program – this one draws a hexagon within a circle of radius R, centre (P,Q). Note that variable names can only use single characters. Note that 'ClrDraw' and 'Line' are found on the 'DRAW' menu ('2nd' 'PRGM'), that 'Degree' is found on the 'MODE' menu, and 'ZDecimal' on the 'ZOOM' menu.

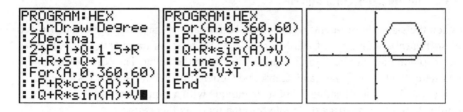

3.3(c) GeoGebra commands

GeoGebra has a long list of commands which can be put together like a program and typed into the input line as an alternative to using the geometric features. You can see details of how to use these if you access the help manual and look at Algebraic Input or by selecting 'view' and 'construction protocol'. 'View' also has an option to see the 'command list'. The commands can be accessed by selecting the 'command' menu on the bottom right of the screen. If you select 'view' and 'navigation bar for construction steps' you can replay the steps in your constructions.

✎ *Can you write a sequence of instructions to produce a row of hexagons using GeoGebra?*

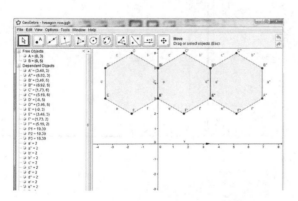

The sequence used here was:
A = (0,3) B = (0,5) P1 = polygon[A,B,6] v = vector[(0,0),(3.46,0)]
P2 = translate [P1,v] P3 = translate[P2,v]

✎ *Can you write a sequence of instructions to produce a tessellation of hexagons?*

In the following section you will find out how sequences of instructions can be put together to define tools.

3.3(d) Scripts, tools and macros

When the same set of operations needs to be repeatedly carried in a particular piece of software it is common for it to provide a tool to record and save the necessary steps so that they can be reapplied just by invoking the name. The common dynamic geometry packages, Sketchpad, Cabri and GeoGebra each have their own means of doing this. We shall illustrate the basic technique with a simple example – given three points A, B, C to construct the circle through them and its centre D.

Sketchpad
First, in Sketchpad we construct three points A, B, C, then segment AB, then its midpoint, then the perpendicular to AB through this point, then repeat the last two steps for segment AC, then find the intersection D of the two perpendiculars and construct the circle centre D through A. Finally, hide the segments and midpoints. Then drag a box around the whole construction to highlight all the visible elements.

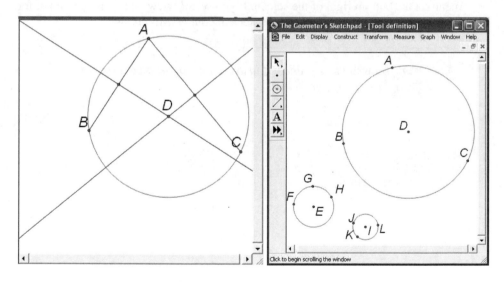

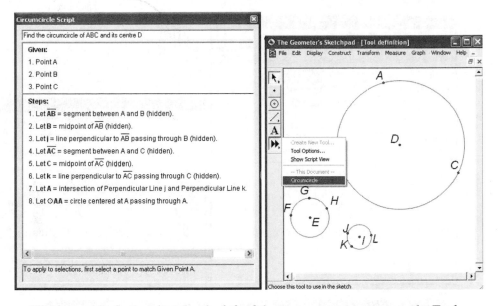

Clicking on the bottom icon on the left of the screen, you can open up the Tool icon, and select 'script view' so that you can read how Sketchpad saves your construction. Once this has been saved you can use this new tool to generate new points and circles wherever you want. Or you can choose three existing points and then replay the construction using them as the inputs.

Cabri

The techniques in Cabri are very similar indeed. Define three points and carry out the same construction as before to find the intersections of the perpendicular bisectors of segments *AB* and *AC*, etc. Then click on the Macro icon. Click on *A*, *B* and *C* to define the Initial Objects. Click on the centre and circle to define the Final Objects. Finally click on Define Macro to name and save it (Circum). If you have the time and inclination you could design your own icon! In order to use it, just define three more points, open the macro menu, click on Circum, then click in turn on the three points to construct the circle and centre. If you save the macro to a File on disk, you can open this file 'circum.mac' using a text editor, such as MS WordPad, to see the way Cabri stores its macros.

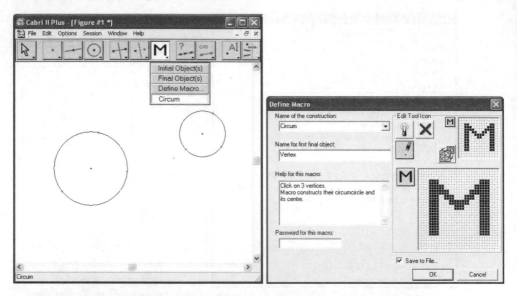

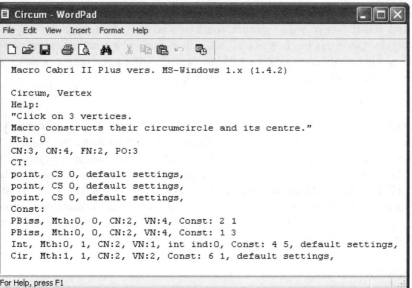

GeoGebra

Finally we show exactly the same process being carried through in GeoGebra. As with the previous examples, you first make your construction, and then the process is virtually identical to the Cabri approach.

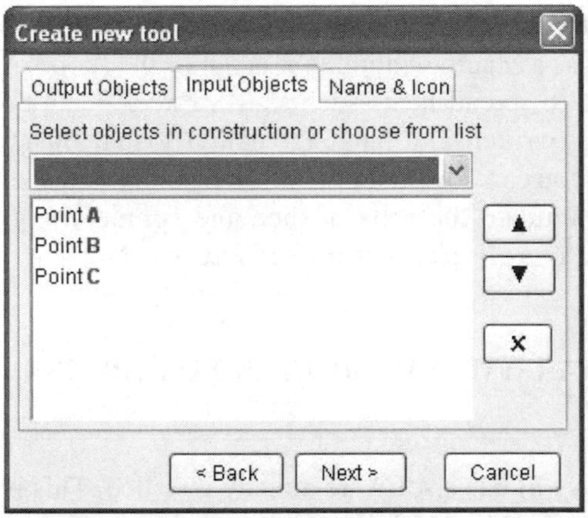

Create new tool

Output Objects | Input Objects | Name & Icon

Select objects in construction or choose from list

Point **A**
Point **B**
Point **C**

< Back | Next > | Cancel

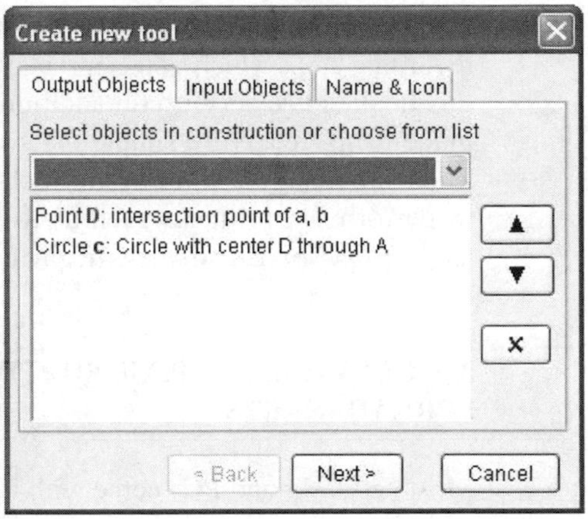

Create new tool

Output Objects | Input Objects | Name & Icon

Select objects in construction or choose from list

Point **D**: intersection point of a, b
Circle **c**: Circle with center D through A

< Back | Next > | Cancel

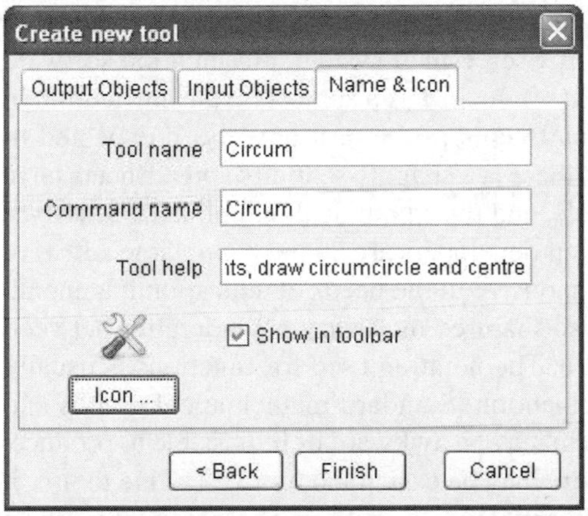

Create new tool

Output Objects | Input Objects | Name & Icon

Tool name   Circum

Command name   Circum

Tool help   its, draw circumcircle and centre

☑ Show in toolbar

Icon ...

< Back | Finish | Cancel

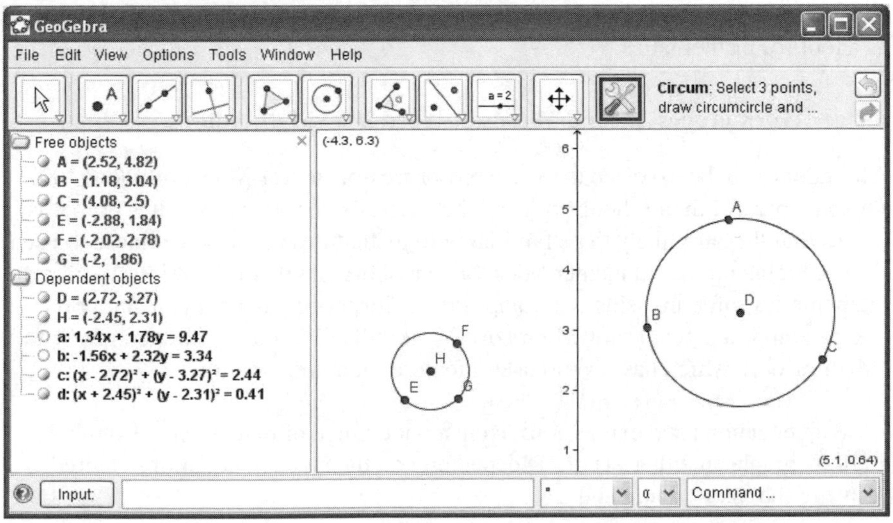

GeoGebra

File   Edit   View   Options   Tools   Window   Help

Circum: Select 3 points, draw circumcircle and ...

Free objects
— A = (2.52, 4.82)
— B = (1.18, 3.04)
— C = (4.08, 2.5)
— E = (-2.88, 1.84)
— F = (-2.02, 2.78)
— G = (-2, 1.86)
Dependent objects
— D = (2.72, 3.27)
— H = (-2.45, 2.31)
— a: 1.34x + 1.78y = 9.47
— b: -1.56x + 2.32y = 3.34
— c: $(x - 2.72)^2 + (y - 3.27)^2 = 2.44$
— d: $(x + 2.45)^2 + (y - 2.31)^2 = 0.41$

(-4.3, 6.3)

(5.1, 0.64)

Input: α   Command ...

So each of these dynamic geometry packages enables you to extend the range of construction and other tools available as you define your own ones – so, like Logo, these systems are *extensible*. Some other software packages also provide means of recording steps which you can replay as a Macro. Although it is out of the scope of this book, some very useful additions to spreadsheets such as MS Excel™ can be made using relatively simple macros, written in a language called Visual Basic. There are many websites from which you can download files which contain macros to perform useful tasks such as to simulate the rolls of dice and spinners: e.g. `http://www.mathsisfun.net/TeachingResources.htm`.

3.4 GENERAL PURPOSE SOFTWARE: WORD-PROCESSORS, ADD-INS, SPREADSHEETS

Most networks and PCs come with a set of basic software already installed. This is often in the form of an integrated package, such as MS Works™, or a suite of software such as Microsoft Office™ incorporating any or all of: a word-processor, spreadsheet, database, graphics package, internet browser, e-mail system, presentation software (such as Microsoft's Office PowerPoint™). As ICT is a subject on the curriculum in most schools, often mathematics departments in the past have been expected to demonstrate uses of spreadsheets. But there is a snag. Essentially spreadsheets have been developed from accountants' tools, and their graphical output usually derives from presentations of sales figures. Their developers are, in the main, large software houses that may not be particularly responsive to the needs of education in general, and of mathematics in particular. Also features may vary considerably between different versions of the same software. The notation used for functions is usually very different from mathematical convention. Standard mathematical graphs and diagrams (such as box-plots in statistics) may be awkward or impossible to produce. Although mathematics-specific software may be easier and more effective to use, it should not be forgotten that a large number of students will have access to spreadsheet software such as MS Excel™ at home and it would be desirable if they could see it as a tool for mathematics.

3.4(a)   Word-processors and Microsoft Word 2007 Math Add-in

All students will be expected to use a word-processor such as Microsoft Word 2007™ for some parts of their school work and they may also have access to it at home. This means that they are likely to be familiar with its features and would choose to use it for producing reports in mathematics. Screen-shots can be inserted into Word from mathematics software using 'Ctrl' and 'Prt Sc' for writing mathematical reports.

One important feature of Microsoft Word 2007™ is that it now comes with a 'Math Add-in' which has several useful features enabling you to:

- write equations and expressions using a wide range of mathematical symbols
- draw graphs in either 2D or 3D depending on the types of equations entered, using the 'plot ' command

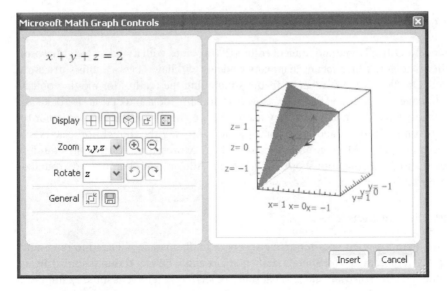

- solve equations and rearrange formulas.

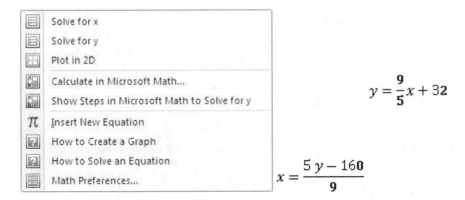

$$y = \frac{9}{5}x + 32$$

$$x = \frac{5y - 160}{9}$$

If you have Microsoft Office 2007 you can download the Math Add-in from Microsoft (just put the above title into a search). Depending on your system, you may be prompted to install one or two other pieces of Microsoft software before this can be completed. This may entail a second search for the named software or the page for its download may be given. Once installed, the add-in can then be accessed from the 'add-ins' tab at the top of a page in Word.

Investigate the different types of graphs and possibilities for solving equations that the Math Add-in offers. How would you use this with students, especially if they had access to this Math Add-in both in school and at home?

3.4(b) Microsoft Office OneNote

Microsoft Office Home and Student edition 2007 comes with a student tool Microsoft Office OneNote which means that many students will have access to this software at home. OneNote has a number of features including the facility for moving objects (text images, etc.) around the page, as well as drawing tools and options to rotate and reflect objects. This makes it a very useful tool for mind-mapping in particular for brainstorming and collaborative learning, and showing the thought processes that have taken place. More complex mathematical expressions and graphs could be copied and pasted in from Word and the Math Add-in, and then moved around as appropriate.

3.4(c) Spreadsheets

While there are good uses for spreadsheets in mathematics, we need to remember that ICT requirements for school mathematics cannot be met through spreadsheets, or other generic software, alone. That said, we shall take a look at some examples of problems tackled using MS Excel™.

Example 1: First we shall show the equivalent of the ITER program at the end of 3.3(a)

Open the spreadsheet application and enter the starting value into a cell, e.g. with the cursor over the cell A1, type '1' and press the Enter key. Now, in cell A2, we want to give a formula involving the cell above: put the cursor on cell A2 and press '=' to start a formula. Enter '1+1/' and then either type 'A1' or move the cursor up to the A1 cell. When you press the Enter key the cell shows the result, i.e. '2', but the 'edit line' above shows the formula: '1+1/A1'.

A2			f_x =1+1/A1				A11			f_x =1+1/A10
Book1							**Book1**			
	A	B	C	D	E		A	B	C	D	E
1	1						1	1			
2	2						2	2			
3							3	1.5			
4							4	1.6666667			
5							5	1.6			
6							6	1.625			
7							7	1.6153846			
8							8	1.6190476			
9							9	1.6176471			
10							10	1.6181818			
11							11	1.6179775			
12							12				
13							13				
14							14				
Ready							Ready				

With the cursor still on cell A2, right click and select 'copy' then press and hold the left mouse button and drag the mouse down to cell A11 and release. Right click and select paste. You will find that you now have a set of successive iterations. If you place the cursor say over A6 you will see the formula '=1+1/A5' has been entered into the edit line. If you now go to cell A1 and type a different starting value, e.g. 2, then when you press Enter, all the values in the cells A2:A11 will be recomputed. This is the key feature of any spreadsheet.

Example 2: In this example a set of heights of 11 students are entered in cells A1:A11 Use the mouse to click on the top of the column, i.e. the box marked A. This highlights the whole A column. Right click and select Copy, then use the mouse to highlight the B columns and right click and select Paste to make B1:B11 an exact copy of A1:A11. Still with the B column highlighted, go to the upper toolbar and choose the 'Sort and Filter' option on the top right. Choose the 'Sort smallest to largest' option, and column B should immediately change to be in ascending order of height.

Now it is easy to pick out, for example, the minimum, median and maximum values of the heights. To calculate the mean, just go to an empty cell, such as B13, press '=' for a formula. Then select the formulas' option from the top toolbar. Selecting 'More functions' and 'Statistical' will allow you to select AVERAGE or of course you can also type this in directly – and then enter (B1:B11) to complete the formula.

Can you now compute the value of the range (max–min) in, say, cell B12?

The Formulas page in Excel™ 2007 has two choices labelled 'Math and Trig' and 'More functions'. What functions can you find here that could be useful for future reference?

3.5 GRAPHING CALCULATORS (GCs)

There have been rapid developments in hand-held technology in recent years. These include the development of 'flash-ROM' which enables both system and application software to be downloaded from the internet. The development of compatible cheap and easy-to-use data-loggers – particularly motion-detectors – makes the acquisition of real data very practicable even in a conventional classroom. Together with the low-cost displays for whole-class teaching, such tools have a place in several subjects in the curriculum and can be vehicles for encouraging cooperation between teachers across subjects. There are examples in our Becta book: Oldknow and Taylor (1998), *Data-capture and Modelling in Mathematics and Science*. The book is out of print but can be downloaded as a pdf file from p. 2 of Adrian Oldknow's website `http://www.adrianoldknow.org.uk/Page2.htm`.

First we show how to solve $x = 1 + 1/x$ graphically using a TI-83 in order to illustrate the general technique. Press 'MODE' and make sure that 'Func' is highlighted in the fourth line. If it is not, then move the cursor to the left to highlight it and press 'ENTER'. Use '2nd' and 'MODE' to 'QUIT'. Now find the blue 'Y=' key immediately below the screen. Press this and enter the functions 1+1/X into Y1 and X into Y2. If any of the 'Plot' areas on the top line are highlighted, then move the cursor over them and press 'ENTER', repeating until all are cleared.

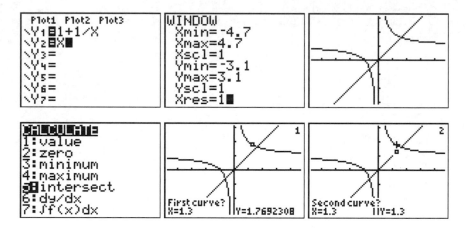

Either press 'WINDOW' and set the values as in the screen-shot, or else press 'ZOOM' and select '4:ZDecimal'. Finally press 'GRAPH' to see the pair of graphs.

Now use '2nd TRACE' for the 'CALC' menu. Select '5:intersect'. You will now have to use the cursor keys to select which functions to use (even though there are only two of them!), and a starting-point for the built-in numerical algorithm to find the intersection.

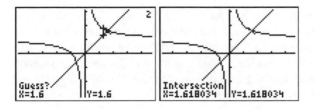

Earlier in this chapter we showed how to program the calculator to draw a hexagon. We can now show an easier way to do this using the TI-83's graphing facilities.

From the 'MODE' screen you need to select both Parametric graphing, and degrees. In the 'Y=' editor enter the parametric equations for a circle of desired centre and radius.

In the 'WINDOW' screen make sure that the parameter T goes from 0 to 360 in steps of 60 degrees. You might want to change the screen's appearance. Use '2nd' 'ZOOM' for the 'FORMAT' screen where you can hide axes, put in grid-points, etc. Try making other polygons, or hexagons, that touch.

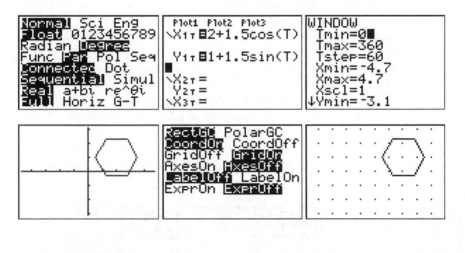

✎ *Try making some polar graphs, e.g. try some variations on*
   $r = 2 + cos(5\theta)$.

Now we can see how the graphing calculator also contains powerful software for statistics.

We will study the familiar 'handshake' problem. That is when there are four people A, B, C, D in a room, and six handshakes are needed to introduce everyone to each other: {AB, AC, AD, BC, BD, CD}. How many handshakes are needed for n people? These are the 'triangle numbers'.

In list L1 we enter the numbers {2,3,4,5,6,7,8} as the numbers of people in a room. In list L2 we enter the corresponding number of handshakes required: {1,3,6,10,15,21,28}, the so-called triangle numbers.

Press 'STAT', select '5:SetUpEditor' and press 'ENTER' twice. Then 'STAT' and '1:Edit' to go into the statistics editor. Type in the number of people in the list L1 and the number of handshakes in the list L2. Then press 'STAT' and move the cursor right to select 'CALC', and choose '5:QuadReg'. The expression 'QuadReg' appears on the home screen. You must tell it which two data-sets to use. So enter 'L1,L2' and press 'ENTER'. 'L1' is found from '2nd' and '1'.

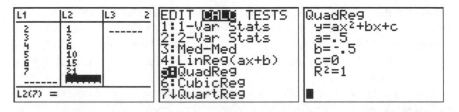

We can show the fit graphically by pressing '2nd' and 'Y=' to get to 'STAT PLOT'. Select '1:Plot1' and highlight 'On' and the symbol for scattergram. Enter the lists 'L1' and 'L2', and highlight the square symbol.

Then choose a suitable 'WINDOW' and press 'GRAPH'. You should see the scattergram with the superimposed quadratic model. Remember, though, that the data here is discrete, yet the fitted function is continuous!

In the 'MATH', 'PRB' menu there are functions for permutations and combinations. If you go back to 'STAT' 'Edit' you can place the cursor over the symbol 'L3' at the top of the third column. Press 'ENTER' to go into the entry line. We shall now enter a formula, similarly as in a spreadsheet, for column L3 in terms of column L1. First find the inverted commas symbol ' by using 'ALPHA' and '+'.

We can then enter the formula "L1 nCr 2', where 'nCr' comes from the 'MATH' 'PRB' menu. When you press 'ENTER' the whole list L3 is now computed in terms of L1.

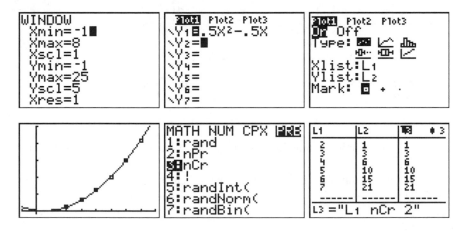

Finally we use the ideas of lists and statistics plots to explore the box-plots of rolls of simulated dice.

From the 'MATH', 'PRB' menu chose '5:randInt(' and enter the line: randInt(1,6,50) STO→L1 to place 50 simulated rolls of a six-sided die into list L1.

Repeat for L2. Then we can add lists L1 and L2 together, term-by-term, and store the result in list L3. From the 'STAT PLOT' screen we can define each of the three plots to be a box-plot of the data in lists L1, L2 and L3 respectively.

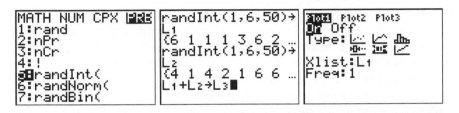

You will need to clear any functions in the 'Y=' editor and choose a suitable WINDOW, e.g. with x from −1 to 13 and any scale for y, e.g. 0 to 4. Pressing 'GRAPH' should now show the three box-plots for comparison. You can trace these to see the medians, quartiles, etc. To see statistics about any one of the three lists use STAT CALC and 1:1-Var Stats followed by the name of the list, e.g. L1.

3.6 MATHEMATICS-SPECIFIC SOFTWARE

This section includes a wide variety of software that is specifically intended for mathematics. Much of it has been and is continuing to be developed with teaching and learning in mind. It has been organized under the following headings.

a. Dynamic geometry software in both 2D and 3D
b. Graph-plotting software (GPS)
c. Computer algebra system (CAS)
d. Data-handling and modelling software (DHS).

Increasingly this type of software has the ability to perform more than one of these functions, sometimes in an integrated way so that features of one aspect are available in another, enabling multiple representations and links between different areas of mathematics. We will try to include examples of this where appropriate. Websites for the software and those which offer support and classroom activities using the software are given in section 3.9 of this chapter.

3.6(a) Dynamic geometry software in both 2D and 3D

Dynamic geometry software enables the user to create geometrical diagrams quickly and accurately and has the facility for the user to drag points and other features of diagrams to look for invariance and other properties. This can enable the discovery of new and exciting results. It also forces the user to think geometrically in order to create diagrams. Images can be inserted into 2D software to explore relative measurements, gradients and fitting geometric shapes.

In 3D solids can be constructed and manipulated to view from a variety of angles and opened to view nets. In both cases, in using the software learners will be introduced to formal geometrical vocabulary and will need to specify details for constructions fully and precisely – both valuable skills. It should be noted, however, that the software does not replace the need for learners to have the kinaesthetic hands-on experience of constructions in 2D and building models in 3D.

3.6(a1) Dynamic geometry software in 2D

Until recently there have been two main dynamic geometry packages in almost equal educational use internationally: Cabri Géomètre™ and The Geometer's Sketchpad™. These are now joined by a third piece of software – GeoGebra which is available free to download or in a web-based version. In addition TI-Nspire™ software and hand-held devices include a simplified version of Cabri.

While these packages were developed specifically to aid geometry teaching, the software is very flexible and versatile, and can be used in many aspects of mathematics as well as in areas such as design and technology. They each also include facilities for dynamic graphing of functions. We shall illustrate their use by exploring the following geometric problem:

If we have three coins, maybe all of different sizes, we can push them together so that they touch each other in pairs, but can we solve the reverse problem?

✎ *Given three points can we always find circles with those points as centres, such that each pair of circles touches each other?*

Cabri

We will first explore this using Cabri.

- We start by fixing three points A, B, C. The toolbar shows 11 icons. The left-hand one, the arrow, is the usual mode where the mouse just moves a pointer across the screen. If you click on the second icon you get a menu dealing with Points. Select the first of these: Point. Now use the cursor to position the pointer over the place you want one of the points, and then click the button to place it there. Repeat to put two other points on the screen. Now click either on the first icon (called the pointer) or anywhere in the grey area of the toolbar. (step 1)
- The next step is to join the points by segments. Go to the third icon and select Segment from the menu. Position the cursor over one of the points (you will see a message saying 'this point') and click, then position it over the other end-point and click to make a segment. Repeat this for the other two sides of the triangle. (step 2)
- Now we shall make a variable point on one of the sides. Open the Point menu again, but this time select the second option: Point on object. Move the pointer to somewhere on one of the segments (such as point P in the diagram), and click. Select the Pointer tool again and check that you can slide this point freely along, but not off, the segment. (step 3)

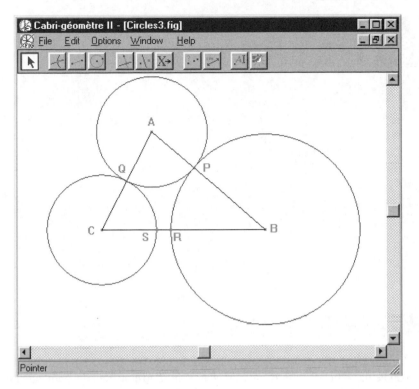

- Now we can construct the circles whose centres are the end-points of this segment (*A,B*) and which pass through the variable point (*P*). Open the menu for the fourth icon and select Circle. Click on a centre-point (*A*) and then on a radius point (*P*). Repeat for the other circle. Return to the Pointer tool and check that, as you slide *P*, both dependent circles change size. (step 4)
- Now we can find their points of intersection with the other two sides (*AC, BC*) of the triangle. Select the Points menu again, but this time the third option: Point at Intersection. Move the cursor to each intersection and click to define a point (*Q,R*). (step 5)
- Finally, we create a circle whose centre is the third vertex (*C*) and which passes through one of the intersection points (*Q*). Create the intersection point (*S*) of this third circle and the remaining segment (*BC*). If you like you can put labels on the point using the tenth icon and selecting Label from the menu. As you click on each point you can enter a label in a little dialogue box. (step 6)
- Now we have seen some of the mechanics of drawing we can use the results for geometry. First drag *P* on *AB* until the intersections *S* and *R* are as close as possible. Now we can try to make some conjectures from the picture. For example, we know that tangents at *P* and *Q* to the circles are perpendicular to the lines of centres *AB* and *AC*.

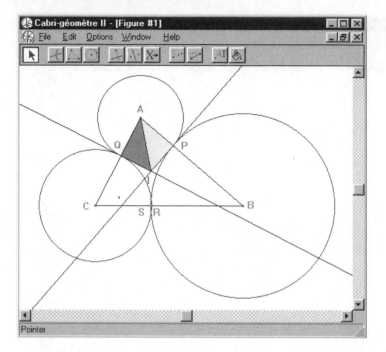

Use the fifth icon to open up the main construction menu and select Perpendicular. Click first on *P*, then anywhere on *AB* to construct the perpendicular to *AB* through *P*. Repeat for the perpendicular to *AC* through *Q*. Create the intersection point and label it *I*. Also create the segment *AI*. Use the third icon and select the Triangle menu item. Click in turn on *A*,*P* and *I*. Repeat for *A*,*Q* and *I*. From the last icon menu choose Fill, select a colour from the palette and click on triangle *API*, repeat to fill *AQI* with a different colour. (step 7)

✎   *What can you deduce about these triangles?*

- You can also use the measurement tool (ninth icon) to select Distance and Length, and then click in turn on segments *IP* and *IQ* to check whether they are equal in this case. The point *I*, which is equidistant from sides *AB*, *AC* must also be equidistant from *BC* in the 'ideal' case. So this gives us another way of characterizing points *P*,*Q*,*R*: they are where the in-circle, centre *I*, touches the sides *AB*, *BC*, *CA*. (step 8)
- Double-click on the point *P* and select Edit Cut. Everything dependent on *P* will now be removed. Construct the angle bisectors of *BAC* and *ABC* (use the Construction tool and click in turn on the three points defining the angle). Create and label their intersection point *I*. Use the Hide/Show menu item of the last icon to hide the angle bisectors. Now create the perpendiculars from *I* to each of the three sides. Then create and label their intersections with the sides. Hide the perpendiculars and create the circle centre *I* through *P*, and each of the three circles centres *A*, *B* and *C*. (step 9)

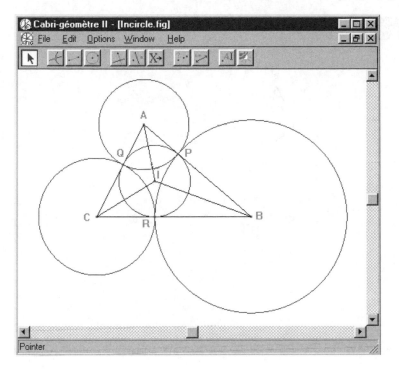

Sketchpad

Now we will see just how similar the approach is using Sketchpad. The major difference is that in Cabri you specify the construction first, and then the objects which are required to define it; whereas in Sketchpad you first highlight all the objects required to define the construction, and then select it from the appropriate menu.

- Again we start by fixing three points *A*, *B*, *C*. The vertical toolbar on the left of the screen shows six icons. The top one, the arrow, is the usual mode where the mouse just moves a pointer across the screen. If you click on the second icon you can create Points. Now use the cursor to position the pointer over the place you want one of the points, and then click the button to place it there. Repeat to put two other points on the screen. Now click on the first icon, the pointer.
- The next step is to join the points by segments. At the moment the most recently drawn point is highlighted. Move the mouse in turn over the other two points and click to highlight these as well. Now open up the Construct menu – the fourth from the left at the top of the screen. Only those constructions which can be made with three points will be highlighted, such as Angle Bisector. Select Segments from the menu. All three sides of the triangle are now drawn and highlighted.
- Now we shall make a variable point on one of the sides. Click on two of the sides to remove the highlighting, leaving just one side highlighted. Use the Construct menu to define a Point on Segment. Check that you can slide this point freely along, but not off, the segment.

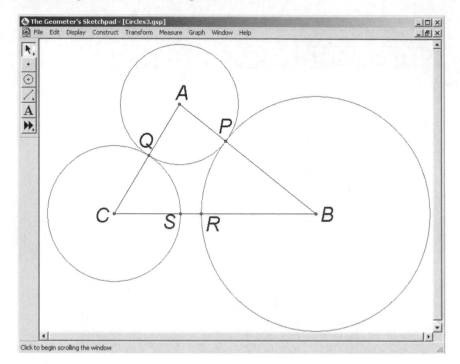

- Now we can construct the circles whose centres are the end-points of this segment (*A*,*B*) and which pass through the variable point (*P*). Click the mouse anywhere on the blank background – this a short way of making sure nothing is currently highlighted. Then click first on the centre point (*A*), and then on the radius point (*P*). From the Construct menu select Circle By Center+Point. Similarly, first click anywhere on the background, then on points (*B*) and (*P*), and construct the circle centre (*B*) through (*P*). Click on the background and then check that as you slide (*P*) both dependent circles change size.
- Now we can find their points of intersection with the other two sides (*AC*, *BC*) of the triangle. Click on the background and move the cursor over the intersection point (*Q*) on (*AC*) – and when the message 'Click to construct the intersection' appears in the bottom left of the screen, click to define (*Q*). Similarly define the point (*R*) on (*BC*). Finally create the circle whose centre is the third vertex (*C*) and which passes through one of the intersection points (*Q*). Create the intersection point (*S*) of this third circle and the remaining segment (*BC*). If you like you can put labels on the point using the fifth icon 'A' in the toolbar. As you click on each point a label will appear. If you double-click on the label a dialogue box appears in which you change the label, as well as specifying font, size, colour, etc.
- So now we have seen some of the mechanics of drawing we can use the results for geometry. First drag *P* on *AB* until the intersections *S* and *R* are as close as possible. Now we can try to make some conjectures from the picture. For example, we know that tangents at *P* and *Q* to the circles are perpendicular to the lines of centres *AB* and *AC*.

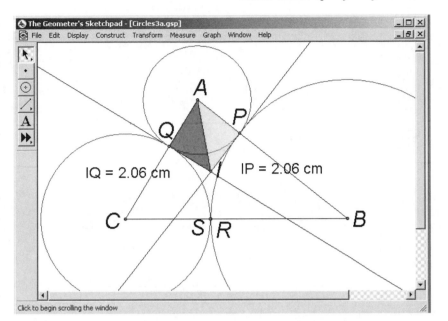

Click on the background and then click on the point P and anywhere on the segment AB. From the Construct menu choose Perpendicular Line to construct the line through P perpendicular to AB. Repeat using the point Q and the segment AC. Construct the intersection of the two perpendiculars and label it I. Construct the segment AI. Click to highlight just A, P, I and use Construct for the Triangle Interior. You can use the Display and Colour menus to change this, e.g. from yellow to blue. Repeat for the triangle AQI.

✏️   *What can you deduce about these triangles?*

- You can select I, P and use the Measure menu to select Distance. This gives the distance IP. Now also measure IQ to check whether they are equal in this case. The point I, which is equidistant from sides AB, AC must also be equidistant from BC in the 'ideal' case. So this gives us another way of characterizing points P, Q, R: they are where the in-circle, centre I, touches the sides AB, BC, CA.
- Highlight point P and select Cut from the Edit menu. Everything dependent on P will now be removed. Construct the angle bisectors of BAC and ABC (highlight the three points in turn that define the angle and from the Construction menu select Angle Bisector). Create and label their intersection point I. Select the two angle bisectors and from the Display menu select Hide. Now create the perpendiculars from I to each of the three sides. Then create and label their intersections with the sides. Hide the perpendiculars and create the circle centre I through P, and each of the three circles' centres A, B and C.

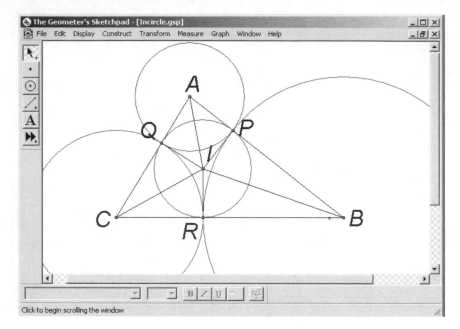

GeoGebra

GeoGebra has many features similar to Cabri. Its construction menu in particular is very similar but there are a few differences:

- To start with a clean geometry page, first close the left-hand algebra window; then select 'View' and deselect 'axes'. Steps 1 and 2 are then the same as for Cabri.
- To place a point on an object (such as a segment in step 3) select 'point' and then move towards the object. When the object (e.g. a segment) is highlighted (goes dark) click on it.
- To get a circle through a particular point (as in step 4), first select the centre then move towards the point until the cursor changes to an arrow.
- To get the intersection of two objects (as in step 5), move towards the point of intersection, and when both objects are highlighted (dark) click to select.
- Points can be labelled (step 6) by right clicking and selecting 'show label'. GeoGebra chooses its own labels for points and lines, but the labels can be changed using 'rename'.
- The main construction menu for perpendiculars and angle bisectors, etc. is the 4th icon. Note that the angle bisector in GeoGebra shows the bisector of both the interior angle and the exterior angle. Obtain the angle bisectors by selecting the two segments in turn that enclose the angle. The angle bisectors have been hidden in the following diagram. This can be done by right clicking on each of them in turn and deselecting 'show object'.
- To construct a triangle (as in step 7) you will need to select polygon and click on all three points and then the first point again to complete the triangle.
- To colour in the triangle, right click on the triangle and select 'properties'.

'Colour' allows you to change the colour; 'style' allows you to select the depth of colour or the thickness of lines. (step 8)
- The measurement tools are on the 8th icon. (step 9)

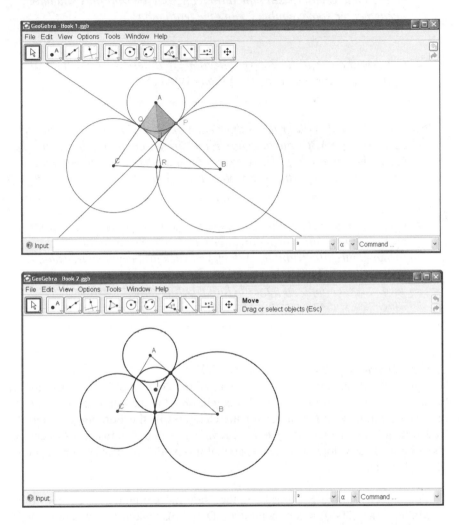

So now we have met the similarities, and a few differences, between Cabri, Sketchpad and GeoGebra as powerful tools for dynamic geometry. Why do you think the term 'dynamic' has come into common use here?

✎ *Can you set up a diagram with a circle and a chord to illustrate circle properties, such as the centre lies on its perpendicular bisector, angles subtended in the same segment are equal, angles subtended in opposite segments add up to 180 degrees, etc.?*

✎ *Experiment with some of the other icons and menus such as the one for working with transformations! For translations you may need to create some vectors, using the third icon, and for rotations you may need to enter some numbers using the tenth icon.*

✎ *Can you show that successive reflections in different mirror lines are equivalent to a single transformation? What is it?*

✎ *Can you set up a diagram to show each of the major centres of the same triangle ABC: the in-centre I, the circum-centre O, the centroid G and the ortho-centre H? As you deform the triangle can you find any invariant properties connecting I, O, G and H?*

✎ *If you are unfamiliar with any of the terms in the previous question try researching them using an internet search. For example, try 'ortho-centre of a triangle'. Which websites are useful sources for this and would be worth remembering for future reference? (You may need to try a couple of pages before you find maths.thesaurus.org which has some interesting features.)*

3.6(a2) Dynamic geometry software in 3D

Visualizing in 3D can be very difficult without the aid of models, at least initially, but it is a very necessary life skill. This is reinforced in the introduction to a paper mentioned earlier in this chapter for the Congress of the European Society for Research in Mathematics Education (CERME), Larnaca, Cyprus, 22–26 February 2007, entitled 'Developing student spatial ability with 3D software applications'. The authors quote:

> The Principles and Standards of the National Council of Teachers of Mathematics (2000) recommend that 2D and 3D spatial visualization and reasoning are core skills that all students should develop. For example, students in grades 3–5 'should become experienced in using a variety of representations for three-dimensional shapes' such as isometric drawings, a set of views (e.g. top, front, and right), and building plans. The field of 3-dimensional geometry is a particularly fertile one for visualization and imagery research. In ascertaining geometric properties of 3-dimensional figures, visual perception plays a major role, and in recalling and describing 3-dimensional figures, image formation is a key ingredient.

The paper deals with middle-school children and the importance of early visualization. Without this experience students are likely to experience difficulties with some aspects of later examination courses and with the expectation in both textbook and examination questions that they can interpret 3D questions. Questions are either given being just in words or with 2D diagrams used to represent 3D situations. Some examples are

- visualizing right-angled triangles in order to use Pythagoras' theorem or trigonometry in 3D;
- visualizing plans and elevations of a 3D object;
- constructing nets of common solids and visualizing which edges or corners connect;
- more advanced work on 3D coordinate geometry such as vectors and equations of lines and planes.

There are applets on the internet to do some of these, some of which have been mentioned earlier in this chapter.

Yenka 3D shapes

Yenka provides educational modelling software from Crocodile Clips in a variety of contexts for mathematics and other subjects. 'Yenka 3D shapes' allows easy access to 3D modelling. You can start by dragging ready-made shapes onto the screen and open them to show their nets using a right-click menu and selecting 'properties' and 'open' under the 'actions' heading. It is also possible to measure lengths, areas and volumes by dragging the measurement tools onto the object. The measurements can also be viewed by right clicking and selecting the 'properties' menu mentioned earlier.

✎ *How many different square-based prisms with integer edges can you find with a volume of 96 cm³? Which has the least surface area? What about other prisms?*

Cabri 3D

Cabri 3D is a 3D dynamic geometry software package that contains many geometrical features similar to the 2D version. Solids can be created and measured, and opened to reveal nets using the 'open polyhedron' feature.

Cabri 3D models can also be easily exported to web-pages or to Microsoft Office 2007 applications (Word and PowerPoint™) where they can be used for live interactions by anyone who has installed the free 'plug-ins' which are available from Chartwell Yorke, along with a free trial version of the software.

✎ *What solid do you get when you join the centre points of each of the faces of a cube?*

✎ *What are the relative volumes of this new solid and the original cube?*

✎ *Can you prove your conjecture?*

A quick way to obtain a cube without a more detailed construction is to use the regular polyhedron menu (2nd from the right) and select 'cube'. Go towards the marked plane and select 'face in this plane' and then move towards the origin and select 'face centred on this point', and finally drag the cube out to a suitable size and select 'a given new point on this plane'.

The next step is to draw in a diagonal for each of the faces of the cube by selecting the 'Line' tool (3rd from the left) and 'segment'. Then go to one vertex of the cube and select 'segment defined by this vertex', move to the opposite corner of that face and select 'and this vertex'. Repeat this for all six faces.

Then select the 'construction' tool (5th from the left) and 'midpoint'. Go to each of the diagonals you have created in turn and select 'midpoint of this segment'.

Finally select the 8th icon from the left and 'convex polyhedron'; systematically select each of your six midpoints in turn and then click on one point again to 'validate polyhedron'.

✎ *What polyhedron have you created? Is this what you expected? Why?*

✎ *You may need to make the cube transparent to view the other polyhedron (see below).*

You can change the appearance of planes, lines and points by using the pointer tool (1st left) and right clicking to change the colour, point size, line thickness or surface style. Small hatches for the surface style will mean that you can see through the solid.

You can add measurements by choosing the far right-hand icon. Choose 'volume' and move first towards the cube and select. Then move towards the polyhedron and select. Drag the measurements to where they are more clearly visible.

Using the pointer tool and selecting 'this cube' and dragging it to resize will give you different volume measurement for both cube and polyhedron.

✎ *What do you notice about the volumes of the cube and polyhedron?*

✎ *Can you prove your conjecture?*

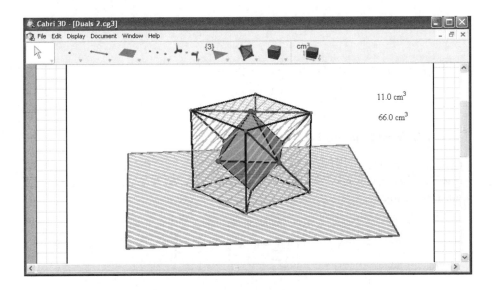

✎ *Can you create a sphere which passes through the vertices of the polyhedron?*

✎ *What is the relationship between the faces of the cube and this sphere?*

✎ *Investigate for other regular polyhedra.*

3.6(b) Graph-plotting software (GPS)

Many of the software packages that plot graphs include other applications as well, such as dynamic geometry or statistical features including lists and spreadsheets. A key feature of these packages is their ability to link more than one application and thus different areas of mathematics. We shall look at a few graphing examples considering the following problem:

> ✎ *How many different graphs or pairs of graphs can you draw that would help you to solve this equation?*
>
> $$x = 1 + \frac{1}{x}$$

> ✎ *Which graphs have been chosen for each of the following examples?*

> ✎ *How are they used to solve the equation?*

Microsoft Word Math Add-in

If you have the Math Add-in, select add-ins and then Math. Enter the equation, then right click and select 'plot in 2D'. If you select trace and trace along the curve you can stop the trace at strategic points to reveal the coordinates.

$$y = 1 + \frac{1}{x} - x$$

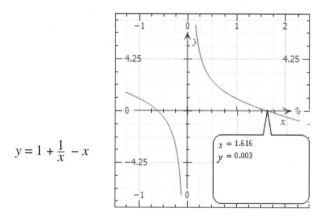

TI-Nspire™

TI-Nspire™ is a hand-held device which resembles a graphing calculator, such as the TI-84, but it has a larger screen and a redesigned keyboard. In fact it is a dedicated hand-held computer running a package called TI-Nspire™ which is also available as a software package for use in a Windows PC. There are two versions of both the hand-held and the software with computer algebra system (CAS) and without, plus a teacher edition of the software which includes an emulator to demonstrate the use of the hand-held. There are five pages that can be added to a TI-Nspire™ document:

- Calculator (this includes symbolic algebra manipulation in the CAS version)
- Graphs and Geometry
- Lists and Spreadsheets
- Notes
- Data and Statistics

A particular feature of TI-Nspire™ is the ability to combine the different features of graphing and geometry. In this case the Geometrical feature to mark intersection points accurately has been used to find the intersection of two graphs.

Hand-held	Software
Select the home key (a house top right). Use the arrows on the central button to move to '6 New document'. Select this using the central button, then in a similar way select the application, in this case 'graphs and geometry'.	Run the software and then on the prompt 'Click here to add an application' select the application, in this case 'graphs and geometry'.
The menu for a particular application page is obtained by selecting the 'menu' key.	The menu for a particular application is shown at the top of the page. The meaning and reference number for each of the symbols is the same as the hand-held one shown on the left.

On both hand-held and in the software, select '3: Graph Type' and 'function'. Then type in the first function in the entry line.
Repeat the procedure and type in the second function.
   You can adjust the axes and scale by selecting '4: Window' and any one of the given options or Window settings to select your own scales.
   To find the intersection point, first select '6: Points & Lines' and then select '3: Intersection Points'. Move to the intersection of the two graphs and select.

The hand-held menu shows:

1: Actions
2: View
3: Graph Type
4: Window
5: Trace
6: Points & Lines
7: Measurement
8: Shapes
9: Construction
A: Transformation
B: Hints

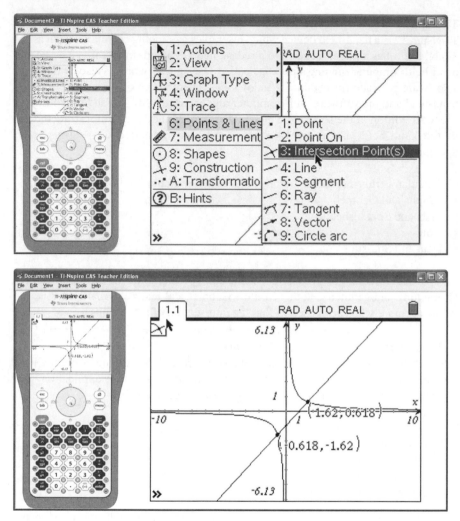

The Mathematical Toolkit

In collaboration with Intel and The Mathematical Association, the Mathematical Toolkit and Number line were designed specifically to support the teaching and learning of mathematics for students. The tools have been developed in Macromedia Flash, so that teachers and students can access them via the internet without needing to purchase any software. The toolkit provides four basic tools: Number line; 2D shapes; Coordinates and graphing; and Charting. The toolkit and supporting materials are available to download free from the 'London grid for Learning' website at `http://lgfl.skoool.co.uk/common.aspx?id=901`

The example below has been done using the graphing tool.

Select 'Graphing', then enter the equations in the boxes for y1, y2, etc., using the calculator pad that emerges when the cursor is placed in the box for each function. Graph window, scales and axes can be adjusted by selecting 'grid settings'.

Select 'Update/Delete coordinates' to place a point at the intersection of the graphs to find their point of intersection.

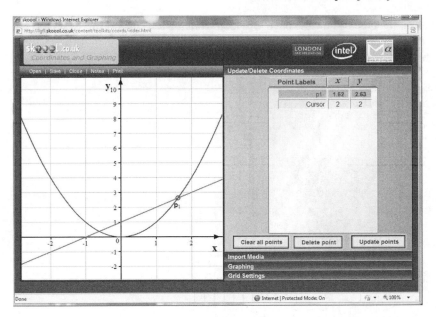

The 'Import media' feature gives you a selection of images or video-clips to import. You can add points to these and fit functions.

Autograph

Autograph is a dynamic graphing package incorporating coordinate and transformation geometry in 2- and 3D, statistical graphing and other data-handling features.

Here a single graph has been entered by selecting 'Equation' on the top menu and then 'enter equation' and typing the equation in the form $y = \ldots$ Hovering near the point of intersection of the graph and the x axis, right click and select solve $f(x) = 0$. The solution appears in the 'results box' on the right. If this box does not appear, select it from the 'view' menu on the top line.

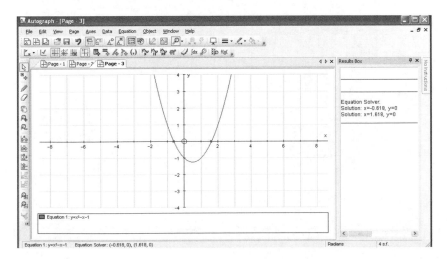

Graphs in 3D: Open a new 3D page (3rd icon from the left); use 'axes' to set the x, y and z axis scales and limits; use 'equation' to enter the equation which for a 3D graph may have more than one line.

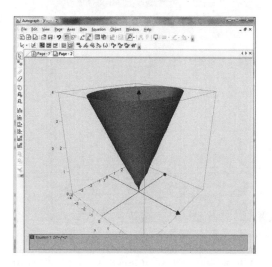

Solids of revolution: Autograph can also be used to generate solids of revolution. On a 3D page select '*x-y* orientation' from the menu on the far left icon. From the 'Equation' menu select 'Enter an equation' type in the equation in the form $y = f(x)$, and in the same window select the 'plot as 2D' option.

Next, click on the graph or two points attached to the graph and right click and select 'Find area'. Select one of the four options rectangle +/− or Trapezium or Simpson's rules and enter the x-limits for the area and the number of steps for the trapezium/Simpson's rule, etc. Select the shaded area and right click and select 'Find volume'. Enter the axis of rotation (this defaults to y = 0). Now return to the far left icon and select '*x-y-z* orientation' to rotate the solid and change the viewing angle.

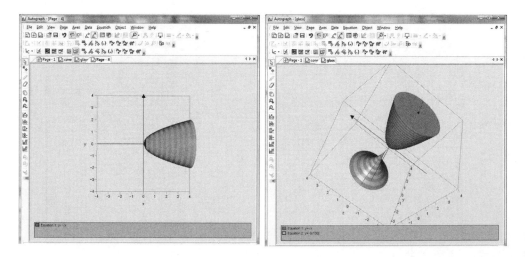

✎   *These Autograph screen-shots show an attempt to model a wine glass.*
Can you improve on this or find suitable curves to model other glasses?

The DALEST applet 'Potter's wheel' mentioned in section 3.2 also looks at visualizing solids of revolution.

✎   *Experiment with graph-plotting packages to find their individual*
capabilities.

✎   *Try to draw graphs of functions defined parametrically, or by polar*
coordinates, or in 3D where the features allow these facilities.

3.6(c) Computer algebra systems (CASs)

TI-Nspire™ has both a CAS and a non-CAS version. Open a 'Calculator' page in TI-Nspire™ then select '3: Algebra' and '1: Solve'. Type the golden ratio equation into the brackets, followed by a comma and an *x* (or the variable used in the equation). The CAS version will give an exact solution.

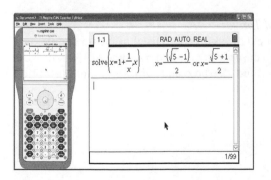

There is much debate around the world about when and whether to introduce students to CAS software. The debate is in many ways similar to the debate about allowing younger students access to basic calculators. Powerful CAS tools are used by engineers and others, both to save tedious algebraic manipulations and to ensure accuracy; however, it is important for students also to develop the necessary skills themselves in order to be able to appreciate the appropriate use of these tools and to check that solutions are reasonable. Using CAS can offer several possibilities for students:

- They give students access to powerful modelling tools enabling them to appreciate and solve more complex problems than would otherwise be possible.
- They can be used as tools for rapidly generating examples to enable investigating algebraic concepts such as finding the coefficients of x^n in the expansion of $(1 + x)^n$. For example, Ti-Nspire CAS™ and the 'Expand' function on the 'Algebra' menu has been used here to develop successive expansions.

$\text{expand}\left((1+x)^2\right)$	$x^2+2{\cdot}x+1$
$\text{expand}\left((1+x)^3\right)$	$x^3+3{\cdot}x^2+3{\cdot}x+1$
$\text{expand}\left((1+x)^4\right)$	$x^4+4{\cdot}x^3+6{\cdot}x^2+4{\cdot}x+1$
$\text{expand}\left((1+x)^5\right)$	$x^5+5{\cdot}x^4+10{\cdot}x^3+10{\cdot}x^2+5{\cdot}x+1$
$\text{expand}\left((1+x)^6\right)$	$x^6+6{\cdot}x^5+15{\cdot}x^4+20{\cdot}x^3+15{\cdot}x^2+6{\cdot}x+1$

3.6(d) Data-handling and modelling software (DHS)

Several of the software packages already mentioned such as Autograph have facilities for entering, displaying and analysing data. In addition, Fathom is a dedicated statistical package with facilities to plot values and functions on top of data and vary them dynamically; build simulations to illustrate concepts from probability and statistics; demonstrate standard statistical analyses; set up populations and sample from them. Here is a selection of easily accessible examples using different software.

Box plots using the Mathematical Toolkit
The charting tool of the Mathematical Toolkit can be used to create simple data charts. In this example the masses (to the nearest gram) of a sample of 15 shells were entered into the first data column and the box and whisker graphing option selected.

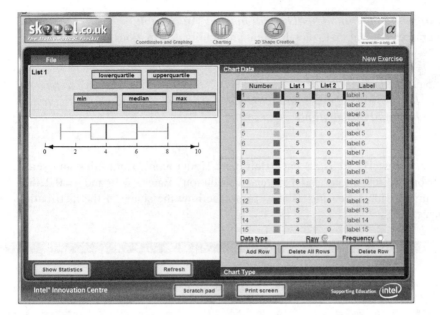

Comparing box-plots using TI-Nspire™

In this example the masses (to the nearest gram) of two samples of 20 shells from two different beaches (a and b) are entered into the columns of a data and statistics page. Each column is selected in turn and then following a right click (or menu selection on the hand-held), select 'quick graph' then right click again and choose 'box-plot'. Repeat for the second column of data. The box-plots can then be compared.

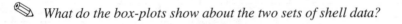

✎   *What do the box-plots show about the two sets of shell data?*

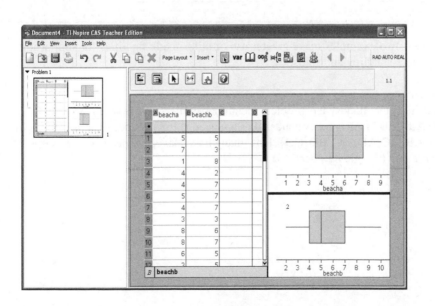

Investigating the binomial distribution using Autograph
Autograph has a feature to plot different probability distributions.

✎   *If the probability of success* (p) = 0.2, *how large does* n *have to be for the Normal distribution to be a reasonable approximation to the binomial distribution?*

Open a new 1D statistics page (left-hand sigma icon), right click and select 'Probability distributions' and 'binomial distribution'. Enter $n = 10$ and $p = 0.2$, then experiment with increasing values of n to see how the shape of the distribution changes.

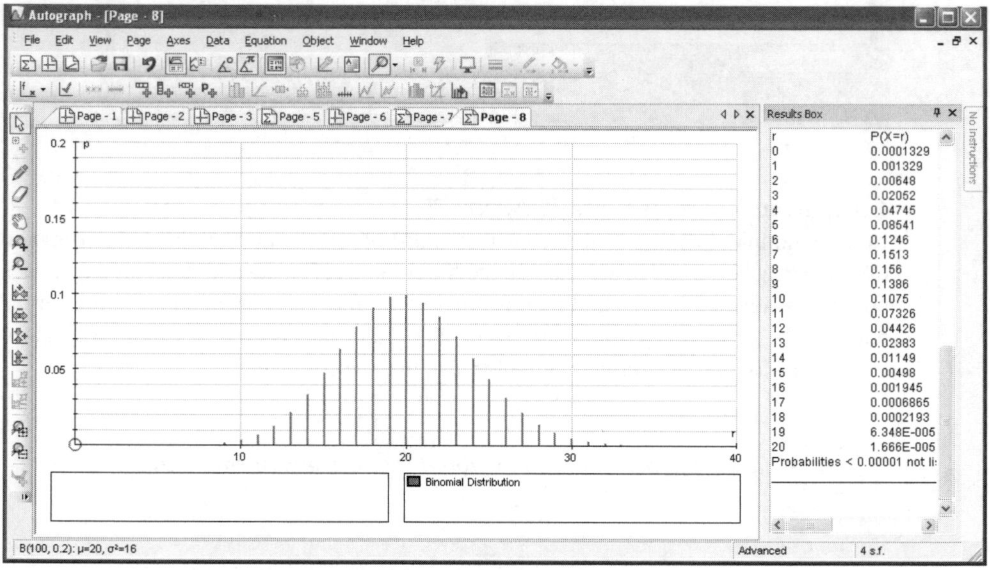

The next two examples make greater use of tailor-made facilities for supporting work in data-handling and statistics.

TI-Nspire™
We will study the 'handshake' problem mentioned earlier. That is when there are four people A,B,C,D in a room, six handshakes are needed to introduce everyone to each other: {AB, AC, AD, BC, BD, CD}. How many handshakes are needed for *n* people? These are the 'triangle numbers'.

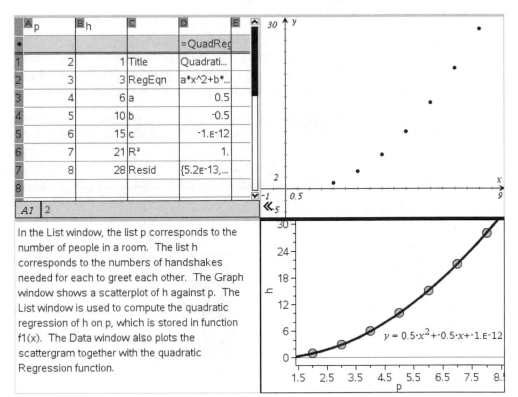

	A p	B h	C		D		E
					=QuadReg		
1	2		1	Title	Quadrati...		
2	3		3	RegEqn	a*x^2+b*...		
3	4		6	a	0.5		
4	5		10	b	-0.5		
5	6		15	c	-1.E-12		
6	7		21	R²	1.		
7	8		28	Resid	{5.2E-13,...		
8							

A1 2

In the List window, the list p corresponds to the number of people in a room. The list h corresponds to the numbers of handshakes needed for each to greet each other. The Graph window shows a scatterplot of h against p. The List window is used to compute the quadratic regression of h on p, which is stored in function f1(x). The Data window also plots the scattergram together with the quadratic Regression function.

First we use a List and Spreadsheet window. In the first column we create a list called '*p*' in which we enter the numbers {2,3,4,5,6,7,8} as the numbers of people in a room. In list '*h*' we enter the corresponding number of handshakes required: {1,3,6,10,15,21,28}.

We can then open a Graphs and Geometry window, and select the Plot type as Scatterplot. In the entry line at the foot of the window we can enter, or select, the list variables to use for the scatterplot, i.e. *p* and *h*. We can use Window Settings to adjust the scales. Back in the List window we can use the Stat Calculations tool to select Quadratic regression, and to specify the lists to be used and where the results are to be displayed and stored.

We could draw the function graph of $y = f1(x)$ over the scatterplot in the Graph window. Instead we have chosen to illustrate another tool from the Data & Statistics window. In this we construct the scatterplot by selecting the list names for the axes. Then from the Regression menu we can select Show Quadratic. Of course we need to remember that our original data was discrete (you can only have a whole number of people!) whereas our new function is continuous and so can be evaluated, e.g. for $n = 3.7$ which doesn't make much sense in the context of our original problem!

Finally we can write comments about our work in a Text Window. So the one screen-shot above illustrates just how versatile the software is, for example for teachers to create students' task sheets, or for students to write their own reports.

Fathom

Fathom, by contrast, has a freer format where different kinds of objects – tables, graphs, texts, etc. – can be placed anywhere on the page. Its main limitation is that it only implements linear regression, and you need to transform the data or adopt a different approach if you want, e.g., quadratic regression, as is illustrated next.

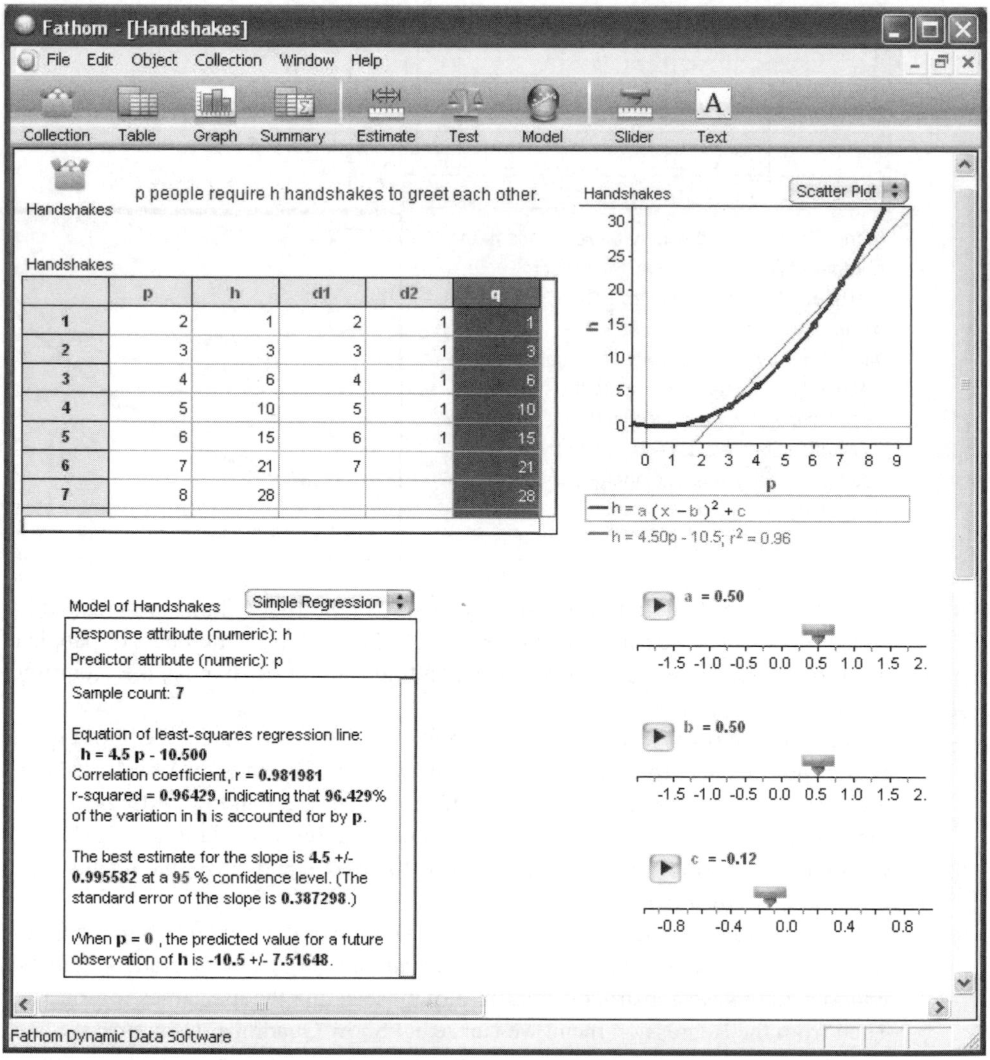

The collection, called 'Handshakes' is formed from a table with a number of 'Attributes' as its columns. The first two of these is the data for people 'p' and handshakes 'h'. In a Graph window we can plot the scattergraph of h against p. In a Model window we can fit a linear regression to h against p, and we can plot the graph of the resulting function as a straight line in the Graph window. We can drag in Sliders and set them up to control the values of the coefficients a, b, c of the function $h = a(x - b)^2 + c$ used to model h. This function is plotted on the graph and used to define the column q in the table.

Mathematical modelling consists of a range of techniques used to predict the future state of a system from current values about its variables and assumptions about the ways in which they are related. For example, radioactive decay is usually modelled by a statement like 'The rate at which the substance loses its radioactivity is proportional to its current level of radiation'. This could be interpreted as a *discrete* model, where we assume that the rate stays constant for small intervals of time dt, or a *continuous* model, where the rate is the instantaneous value of the derivative:

Discrete: $dr = -k*r*dt$ giving the sequence: $r(n+1) = r(n) + dr = r(n) - k*r(n)*dt$

Continuous: $dr/dt = -k*r$ giving the solution: $r = r_0*e^{-kt}$

Many of the more interesting continuous models produce differential equations which cannot be solved analytically, and so require a numerical technique, such as a Runge-Kutta method. Using modelling software we can express the relations between variables using algebra, as well as setting values for constants and for the initial values of variables. It also gives us tools to make the creation of representations such as graphs, tables and animations easier.

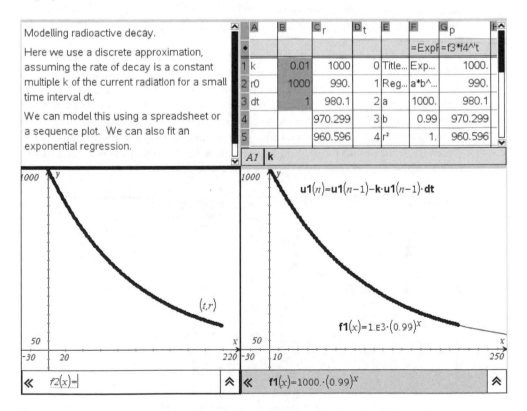

A very powerful modelling system is provided by the free Modellus software, `http://modellus.fct.unl.pt/`, used in the Advancing Physics course: `http://advancingphysics.iop.org/`.

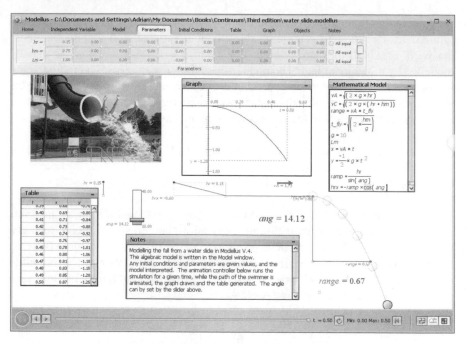

The model is entered using mathematical notation in a Modelling window. You define the Parameters and Initial Conditions needed to complete it, and then, when the model has been validated, you can build animations and display graphs and tables which change dynamically when the animation controller is reset and run (at the foot of the screen). For those who want to produce their own animations, the US Open Source Physics project has produced a package called Easy Java Simulations. The screen below illustrates its use. You can find out more at `http://www.compadre.org/osp/search/categories.cfm?t=Overview`.

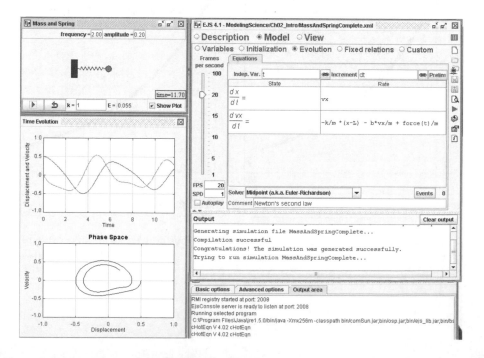

3.7 DATA-CAPTURE SOFTWARE

Many of us have had to become familiar with the ways in which our developing technological world gathers data about us, from CCTV surveillance in buildings and towns to swipe cards for access to buildings and transport. Many of the technological artefacts on which we rely, not just cars and central heating but also washing machines and fridges, are constantly monitoring gathered data both to improve performance and to help with diagnosis in case of breakdown. A long vehicle, such as a coach, may have several aids to help the driver when reversing other than the conventional optical mirrors – for example one or more video cameras to cover the 'blind spots', and also distance sensors to detect the range of the nearest object. Sometimes data is gathered at a distance and transmitted wirelessly to a control point, such as is the case with *telemetry* used on F1 racing cars. Here data is captured from sensors around the car, e.g. temperature, tyre pressure and fuel usage, and transmitted by radio to the race team HQ in the pits. At the same time, small wireless cameras can be sending TV pictures from the car of both the track and the driver. Recent domestic examples of this technology are to be seen in the way 'game stations' such as Wii, PlayStation Portable and X-box now use sensors and/or video capture to monitor the motions of players simulating rolling balls down skittle alleys, hitting golf balls down a fairway or participating in other sports such as football, tennis or cricket. We can use many simple examples of these kinds of technology to enliven mathematics teaching as well as to make it more relevant to the world inhabited by modern learners!

3.7(a) Data-logging

Here there are three main components to consider. The first, known as 'probeware', is the range of sensing devices that are available and practical for schools' use. The second is the hardware/software combination needed to capture data from the probes and sensors and then with which to process, analyse and communicate. The third, often the most frustrating, is the means of connection between the devices! For convenience we will treat imaging devices, such as webcams, cameras and video recorders as a separate type of data-logging – at least for the moment.

There is a pretty wide range of suppliers of educational probes and sensors: Data Harvest, Deltronics, Fourier, LogIT, Philip Harris, Pasco, Sciencescope, Texas Instruments, Valiant, Vernier and XLogger. A useful review of their products can be found at `http://rogerfrost.com/equipment.html`. Those of particular importance for mathematics are distance (or motion-detectors), temperature probes, force gauges, microphones, light gauges, accelerometers, voltage probes, pressure gauges and heart-rate sensors. More recently, we have seen a proliferation in devices using data from GPSs. So now, when you capture a piece of datum, such as a temperature, you can also keep with it data about the time, latitude, longitude and altitude at which it was recorded. This opens up completely new aspects of graphical representation and interpretation, with large implications for cross-curricular work.

There are also many choices of equipment for processing the data. At the simplest is a device (PC or hand-held) into which you can plug one or more probes directly, e.g. a laptop with probes connected through the USB ports. Among hand-held devices are graphing calculators from Casio, HP and Texas Instruments, the TI-Nspire™ hand-held, and special purpose data-logging devices, e.g. from Fourier, Sciencescope and Vernier. The hand-held devices also have their own special purpose software for data-processing already installed. We will illustrate examples for TI-Nspire™ and the TI-84 graphing calculator. For the PC there is also quite a choice of software – and from that available we will illustrate examples for Vernier's Logger Lite and Logger Pro.

Each brand of sensor will have its own (sometimes unique) choice of connector, e.g. BT connector, DIN plug, phono connector or USB plug (mini, normal or square). Sometimes these can be connected directly to the PC, or else they need to be connected via a hub or interface box. Some will connect wirelessly to the PC, using e.g. Bluetooth.

While that may sound a bit bewildering, in practice, once you have decided what sorts of experiments you want to build into your scheme of work, they should be easy and reliable to set up. See, for example, the uses of the CBR motion-detector documented in the next chapter. Ideally, any new acquisition of data-capture systems should be discussed with science and technology colleagues to ensure maximum usage, as well as curriculum coherence and cost-sharing!

The use of a very portable motion-detector, such as Texas Instruments' Calculator Based Ranger (CBR2™), provides a simple means of getting real data, gathered first hand, for analysis in mathematics classes. The CBR2™ can be set up for use either controlled by a GC or a PC. Here we give examples of its use both with the TI-83/4 and with TI -Nspire™.

The TI-84 Plus comes with a ready loaded application called CBL/CBR. If you are using a model which does not have it pre-loaded then you can download and install it, using TI-Connect and suitable cable, from `http://education.ti.com/educationportal/sites/US/productDetail/us_cbl_cbr_83_84.html`. Just press the purple (or blue) APPS key, select the CBL/CBR application, and select 3:Ranger from the first menu.

Use 'EXEC' and cursor down to 'RANGER', then press 'ENTER' twice. From the Main Menu select 1:SETUP/SAMPLE, and then adjust the settings as below. For example, to cycle through the possibilities for 'BEGIN ON' just place the cursor on that line and press 'ENTER' repeatedly to see the options available. When you have set it up, cursor to the top line of the screen next to 'START NOW' and press 'ENTER'. Now you can take your TI-84 and CBR for a walk. Point the CBR at a wall, press 'ENTER' on the TI-84, and walk back and forwards until the CBR stops ticking (15 seconds).

As you walk, the distance–time graph is shown at the same time. Can you interpret the graph above? Can you explain the little 'spike' around 15 seconds? Press 'ENTER' to get to the next menu. If you go back to the main menu and change the settings to read 'REALTIME: NO' then you can sample over longer or shorter periods. Then you can also change the representation to velocity–time or acceleration–time graph.

TI-Nspire™ computer software also provides facilities to capture data directly from the CBR2™. Plug the connector cable into the square socket on the left-hand side of the CBR2™. Run TI-Nspire™ on your computer and then plug the free end of the cable into a USB port. You will be asked which application should be opened to capture the data. Select Lists & Spreadsheet. The window at the bottom of the screen will show the current distance measurement read from the CBR2™. When you are ready to collect data just press the green arrow in this window.

The system is set up initially to capture data at intervals of 0.05s for 5s. You can use Setup Experiment to change these values. Now, as you move in front of the CBR2™ so the data is logged in the CBR2™ and also transferred to the computer.

	A dc01.ti...	B dc01.d...	C dc01.v...	D dc01.a...	E
◆					
1	0.	0.719634	-0.35579	-0.154942	
2	0.05	0.701948	-0.363271	-0.144635	
3	0.1	0.683641	-0.370758	0.084519	
4	0.15	0.664141	-0.347504	0.406471	
5	0.2	0.648407	-0.299778	0.384903	
6	0.25	0.634382	-0.251103	0.429934	
7	0.3	0.62281	-0.18731	0.420582	
8	0.35	0.615867	-0.130112	0.548733	
9	0.4	0.610081	-0.083222	0.560122	
10	0.45	0.607231	-0.02467	0.863882	
11	0.5	0.607421	0.0454	1.53373	
12	0.55	0.611705	0.118715	2.00276	
13	0.6	0.619425	0.186817	1.95786	
14	0.65	0.630444	0.248248	1.42379	
15	0.7	0.644555	0.296583	1.14132	
16	0.75	0.660134	0.338353	0.922936	

A9 =0.40000000596046

▷ Dist   **0.3 m**   ☒

It is stored in the four lists shown. By splitting the screen vertically you can add a Data & Statistics window and display the scattergram of distance against time.

The CBR2™ is a special purpose device for sensing distances. There are other probes, such as Vernier's EasyTemp, which connect directly to the mini-USB port of hand-held devices, like the TI-Nspire™ and TI-84 Plus units, and also ones, such as

Vernier's GoTemp!, which connect to USB ports on a PC. In order to connect a sensor with a BT connector, such as a light probe or voltage probe, there are adaptors for use either with hand-helds (EasyLink) and PCs (Go!Link).

In the first experiment we shall place the temperature probe in a mug of hot water for a minute or so to heat up. Then when we click on the green arrow in the Data Capture window we can remove the sensor from the liquid and let it cool in air. The resulting decay data can be captured and graphed, just as before. This time we use a couple of Sliders in the Data & Statistics window to experiment modelling with exponential decay.

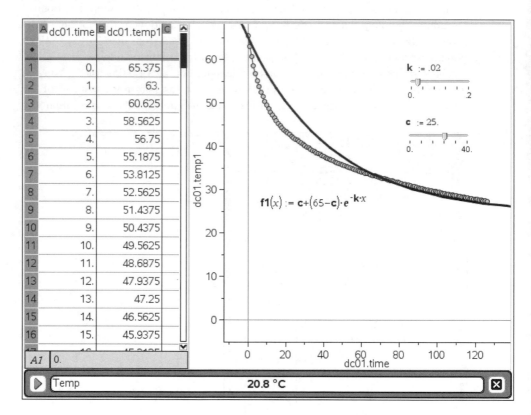

For our final example in this section we will use a voltage probe with BT connector in conjunction with a Vernier Go!Link connector. Here we have set up a very simple circuit consisting of a 220μF capacitor wired in parallel to a 100Ω resistor across a 9V cell. After the capacitor has charged up, the cell is disconnected and the data-capture begins, this time using Vernier's free Logger Lite software. Once the data is collected in the lists they can be copied and pasted into another application for subsequent analysis and modelling.

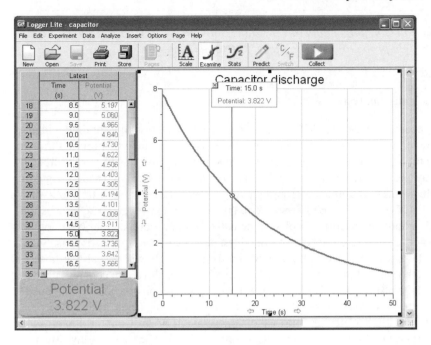

Here we have pasted the data into MS Excel™, and used it to draw a scattergram. Using Excel™'s 'trendline' tool we can see that we have an excellent exponential decay-model fit.

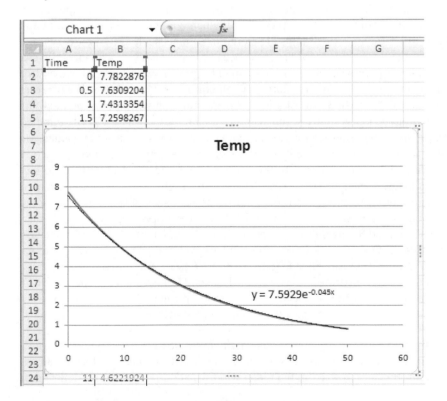

✎ *You can collect data at very short time intervals. Can you set up the light probe to show the flicker rate of a neon tube?*

3.7(b) Video analysis

Until recently we have tended to regard ICT as a presentation tool for digital images – allowing us to capture, edit and store them, as well include them in multimedia presentations, such as MS Powerpoint™. In some ways this has been reinforced by the way personal technology enables easy capture of images and video, e.g. with mobile phones, and uploading and sharing to websites such as `http://www.flickr.com` and `http://www.YouTube.com`. However, these images may contain important information of a mathematical nature! For example, a photograph taken with a camera, digital or not, contains a perspective view of its objects. So, for example, a photograph of a building taken from an angle will reveal that lines we know to be parallel in space, e.g. the horizontals in one elevation, actually meet in a point in the plane of the 2D picture. Similarly, a photograph of a water-fountain will 'freeze' the positions of lots of droplets of water all pursuing (more or less, depending on the wind and water pressure) the same trajectory. In Chapter 1 we used a photograph of an innocuous chain as a stimulus for a mathematical investigation. Even more information can be extracted from a video-clip, such as of the trajectory of a ball, or the movement of a mechanism like that of a water-sprinkler.

You can locate images and clips on the internet, buy them on CD/DVD, or take your own using digital cameras and/or camcorders. Images stored on computers use one of a number of types of compression of which common ones are called: bmp, jpg and tiff. Similarly, video-clips are stored in formats such as avi, mov, swf and wmv. Because each frame of video can consist of many pixels, and a video-clip can consist of many frames, video files can quickly become very large. However, for mathematical analysis a low-resolution avi clip of 320 × 240 or 640 × 480 pixels at frame rates of 20, 25 or 30 fps of a few seconds' duration will often contain all the information needed. Usually when you buy a camera there is a CD of 'bundled software' including tools to edit video so you can extract just the set of frames you want to analyse. With the advent of consumer cameras capable of taking video at frame rates between 200 and 1,000 fps we now have the capacity to collect information faster than the eye can see. High-quality, high-speed video has been used to capture sporting events, and to help improve performance of sportsmen, for some time – and some powerful software tools have been developed e.g. Dartfish, Quintic, Silicon Coach and Swinger Pro. With the support of the National Science Foundation in the USA, its Open Source Physics project has produced its own innovative tools, called Vidshell 2000 (download from: `http://www.webphysics.ccsnh.edu/vidshell/vidshell.html`) and Tracker 2 (a Java applet from: `http://www.cabrillo.edu/~dbrown/tracker/`). Vernier's Logger Pro 3 software also includes tools for video analysis, which can be synchronized with data captured from other probes.

For the first example we have taken a high-speed video of a fast bowler during a cricket match. With the Tracker 2 software we use the Video menu to load in our avi video-clip. It can be resized in the video window, and the clip can be replayed or single-stepped using the controller at the foot of that window. You can also select a starting and finishing clip for more precise analysis. Using the Tape-measure icon you can drag the arrow heads to an object of known proportions, such as the stumps, and a measurement given e.g. 0.711 m for their height. Using the Axes icon you can drag these to a sensible origin and change the direction of the axes to suit the action. When you select the Tracks menu you can choose Point Mass, and then use Shift-click to mark the current position of the ball, at which the data will be entered in the table and on the graph, and the video advanced by a frame. You can step forward another frame or two, if you wish, between collecting data. Clicking on either axis of the graph you can enter a different variable, but horizontal displacement x against time t is fine for now.

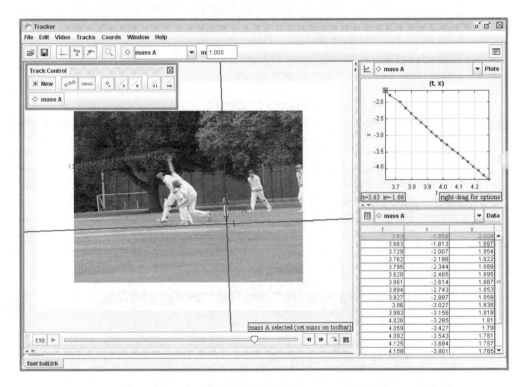

Of course you can copy the data out from the table to paste in another application for further analysis and modelling, or you can right click in the graph window and select Analyze to open up Trackers own analysis window. Here we can find that a very good approximation to the slope of the graph is 3.9. In fact the frame rate of the original video was 210 fps, although it is recognized by video software to play in slow motion at 30 fps. So time has been slowed down by a factor of 7, and this slope represents a speed of nearly 28 ms^{-1}.

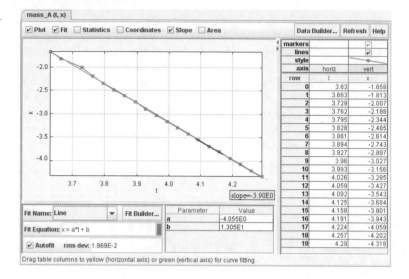

The final example shows Vernier's Logger Pro 3 used for both video-capture and data-logging for a dropped ball in a laboratory. A CBR2™ is mounted on a clamp on the retort stand above the point of release of the ball. As the ball moves, so its displacement is logged by the CBR2™. During the experiment the motion of the ball is captured on video using a camera on a tripod. From the Insert menu, this video-clip can be imported. The frame at which the video shows the release of the ball can be found, and synchronized with the distance-capture data. Using similar tools to the Tracker example above, the top point of the ball can be tracked frame by frame, and the data stored. Graphs can be drawn both from the logged data and from the video data. Using the modelling function, quadratic fits can be made to either graph, and used to estimate *g*, the acceleration due to gravity, with an accuracy of around 5 per cent.

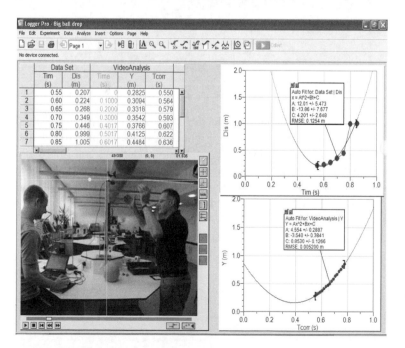

✎ *Can you suggest possible explanations for any inaccuracies in the measurements recorded from the CBR2™ and/or captured from the video?*

3.8 MULTIMEDIA TOOLS

This section describes a variety of more general tools which we feel could be useful for teachers and learners of mathematics, as well as other subjects, but which do not fall into the other more specific categories in this chapter.

3.8(a) Whiteboard tools

The Mathematical Association (MA) website has a link to a booklet offering advice on maximizing the potential of the features of interactive whiteboard `http://www.m-a.org.uk/jsp/index.jsp?lnk=140`. Although the materials that accompany the booklet are written specifically for SMARTboards, the booklet itself is a Word document which contains useful advice about general use of IWB tools. The booklet uses quotes from a variety of organizations to illustrate advantages of learning with IWBs.

Learners can interact with the board by being invited to solve a mathematical problem on it (`http://www.curriculumonline.gov.uk`).

Encourages more varied, creative and seamless use of teaching materials.

Engages students to a greater extent than conventional whole-class teaching, increasing enjoyment and motivation (`http://www.becta.org.uk`).

There are immediate gains in terms of student motivation, increased engagement in lessons, greater opportunities for student interactivity and a better understanding of concepts taught through the use of mixed learning styles – visual, aural and kinetic (`http://www.standards.dfes.gov.uk`).

Notes, diagrams and entire lessons can be saved, archived and added to the school intranet or similar centralized teaching resource (`http://www.kented.org.uk`).

Key features for mathematics lessons are the facility to be able to interact with dynamic software objects. Students can actively participate by physically manipulating images in dynamic geometry (2- and 3D) and graphing software. Examples of this can be seen in the Teachers TV programme *Hard to Teach Secondary Maths using ICT* (`http://www.teachers.tv/video/29853`).

3. 8(b) Screen-capture tools

There is now a variety of screen-capture tools available to make short movie clips demonstrating how a piece of software can be used for particular applications. They capture both the screen display and the movements of the mouse, and usually have sound-track facilities so that an audio explanation can be added.

The advantage of using this type of software is that it increases the speed and accessibility of explanations about how to use software, it is much more visual and kinaesthetic and it avoids lengthy and wordy explanations of processes with multiple screen-shots.

Professional software such as Camtasia allows the final movie to be produced in a variety of formats, e.g. for exporting to YouTube, or in a flash format, or to be played with Windows media player.

Jing is free screen-capture software which allows you to make short clips and to share them with others. The Jing project web page also has links to more professional software including Camtasia (`http://www.jingproject.com/`).

While some teachers are now beginning to use this technology to enhance their lessons and to help students to access software tools more easily, one school in the QCA project 'Engaging mathematics for all learners' `http://www.qcda.gov.uk/22221.aspx` had their students using the screen-capture software to make an instructional video for use by other students and by teachers. The software in question was for video analysis and was unfamiliar to most of the teachers as well as the students. There is also an increasing number of companies and others who are producing video-clips about specific software that are available on the internet. One such company is Atomic learning (`http://www.atomiclearning.com/uk/en/browse?page=tutorials`).

3.8(c) Design tools

Students increasingly have access to computer-aided design tools (CAD) in other subjects such as design technology, which could also enhance their mathematics, particularly in visualizing in 3D. Whilst CAD software can be expensive and sophisticated, and it may be difficult for the mathematics department to access it, there are some simple free-design tools available over the internet. One example is the IKEA Home Planner which allows users to put in the dimensions of their room, mark objects such as windows and doors and then to drag in items or furniture and rearrange them. It is possible to view the room in 3D and rotate to change the viewing angle, or to view from above. This real-life application could help to improve functional skills and could be suitable for students with learning difficulties (`http://www.ikea.com/ms/en_GB/rooms_ideas/splashplanners.html`).

3.8(d) Satellite imaging and mapping

There is a variety of mapping websites which show scales and have the facility to zoom in and out. These can be used to make otherwise difficult concepts such as relative areas with different scale factors more accessible. Satellite imagery adds another dimension to this. Google earth, for example, comes with some tools such as a measuring tool and direction-finder. There are lots of possibilities for using this. One example where a curve is fitted to a satellite image is given in Chapter 4. Some simple examples would be zooming in on the local tennis courts or a school football pitch or running-track to find measurements in order to be able to draw accurate scale plans of them; measuring the plot that your house stands on and finding the direction it faces; planning the track distance and course directions (bearings) for a round-an-island trip (`http://earth.google.co.uk/`).

Some software can output to Google earth to track movement.

3.8(e) Learning platforms

Many schools and colleges now have a virtual learning environment (VLE) and it is a target of the UK government that all schools should be making use of a full managed learning environment by 2010. Previously, local authorities have provided this service to some degree. One example is the London Grid for learning (LGfL) which created an online community to which any London teacher or student could belong and contribute and with shared access to digital resources (`http://www.lgfl.net`).

The existence of a virtual learning environment in schools is not a guarantee that it will be used creatively. It would be a great pity if having a shared online community that teachers and students can contribute to both in school and at home was simply used as a convenient means for storing, sharing and accessing worksheets and homework assignments. In the QCA project 'Engaging mathematics for all learners' there are examples which show how schools have used their VLE more creatively. One large school makes extensive use of the school's VLE to share activities and ideas between staff. They are particularly keen to show and share students' work in a variety of forms such as a video made jointly between students and the school's technician about the mathematics the students had found during a 'Playground project'. Another school encouraged students to do their own internet research on aspects of the golden ratio and Fibonacci sequence that particularly interested them and to share these with others on the VLE (`http://www.qcda.gov.uk/22221.aspx`).

3.8(f) Video-conferencing and real-time online classrooms

There is a variety of circumstances where face-to-face teaching is either impossible or impractical:

* For students not at school for a variety of reasons such as ill health or emotional or behavioural difficulties.
* For students of minority subjects such as Further Mathematics where there are not enough students in an institution to form a viable group.
* In remote sparsely populated areas of the world such as Alaska or Queensland in Australia.

In these situations video-conferencing or online classrooms provide a real opportunity for students to participate in a classroom situation and to interact with a teacher and other students in ways that would not have been possible before the widespread availability of fast broadband internet connections. Students can access live interactive tuition at flexible times and locations. Elluminate (`http://www.elluminate.com/`) and iLinc (`http://www.ilinc.com/`) are examples of providers of video-conferencing and online classroom facilities.

The Further Mathematics network delivers lessons to students from schools where it is not possible to offer the subject. It uses Elluminate which provides an online classroom with an IWB that both teachers and students can use; facilities to up-load documents such as PowerPoint™ presentations; lesson-recording and playback for absent students or for revision; application-sharing capability for working together on mathematical applications such as spreadsheets, dynamic geometry or graphing software. Communication happens via keyboard, via microphone and headset and through handwritten mathematics via a graphics tablet. The Further Mathematics network also provides in-service training courses for teachers which can be in an online classroom (`http://www.furthermaths.org.uk/`). Accipio Learning is another organization providing live, online teaching. They work in partnership with local education authorities and schools in the UK to provide education for students who are out of the mainstream classroom for a variety of reasons (`http://www.accipio-learning.com/`). Another such provider is the Nisai Virtual Academy (`http://www.nisai.com/`).

3.9 INTERNET RESOURCES

The range and variety of resources available to mathematics teachers via the internet are expanding so rapidly that all we can hope to do in this section is to highlight some resources that we know have already proved useful and to mention others that we think give a flavour of the variety available. We would encourage teachers to keep their own record of useful web references either by saving the URLs to organized folders in 'favourites' or in one or more Word documents or spreadsheets so they could be used on more than one PC. The advantage of using a Word document is that you can add a brief sentence about the URL to act as a reminder later. We have found it useful to separate an otherwise lengthy list under four headings:

- Sources of data and data-handling activities
- Sources of software, including freeware, and software specific support and activities
- Sources of interactive and online activities
- Classroom activities and pedagogical support.

It is the nature of web links, particularly to documents, that they go out of date quickly, so we have included titles that could be used as the basis of a search should the link prove unavailable at some time in the future. This section (3.9) will be included as a pdf (portable document format) file on the website so that it can be downloaded and saved, and the links can be used directly from the text.

One last but very important point: in choosing to use internet resources in lessons we hope that teachers will consider carefully the reasons for using a particular resource and how the use of that resource enhances the learning experience.

3.9(a) Sources of data and data-handling activities

There is a wealth of data available on the internet which enables the making and testing of statistical hypotheses relating to large data-sets without the time-consuming process of collecting and organizing the data. The use of real-world data and topical contexts adds a richness and relevance to data-handling activities. The web references given below fit into one or more of these categories

- sources of data
- sources of classroom activities and lesson-plans for data-handling activities
- websites with simulation applets that can be used to capture data such as the reaction-timers mentioned in section 3.2.

It should be noted that there are also many opportunities to use data-sets in mathematics lessons which are related to other subjects in the curriculum, such as science, geography, design technology, etc.

CensusAtSchool is an international children's census, collecting and disseminating real data for use by teachers and students in data-handling, ICT and across the curriculum for learning and teaching. The Census at School project collects data from students and provides classroom activities using the data (`http://www.censusatschool.org.uk/`).

Experiments at school This website has a number of experiments to carry out. 'Live Experiments' collect your data into a database and you can download the data from your school in the 'Retrieve Data' section for analysis. You can also download a random sample of data from all schools for comparison (`http://www.experimentsatschool.ntu.ac.uk/main/`).

The London Grid for Learning (LGfL), mentioned in section 3.8 (e), provides a number of useful resources including a Networked Weather Station which provides real-time monitoring of weather variables and an archive of data which allows climate trends and patterns to be analysed (`http://weather.lgfl.org.uk/`).

The Office for National Statistics provides information and data on society and the economy of the UK together with some government statistics (`http://www.ons.gov.uk`).

Royal Statistical Society Centre for Statistical Education There are resources, information and links on this website (`http://www.rsscse.org.uk/`).

QCA – RSS Centre Review of Handling Data and Statistics in GCSE Mathematics consists of eight case-studies with teacher's notes and links to appropriate data-sets (`http://www.rsscse.org.uk/qca/resources0.htm`).

Stats4schools is a website aiming to help teachers and pupils to get more from statistics. For pupils, there are data-sets to download and include in projects, free of charge. For teachers, there are lesson-plans and worksheets, which are free to download and use in class. Stats4schools is managed by the independent Office for National Statistics, and includes data from across government (`http://www.stats4schools.gov.uk/default.asp`).

TSM RESOURCES (`http://www.tsm-resources.com/index.html`) Douglas Butler's website contains useful links to data-handling sources such as 'The Met Office historical weather data' on the mathematics page, section 4 (`http://www.tsm-resources.com/mlink.html#stats`).

Understanding Uncertainty is a website produced by the *Winton programme for the public understanding of risk*, based in the Statistical Laboratory in the University of Cambridge. The aim is to help improve the way that uncertainty and risk are discussed in society, and show how probability and statistics can be both useful and entertaining (`http://understandinguncertainty.org/`).

United Nations Cyberschool Bus This website allows you to view and compare United Nations data from countries around the world (`http://cyberschoolbus.un.org/`).

UNICEF publications have a number of documents with statistical information which can be downloaded in PDF format (`http://www.unicef.org/publications/index.html`). In particular *The State of the World's Children* is an annual publication containing tables of statistical data relating to children and mothers. This can be downloaded from the above link or from `http://www.unicef.org/publications/index_51775.html`.

Additional sources
Applets: Several of the websites mentioned later in the section on interactive and online resources contain data-handling activities. Some also contain applets that will collect data such as reaction times, or from simulations such as coin-tossing.

Two resources mentioned in more detail later in this section also contain data-handling activities: the *Practical Support Pack and Lesson and Support Materials for the DfES KS3 Offer.*

3.9(b) Sources of software, including freeware, and software specific support and activities

Autograph is a dynamic graphing package incorporating coordinate and transformation geometry in 2D and 3D, statistical graphing and other data-handling features. The website has videos of Autograph in action (`http://www.autograph-math.com/`).

Cabri Geometry II plus is a dynamic geometry software package that allows the user to create geometric and numerical constructions, transformations and graphs and to manipulate or animate these dynamically. Cabri Jnr a version of Cabri is available on TI-Nspire™ and some Texas graphing calculators (`http://www.cabri.com/cabri-2-plus.html`).

For additional information and video demonstrations, go to `http://www.chartwellyorke.com/cabri.html`. Demonstrations of some constructions are at `http://www.mathsnet.net/cabri/index.html`.

Cabri 3D allows the user to create, transform, measure and investigate dynamically 3D objects and space (`http://www.cabri.com/cabri-3d.html`).

Further information and video footage of Cabri 3D in action is from the Chartwell-Yorke website (see below) (`http://www.chartwellyorke.com/cabri3d/cabri3d.html`).

Note: Cabri (both 2D and 3D) documents can be included as fully interactive figures in Windows applications and on the internet since it is now possible to export a screen-shot as a png file, or as an embedded XML object in an html web-page. To be able to use these images interactively the user will need to have installed the free plug-ins from the CabriLog website (`http://www.cabri.com/download-cabri-2-plus.html1#plugin`).

Chartwell-Yorke is a publisher whose website provides information about a wide variety of dynamic mathematics software, including data-handling software such as Fathom 2 and Tinkerplots and other software already mentioned in this section. Chartwell Yorke act as distributors for Autograph, Cabrilog and Key Curriculum Press software (The Geometer's Sketchpad, Fathom and TinkerPlots) . They also supply trial versions of software and related books (`http://www.chartwellyorke.com/cabri.html`).

The DALEST project (Developing an Active Learning Environment for the Learning of Stereometry) aims at enhancing middle-school students' 3D geometry understanding and spatial visualization skills. The project is co-funded by the European Union under the Socrates Program, MINERVA. There are a number of applets available to download from Elica including 'Cubix Editor', 'Potter's wheel', 'Stuffed toys' and 'Origami nets' (`http://www.elica.net/site/index.html`).

GeoGebra is dynamic mathematics software aimed at all levels of education that joins arithmetic, geometry, algebra and calculus. The software can be used in a web-based version or it is free to download (`http://www.geogebra.org/cms/`).

On the GeoGebra website you will also find: **GeoGebraWiki!**, a free pool of teaching materials for the software to which anyone can contribute, and **GeoGebra User Forum,** an international user forum where you can get help and support others.

The Geometer's Sketchpad is a dynamic geometry software package that allows the user to create geometric and numerical constructions, transformations and graphs and to manipulate or animate these dynamically. It has the facility for multiple pages (`http://www.dynamicgeometry.com/`). Additional information is available

from `http://www.chartwellyorke.com/sketchpad.html` and sample
tutorials at Atomic Learning `http://movies.atomiclearning.com/uk/`
`geomsketch_pc`.

Grid Algebra by Dave Hewitt provides a visual and kinaesthetic way to develop
number concepts and algebraic ideas. Algebraic expressions can be created and
interpreted with physical movements around a grid. Grid Algebra can be bought from
the Association of Teachers of Mathematics (ATM) which also provides a range of
free resources and a video demonstration (see below).

Logger Pro 3 and **Logger Lite** are data-capturing software from Vernier to go with
data-logging equipment. Synchronize data-capture with video analysis using Logger
pro. Examples of this are given in Chapters 2, 3 and 5 (`http://www.vernier.`
`com/soft/lp.html`).

The Mathematical Toolkit In collaboration with Intel and The Mathematical
Association, the Mathematical Toolkit and Number line have been designed
specifically to support the teaching and learning of mathematics for students. The
tools have been developed in Macromedia Flash so that teachers and students can
access them via the internet without needing to purchase any software.
   The Toolkit has four tools: Number line; 2D shapes; Coordinates and graphing;
Charting. For each of these tools you can also download a full user guide, activities
for teachers and students to follow when using the tool, and a troubleshooting guide.
The toolkit and supporting materials are available to download free from the 'London
Grid for Learning' website. The latest online version 3 of the toolkit is at `http://`
`lgfl.skoool.co.uk/common.aspx?id=901`.

MSW Logo™ is a programming language that allows you to create procedures. These
are most commonly used to create shapes or paths using the screen turtle. MSW Logo™
is a free download from `http://www.softronix.com/logo.html`.

Turtle geometry from the **NLVM** (see section 3.9(c)) can perform some simple
procedures similar to Logo.

MATHSNET website (see section 3.9(c)) has further information about Logo and
some animations.

The ATM website (see section 3.9(d)) has a number of Logo resources and some
articles in their Micromaths archive.

Texas Instruments – graphing calculators and TI-Nspire™
The UK home page of Texas Instruments has a series of drop-down menus from six
tabs (Technology, Learners, Teachers, Support, Research and Downloads) at the top
of the page. These give a full picture of the resources and support material available
on this site for both TI-Nspire™ and graphing calculators as well as data-logging.
There are links to downloads of trial versions of TI-Nspire™ software plus resources,
and other documents such as reports on case-studies and research findings

(`http://education.ti.com/educationportal/sites/UK/ homePage/index.html`). There is an option (top right) to change the country – the USA site has a large range of activities and links to tutorials for using TI devices.

`http://www.nspiringlearning.org.uk/` is a newly developed site which is constantly being updated. It has classroom activities, downloads and tutorials.

Trial versions of the new teacher edition software for TI-Nspire™ which includes an emulator for the hand-held version are available from `http://education. ti.com/html/nspire/te.html`.

Formulator Tarsia is an activity template software to create matching puzzles for example for algebraic expressions. This is available on the CD in the Standards unit's 'Improving Learning in Mathematics' (see later in this section). Originally known as Jigsaw it has been developed by Hermitech Laboratory of Mathematical and Modelling Software in the Ukraine. It is free software that you can download from the site (`http://www.mmlsoft.com/index.php?option=com_conten t&task=view&id=4&Itemid=5`). Further information about the software can also be obtained from the Mathsnet website (`http://www.mathsnet.net/ jigsaw/index.html`).

Tracker is a free video analysis Java Applet, from `http://www.cabrillo. edu/~dbrown/tracker/`.

Adrian Oldknow has a folder of new documents in the 'ICT in Mathematics community' on the NCETM portal (see below). In particular 'Analysing projectile motion' which uses Tracker is in the STEM sub folder (`http://www.ncetm.org. uk/Default.aspx?page=14&module=com&mode=102&comcid=241`).

Yenka is a range of educational modelling software from Crocodile Clips, which lets you simulate concepts. It is developing all the time and currently includes applications in science, computing, mathematics and technology. The mathematics software consists of 3D shapes, statistics and coordinates. Yenka 3D Shapes is a fast and easy to use tool to aid 3D visualization. It is possible to try the software free at home (`http://www.yenka.com/en/Mathematics_products/`).

Further sources of activities or help for using dynamic software
Adrian Oldknow's website (`http://www.adrianoldknow.org.uk/`).
Adrian Oldknow has written extensively about the use of ICT in teaching mathematics, in particular about the use of dynamic geometry software such as Cabri Geometry II Plus, Geometer's Sketchpad and Cabri 3D (version 2) His website contains links to an enormous variety of resources including articles that he has written, publications, sources of information and prepared software files.

Atomic Learning This website provide video demonstrations of a number of different dynamic software packages in action such as *Sketchpad*, Texas Instruments calculators and TI-Nspire™ (`http://movies.atomiclearning.com/k12/ tutorials/en*/pc/0/0`).

Teachers TV programmes
Hard to Teach – Secondary Maths Using ICT (`http://www.teachers.tv/video/29853`). A group of maths teachers use ICT as they tackle three traditionally hard to teach topics with their students.

Hard To Teach – Secondary Maths (`http://www.teachers.tv/video/19119`). Shows sports videos and dynamic geometry software being used to explore quadratic functions.

KS3/4 Maths – Using Dynamic Geometry (`http://www.teachers.tv/video/3081`).

KS3/4 Maths – Demonstrating Dynamic Geometry (`http://www.teachers.tv/video/3080`).

KS3/4 Maths – New Maths Technology – In the Classroom (`http://www.teachers.tv/video/154`). A maths department embarks on a project to make maths more stimulating by making better use of ICT in the classroom. The teachers are introduced to some of the new technology and try out their newly acquired skills.

Resource Review – Secondary Maths 2 (`http://www.teachers.tv/video/4872`). Reviews three resources including the 'Calculator Based Ranger CBR2' from Texas Instruments – a motion sensor used to collect real-time data and 'The Mathematical Toolkit' a free resource from Skoool which offers four tools to help in mathematics teaching.

Integrating ICT into the Mathematics Classroom Book and CD are available from ATM (see section 3.9(d)). The CD contains a variety of dynamic geometry support materials.

3.9(c) Sources of interactive and online activities

Bowland Maths is a new initiative providing a series of innovative case-studies to appeal to students aged 11–14, each supporting three to five lessons. These use key mathematical concepts and emphasize key processes. The case-studies are interactive, with open questions requiring problem-solving skills, imagination and a degree of teamwork. They are complemented by five professional development modules for teachers which cover the pedagogical challenges in working with students to tackle non-routine unstructured problem-solving. Included with the professional development materials is a number of short computer programs. The Bowland player can be run online or from a DVD and the professional development modules can be downloaded (`http://www.bowlandmaths.org.uk/`).

Maths-it.org This website was set up as part of a Gatsby Fellowship Project. It contains a range of ideas and resources for using ICT in mathematics (`http://www.maths-it.org.uk/index.php`).

MathsNet is an independent educational website providing free mathematics resources to the education community. As well as games, puzzles and interactive activities, it has a wealth of information on resources including most dynamic mathematical software and graphing calculators. It also hosts discussion forums with feedback on these resources (`http://www.mathsnet.net/`).

Maths thesaurus This website has explanations of a wide range of mathematical terms in many languages. Type the word or phrase into the search facility. Some searches have the opportunity to 'show graph' (a Java application) which is like a mind-map connecting different related topics (`http://thesaurus.maths.org/`).

The National Library of Virtual Manipulatives (NLVM) is a project that began in 1999 based at Utah State University to develop a library of uniquely interactive, web-based virtual manipulatives or concept tutorials, mostly in the form of Java applets, for mathematics instruction. There is a vast range of useful applets on this website some of which have been mentioned earlier in this chapter (`http://nlvm.usu.edu/`).

NRICH is the main website of the Millennium Mathematics Project at Cambridge University. It is a joint project between the Faculties of Mathematics and Education. It has an extensive resource bank of rich activities (some interactive), games, problems and articles for all learners from 5–19.

   AskNRICH is an online discussion and mentoring service staffed by Cambridge University student volunteers, which answers mathematical queries from students of all ages and provides a forum for an online mathematics community (`http://nrich.maths.org/public/index.php`).

WaldoMaths There are many applets on this site. Following are some examples:
- Histograms: Investigate the effect on histograms of changing the width of columns and using frequency density.
- Scatter diagrams: Create your own scatter diagram. See if you are as good as the computer at drawing the line of best fit.
- Investigating quadratic sequences: This is a tool for investigating quadratic sequences (`http://www.waldomaths.com/index1116.jsp`).

Wisweb is the website of the Freudenthal Institute for Secondary Education. The main focus of the site is applets – small computer programs that run over the internet. A selection of applets, software, instructional materials and other information is available in English. Some have been mentioned already in this chapter. Here are a few more examples:
- *Broken calculator*: Obtain a target total using brackets and only specified numbers and operations.
- *Solving equations with balance strategy game* allows students to score points for their strategies and solutions.

- *Shooting balls* is a target game involving gradients and y-axis intercepts.
- *Growth* allows you explore different models of growth and decay (`http://www.fi.uu.nl/wisweb/en/`).

3.9(d) Classroom activities and pedagogical support

Subject associations

The Association of Teachers of Mathematics (ATM) believes in providing teachers with the resources to help them develop their mathematics teaching in creative and broad-thinking ways (`http://www.atm.org.uk/`). The website contains a number of different types of resources, some of which are free. The main resource page contains many links to activities (`http://www.atm.org.uk/resources/`).

Two resources available to purchase from ATM are:

1. *Integrating ICT into the Mathematics Classroom* Book and CD contain a selection of articles from the last five years of *Micromath*, the journal of the ATM, including dynamic geometry; logo and graph plotting; spreadsheets; graphing calculators; interactive whiteboards; and the internet. The CD contains a range of resources, including a Micromath archive, A **Maths Gallery** of Richard Phillips' photos (UK only), files of ATM published resources (such as Active Geometry and Interactive Mathematics), Graphing calculator resources, **Becta documents**, a set of research bibliographies and *Furbles*, which is random population-generating software. Among many other useful resources in the Becta documents folder is one labelled '**Project A07**' which contains lesson-plans and materials for six mathematical activities which encourage the use of ICT and are aimed at 11–14 year old students. These were produced as part of the *Lesson and Support Materials for the DfES KS3 Offer* (`http://www.atm.org.uk/buyonline/products/rea025.html`).
2. Grid algebra software (`http://www.atm.org.uk/buyonline/products/sof071.html`), this page has links to free resources and demonstrations.

The Mathematical Association (MA) website has links to resources for teaching mathematics using ICT and professional development materials. At the time of writing this book the website is in the process of reorganization so it has not been possible to give many links here, but more may be included on the book's website (`http://www.m-a.org.uk/jsp/index.jsp?lnk=000`).

The MA has worked with Steljes plc to develop a half-day professional development course designed to help teachers use the power and functionality of the SMART Board IWB to enhance teaching and learning in mathematics. The guide is entitled *Winning with the Smart Board Interactive Whiteboard in the Mathematics Classroom*. The MA has also developed a series of Smart NoteBook resources and accompanying lesson-plans, all of which can be freely downloaded from the Smart Exchange website via this link, `http://www.m-a.org.uk/jsp/index.jsp?lnk=140`.

The National Association for Numeracy and Mathematics in Colleges (NANAMIC) is an association of further education, tertiary and sixth form colleges which aims to assist colleges nationally to develop quality in all aspects of their work in mathematics and numeracy. Its website contains links to Tarsia software and examples its use (`http://www.nanamic.org.uk/`).

Curriculum websites

The Qualifications and Curriculum Development Agency (QCDA, formerly QCA) is responsible for developing the curriculum in England as well as assessments and qualifications. It has links to information and resources for mathematics at `http://www.qcda.gov.uk/6657.aspx`. A pdf copy of the guidance booklet for the 'Engaging mathematics for all learners' project is available at `http://www.qcda.gov.uk/22223.aspx`.

The curriculum website of the QCDA has details of mathematics programmes of study and details and short video-clips of case-studies, including some mentioned earlier in this chapter, available from links on the page `http://curriculum.qca.org.uk/key-stages-3-and-4/subjects/index.aspx`.

The UK government Department for Children, Schools and Families (DCSF formerly DFES) now houses the Practical Support Pack on its website (`http://www.dcsf.gov.uk/psp/`). This pack includes lesson-plans, classroom resources and practical advice written by experts in teaching mathematics using ICT, developed with the support of the Mathematical Association. There are 28 activities available from `http://www.dcsf.gov.uk/psp/subject.aspx?t=2&s=10`.

Teachernet (`http://www.teachernet.gov.uk/`) has information about teaching and learning, and links to thousands of resources. Included in their resources is the booklet aimed at 11–14 year olds '*Key Stage 3 National Strategy ICT Across the Curriculum – ICT in Mathematics*' which focuses on how information and computer technology can help in the teaching of mathematics (`http://publications.teachernet.gov.uk/default.aspx?PageFunction=productdetails&PageMode=publications&ProductId=DfES+0176+2004G&`).

Communities of practice

The National Centre for Excellence in the Teaching of Mathematics (the NCETM) (`https://www.ncetm.org.uk/`) states that it 'aims to meet the professional aspirations and needs of all teachers of mathematics and realize the potential of learners through a sustainable national infrastructure for mathematics-specific continuing professional development (CPD)'. The NCETM portal offers an online community for mathematics teachers with a wide variety of facilities including a personal space, professional development advice, discussion forums (communities) on a variety of topics, spaces to store and share documents, advice on resources and much more. One NCETM community is 'ICT in mathematics' and the documents folder of this community contains a variety of useful documents including a number produced in combination with Becta.

The **ICT Enriched Curriculum Grid** which links the 14–16 mathematics curriculum to activities and resources involving the use of ICT is one of the resources in the Becta folder. To access this you first need to join the NCETM (available to anyone, at `http://www.ncetm.org.uk/`). Remember your log-in name and password for future use. Once you have joined and logged in, select 'community' then 'view all communities' and then 'ICT in Mathematics'. You need to apply to join the community, but any logged-in users of the site can do this. Finally select the documents tab and 'Becta ICT products'.

The NCETM website also provides a link to 'Improving Learning in Mathematics' a multi-media resource where learners are encouraged to become more independent, to learn to think mathematically rather than simply learning rules and most importantly, to enjoy their mathematics. The pack includes some activities making use of ICT on CD-ROM 6. For more information or to download a copy of Malcolm Swan's book *Improving Learning in Mathematics: challenges and strategies*, which explains more about the approaches and background research, go to `https://www.ncetm.org.uk/resources/1442`.

The National Education Network (NEN) is the UK collaborative network for education, providing schools with a safe, secure and reliable learning environment and direct access to a growing range of online services and content (`http://www.nen.gov.uk/`).

London Grid for Learning (LGfL), mentioned in section 3.8(e) is just one of the Local Area Networks that are part of NEN. The LGfL provides a number of useful resources including the Mathematical Toolkit mentioned in section 3.9(b) and a Networked Weather Station mentioned in section 3.9(a) (`http://cms.lgfl.net/web/lgfl/homepage`).

Others

Becta is a UK government agency leading the national drive to ensure the effective and innovative use of technology throughout learning (`http://www.becta.org.uk/`).

Some resources produced by the MA with the support of Becta are included in a folder on the *Integrating ICT into the Mathematics Classroom CD* available from the ATM (above), and other more recent ones are in a folder on the NCETM website.

Becta Schools' website offers advice and guidance to school leadership teams on how technology can be built into teaching, learning and management (`http://schools.becta.org.uk/`).

ITE Maths has materials for Initial Teacher Education (`http://www.itemaths.org.uk/`). Resources for using ICT to teach mathematics, including dynamic geometry and graphing calculators, are at `http://www.itemaths.org.uk/using-ict.html`.

Problem Pictures In this website Richard Phillips presents a number of photographs, some of which are available free as examples. The pictures can be used in many different ways. Some images are suitable for copying and pasting into software that allows a graph to be superimposed. Others are presented with activities and questions for discussion. There is a file of 125 of these pictures on the 'Maths Gallery' of the CD which accompanies the book *Integrating ICT into the Mathematics Classroom*, published by ATM (see above) grouped into themes (`http://www.problempictures.co.uk/index.htm`).

Schoolzone houses many teaching resources but also evaluates new products particularly software (`http://www.schoolzone.co.uk`).

TEEM (Teachers Evaluating Educational Multimedia) also evaluates products such as software (`http://www.teem.org.uk/`).

The Teacher Resource Exchange (TRE) is a moderated database of resources and activities created by teachers (`http://tre.ngfl.gov.uk/`).

Teachers TV More detail of some Teachers TV programmes is given earlier in this section. A full list can be found at `http://www.teachers.tv/video/browser/811/964`.

3.10 SUMMARY

We have tried to give you a practical introduction to the features of many of the main types of ICT tools which have potential benefits for mathematics teachers with details about where to find these tools and further support for using them in the classroom. Once you have started to get familiar with the features of such tools, you should then review their potential to offer you pedagogical, mathematical and/or organizational support.

A few further activities are suggested here that could extend your ideas and use of the software tools mentioned in this chapter.

Problems and activities (you choose the tool!)

✎ *Fibonacci sequence, golden ratio, pentagons and pentagrams: find out as many links between them as you can and use ICT tools to explore them. For example, given that the ratio between the lengths of the sides and diagonals in a pentagon is golden ratio ϕ, can you find a way to construct a pentagon using 'straight edge and compasses' only? Can you locate interesting information about Fibonacci and golden ratio on the internet?*

✎ *Investigate the intersections of* $y = x$ *with* $y = kx$ *for different values of* $k > 0$. *For what value of* k *is the line tangent to the curve, and at what point does this occur? Investigate the iteration given by* $x_0 = 1$, $x_n + 1 = kx_n$ *for* $n = 0,1,2, \ldots$ *What is the largest value of* k *for which this sequence does not diverge?*

Read about ways of testing for prime numbers, and for generating sequences of prime numbers and implement them as algorithms using ICT tools.

 The neat result linking three touching circles to the in-centre was known to the ancient Greeks. Many more interesting results and ideas for explanation can be found in books by Coxeter and Wells. Can you find any that lend themselves to use in the classroom?

Chapter 4

Chapter 4

How to plan effective use of ICT

4.1 USING ICT IN THE SECONDARY MATHEMATICS CLASSROOM

In Chapters 2 and 3 you have met the ICT tools – hardware and software – that are most likely to impact on your work as a teacher of mathematics. In thinking about your use of ICT to support teaching it is useful to have a framework within which to check your progress. Fortunately this work has already been done by the UK's Teacher Training Agency both in connection with the lottery-funded ICT training for all teachers (1999–2003) and the ongoing preparation for students in initial teacher training (ITT) to use ICT in their subject teaching. This still applies today, and for convenience we reproduce the first section of the TTA's (now the TDA) document: *The Use of Information Technology in Subject Teaching: Identification of training needs.*

Overview of the use of ICT in teaching secondary mathematics
There are many possible uses of ICT in teaching and, as with all materials and methodologies, some have a greater potential to contribute to the teaching of different subjects. This section highlights the aspects of mathematics teaching where ICT has the potential to make a significant contribution to teaching and learning.

When making decisions about the use of ICT in subject teaching, there are three key principles which you may find useful to apply.

- Decisions about when, when not, and how to use ICT in lessons should be based on whether the use of ICT supports good practice in teaching the subject. If it does not, it should not be used.
- In planning and teaching, decisions about when, when not, and how to use ICT in a particular lesson or sequence of lessons must be directly related to the teaching and learning objectives in hand.
- The use of ICT should either allow the teacher or the student to achieve something that could not be achieved without it; or allow the teacher to teach or the students to learn something more effectively and efficiently than they could otherwise; or both.

These principles are important, whether ICT is to be used by:

- *all the students*, individually, in groups or as a whole class;
- *some students only*, e.g. for support or extension work;
- *the teacher*, e.g. where the teacher uses the ability of a spreadsheet to calculate the results of varying factors and demonstrate the results in graphical form to the full class with the help of a large screen or display; where the teacher downloads lesson-plans, or where the teacher downloads selected resources from the internet in advance of the lesson so that students can browse through them.

Practical considerations may also play a part in decisions about whether or not ICT should be used. These will include the nature of the available resources, e.g. teaching objectives that could be met very effectively if a suite of computers were available in the classroom might not be attainable if there is just one stand-alone computer.

Using ICT in secondary mathematics lessons

ICT has the potential to make a significant contribution to students' learning in mathematics by helping them to:

- *practise and consolidate number skills*, e.g. by using software to revise or practise skills and to give rapid assessment feedback;
- *develop skills in mathematical modelling through the exploration, interpretation and explanation of data*, e.g. by choosing appropriate graphical representations for displaying information from a data-set; by experimenting with forms of equations in trying to produce graphs which are good fits for data-plots; by using a motion sensor to produce distance–time graphs corresponding to students' own movements;
- *experiment with, make hypotheses from, and discuss or explain relationships and behaviour in shape and space and their links with algebra*, e.g. by using software to automate geometric constructions, to carry out specified geometric transformations, to perform operations on coordinates, to draw loci;
- *develop logical thinking and modify strategies and assumptions through immediate feedback*, e.g. by planning a procedure in a sequence of instructions in a programming language, or a sequence of geometrical constructions in geometry software or a set of manipulations in a spreadsheet;
- *make connections within and across areas of mathematics*, e.g. to relate a symbolic function, a set of values computed from it, and a graph generated by it to a mathematical or physical situation, such as the pressure and volume of a gas, which it models;
- *work with realistic and large sets of data*, e.g. in using box and whisker diagrams to compare the spreads of different data-sets; to carry out experiments using large random samples generated through simulation;
- *explore, describe, and explain patterns and relationships in sequences and tables of numbers*, e.g. by entering a formula in algebraic notation to generate values in an attempt to match a given set of numbers;
- *learn, and memorize, by manipulating graphic images*, e.g. the way the graph of

a function such as $y = x^2$ is transformed by the addition of, or multiplication by a constant: $y = a . x^2$, $y = x^2 + a$, $y = (x + a)^2$, etc.

ICT also has the potential to offer valuable support to teachers of secondary mathematics by:

- *helping them to prepare teaching materials*, e.g. downloading materials for classroom use from the internet, such as mathematical problems for students to solve with accompanying teachers' notes, software for computers and graphing calculators, reviews of published resources;
- *providing a flexible and time-saving resource that can be used in different ways and at different times without repetition of the teachers' input*, e.g. by enlarging fonts, adding diagrams or illustrations, adapting parameters used in problems;
- *providing a means by which subject and pedagogic knowledge can be improved and kept up to date*, e.g. accessing websites such as the ATM, DCSF, MA, NCETM, Teachers TV, to obtain practical advice, to exchange ideas with peers and 'experts' outside the school;
- *aiding record-keeping and reporting*, e.g. storing and regularly updating formative records which can form the basis of a subsequent report.

✎ *Having read the previous chapter you should now be able to identify which type or types of software would be likely to be helpful in each of the above aspects. In this chapter we get down to detail in looking at applications of the resources met in earlier chapters to the content of the secondary school mathematics curriculum. Before starting this, now would be a good time (if you haven't already done so) to set out what you think are your main needs at the moment in improving your ability to deploy ICT effectively. The set of criteria used in the TTA (TDA) identification of needs document is reproduced for your convenience.*

Individual training needs

1. Planning
In planning to use ICT to achieve subject teaching objectives, you might consider the following aspects of the TTA's Expected Outcomes as possible training needs:

a. understanding and considering the advantages and disadvantages of using ICT;
b. planning to use ICT so as to provide access to the curriculum for those students who might otherwise have difficulties because of their special educational needs;
c. preparing for lessons using ICT by selecting and preparing appropriate sources of information, relevant software and the appropriate technology, and deciding on the most effective organization of the classroom and students.

2. Teaching
In using ICT effectively in your teaching, you might consider the following aspects of the Expected Outcomes as possible training needs:

a. extending students' learning in the subject through the use of ICT;
b. intervening and posing questions to stimulate, direct, monitor and assess the learning of students who are using ICT;
c. employing the use of ICT with other resources and methods to achieve your teaching objectives.

3. Assessing and evaluating
In assessing students' progress in the subject and evaluating the effectiveness of using ICT, you might consider the following aspects of the Expected Outcomes as possible training needs:

a. enabling students to demonstrate their knowledge, understanding and skills in the subject while using ICT;
b. ensuring that students' learning in the subject is not masked by the technology being used;
c. judging how the use of ICT can alter expectations of students' attainment;
d. judging the effectiveness of using ICT in achieving teaching objectives.

4. Personal, professional use of ICT
In the context of the subject(s) that you teach, and to increase professional efficiency and reduce administrative burdens, you might consider the following aspects of the Expected Outcomes as possible training needs:

a. using generic and/or subject-specific hardware and software, e.g. databases, internet, presentation tools, scanners, printers, etc.;
b. using ICT to aid record-keeping, analysis of data, target-setting, reporting, transfer of information, etc.;
c. accessing and using resources, including from the NCETM and the professional associations;
d. accessing research and inspection evidence.

✎ *Can you identify which of the above 14 points are ones you already feel reasonably confident with?*

✎ *Can you identify, say, four of the remaining points you would class as immediate priorities?*

✎ *Can you identify, say, another four of those points which are left as longer-term goals?*

Finally we suggest you review the Teachers TV video *New Maths Technology – In the Classroom* (`http://www.teachers.tv/video/154`) to see, for instance:

- which ICT tools the teacher has chosen to use;
- how the choice of ICT has affected the organization of the lesson;
- what preparation was required to use the ICT.

In this programme, the maths department at Tanbridge House School in Horsham embarks on a project to improve its teaching and make maths more stimulating by making better use of ICT in the classroom.

The teachers are introduced to some of the new technology and try out their newly acquired skills in front of their students for the first time. Each class then gets the opportunity to experiment with the new ICT resources:

- Year 7 investigates algebraic expressions using an interactive number line.
- Year 8 has fun with time and distance graphs using a data-plotting range-finder.
- Year 9 explores rotational symmetry with dynamic geometry software.
- Year 10 investigates a problem using graphing calculators.

Year 7 investigates algebraic expressions using an interactive number line

In this lesson students and teacher use an interactive number line to explore simple linear and quadratic expressions and, in particular, the functions $2n$ and n^2 which often give rise to confusion. The teacher uses an interactive whiteboard and invites several students from the class to move the 'defining' point along the line, observing the effect on other dependent points. Giving students control of the IWB allows the teacher more opportunity to question the whole class, e.g 'For what values do the expressions coincide on the number line . . . ?', 'Describe what happens to n^2 for positive and negative values of n . . . .' Students also keep a written record of values of the functions for different values of n – helping to reinforce the ideas they have explored in the lesson.

How did the dynamic number line and the teacher's approach support students' understanding of algebra and algebraic notation?

Year 8 has fun with time and distance graphs using a data-plotting range-finder

This is a low-ability Year 8. The students are using a data-plotting range-finder to draw time and distance graphs. As they move towards and away from the sensor it automatically draws a graph on a whole-class display. They are then asked to interpret some ready-made time and distance graphs. Later on they are challenged to match their physical movement to some given graphs.

What difficulties do early secondary (11–13 year old) students have when interpreting distance-time graphs? What are the common errors? How does this activity help students' understanding and interpretation of graphs?

Year 9 explores rotational symmetry with dynamic geometry software

This low-ability Year 9 group is using dynamic geometry to explore rotational symmetry. The students create their own designs using the built-in commands of the software. Having personal access to ICT helps to motivate this group of students on a warm summer afternoon.

 How do the commands and tools in the dynamic geometry software compare with everyday and mathematical language?

Year 10 investigates a problem using graphing calculators

This high-attaining Year 10 set is challenged to produce a 'tilted square' using the equation editor and Cartesian axes on their graphing calculator. The teacher uses a software emulator of the graphing calculator on the IWB as an aid to getting the students started and for familiarizing the class with the key strokes and facilities of the graphing calculator.

✎ *What functions would you use to produce a 'clown's face'?*

Part 2 of the this video *KS3/4 Maths – New Maths Technology – Managing Change* is at `http://www.teachers.tv/video/155`.

The programme looks at:

- how the initiative was planned and introduced
- how staff and students are reacting to it
- why changes were needed in the first place
- how the school set about introducing the changes
- how the new technology was introduced to the staff
- the wider impact it had on the staff's teaching techniques and on their students' learning

---

 You might like to look at this before considering your own and/or your department's training needs. What were the key elements of the professional development of this mathematics department?

4.2 TRAINING NEEDS – EXPECTED OUTCOMES

The TDA provides a useful résumé of what mathematics teachers need to know about ICT in order to be able to embed it fully into their teaching. Of course this is something that most of us aspire towards, but it will be useful if you read through these and rate your own current capacity.

Expected Outcomes for training in the use of information and communications technology in secondary mathematics

A. *Effective teaching and assessment methods*

1. Teachers should know when the use of ICT is beneficial to achieve teaching objectives in secondary mathematics, and when the use of ICT would be less effective or inappropriate. In making these decisions, they should know how to take account of the functions of ICT and the ways that these can be used by teachers in achieving mathematics teaching and learning objectives. This includes:

(a) how the speed and automatic functions of ICT can enable teachers to demonstrate, explore or explain aspects of mathematics to make pupils' learning more effective;
(b) how the capacity and range of ICT can enable teachers and pupils to gain access to historical, recent or immediate information;
(c) how the provisional nature of information stored, processed and presented using ICT allows work to be changed easily;
(d) how the interactive way in which information is stored, processed and presented can enable teachers and pupils to explore models, communicate effectively with others and present and represent information effectively for different audiences.

2. Teachers should know how to use ICT effectively to achieve mathematics teaching objectives, including:

(a) using ICT because it is the most effective way to achieve teaching and learning objectives, not simply for motivation, reward or sanction;
(b) avoiding the use of ICT for simple or routine tasks which would be better accomplished by other means;
(c) where ICT is to be used, what appropriate preparation of equipment, content and methodology is required;
(d) avoiding giving the impression that the quality of presentation is of overriding importance and supersedes the importance of content;
(e) structuring pupils' work to focus on relevant aspects and to maximize use of time and resource;
(f) having high expectations of the outcomes of pupils' work with ICT, including:
    i. expecting pupils to use ICT to answer valid questions appropriate to the subject matter being taught;
    ii. when appropriate, requiring pupils to save work, and evaluate and improve it;

(g) making explicit the links between the ICT application and the subject matter it is being used to teach as well as the impact of ICT on everyday applications.

3. For those aspects of lessons where ICT is to be used, teachers should be able to identify in their planning:

(a) the way(s) in which ICT will be used to meet teaching and learning objectives in mathematics;
(b) key questions to ask and opportunities for teacher intervention in order to stimulate and direct pupils' learning;
(c) the way(s) in which pupils' progress will be assessed and recorded;
(d) criteria to ensure that judgements about pupils' attainment and progress in mathematics are not masked because ICT has been used;
(e) any impact of the use of ICT on the organization and conduct of the mathematics lesson and how this is to be managed;
(f) how the ICT used is appropriate to the particular mathematical objectives in hand and to pupils' capabilities, taking account of the fact that some pupils may already be very competent, and some may need additional support.

4. Teachers should know how to organize classroom ICT resources effectively to meet learning objectives in mathematics, including how to

(a) use ICT with the whole class or a group for introducing or reviewing a topic and ensuring that all pupils cover the key conceptual features of the topic;
(b) organize individuals, pairs or groups of children working with ICT to ensure that each participant is engaged, that collaborative effort is balanced, and that teacher intervention and reporting back by pupils takes place where appropriate;
(c) make ICT resources available to pupils for research or other purposes that may arise either spontaneously during lessons or as part of planned activity, ensuring that the resource is used profitably to achieve mathematics-related objectives;
(d) position resources for ease of use, to minimize distraction, and with due regard to health and safety;
(e) ensure that work done using ICT is linked to work away from the screen, allowing ICT to support teaching rather than dominate activities.

5. Teachers should be able to recognize the specific contribution that ICT can make to teaching pupils with special educational needs in mainstream classrooms based upon the need to provide access to the curriculum in a manner appropriate to pupils' needs, and to identify where ICT can provide mathematics-specific support.

6. Teachers should be able to choose and use the most suitable ICT to meet teaching objectives, by reviewing a range of generic and mathematics-specific software critically.

7. Teachers should know how to contribute to the development and consolidation of pupils' ICT capability within the context of mathematics through

(a) explicit discussion and, where necessary, teaching of the ICT skills and applications which are used in mathematics;
(b) using terminology accurately and appropriately, and explaining to pupils any terminology that arises from the application of ICT to mathematics;
(c) using ICT in ways that provide models of good practice for pupils, and ensuring that pupils employ correct procedures when using applications.

8. Teachers should understand how to monitor and assess pupils' learning in mathematics when ICT is being used, and how to evaluate the contribution that ICT has made to the teaching of mathematics. They should be able to:

(a) monitor pupils' progress by
   i. being clear about teaching objectives and the use of ICT in achieving them;
   ii. observing and intervening in pupils' ICT-based activities to monitor and support their progression towards the identified objectives;
   iii. asking key questions which require pupils to reflect on the appropriateness of their use of ICT.
(b) recognize standards of attainment in the mathematics when ICT resources are used, including:
   i. recognizing how access to computer functions might change teacher expectation of pupil achievements;
   ii. identifying criteria by which pupils can show what they have learnt as a result of using ICT-based resources from the internet or CD-ROM, and insisting that pupils acknowledge the reference sources used in their work;
   iii. how to determine the achievement of individuals when the 'product' is the result of a collaborative effort, for example through observation, record-keeping, teacher intervention and pupil–teacher dialogue;
   iv. knowing how to ensure that assessment of ICT-based work reflects pupils' learning and the quality of their work within mathematics rather than just the quality of presentation or the complexity of the technology used;
(c) use formative, diagnostic and summative methods of assessing pupils' progress in mathematics where ICT has been used, including how to set up ICT activities with targeted objectives for assessment and make provision in those activities for all pupils to demonstrate achievement, conceptual understanding and learning through the use of ICT.

9. This section of the Expected Outcomes has been omitted since it refers only to pupils aged 3–8 and 3–11.

B. Teachers' knowledge and understanding of, and competence with, information and communications technology

10. In relation to the ICT content set out in paragraphs 11 to 18, teachers should be able to:

(a) evaluate a range of information and communication technologies, and the content associated with them, justifying the selection and use of ICT in relation to aspects of their planning, teaching, assessment and class management, including for personal professional use;

(b) understand and use correctly the specialist terms associated with the ICT used in the mathematics that are necessary to enable them to be precise in their explanations to pupils, to discuss ICT in relation to mathematics at a professional level, and to read inspection and classroom-focused research evidence with understanding.

11. Teachers should be competent in those areas of ICT that support pedagogy in every subject, including that they:

(a) can employ common ICT tools for their own and pupils' benefit and can use a range of ICT resources, at the level of general users (rather than as network or system managers), including:
    i.   the common user interfaces, using menus, selecting and swapping between applications, cutting, pasting and copying files, and cutting, copying and pasting data within and between applications;
    ii. successfully connecting and setting up ICT equipment, including input and output devices;
    iii. loading and running software;
    iv. file management;
    v.   seeking and using operating information, including from online help facilities and user guides;
    vi. coping with everyday problems and undertaking simple, routine maintenance, with due consideration to health and safety;
    vii. understanding the importance of passwords and the general security of equipment and access to it;

(b) know and understand the characteristics of information, including:
    i.   that information must be evaluated in terms of its accuracy, validity, reliability, plausibility, bias;
    ii. that information has to be stored somewhere, it takes up memory (storage space) and that there are implications when saving and compressing files;
    iii. that ICT systems can present static information or changing information;
    iv. that information can be directly and dynamically linked between applications;
    v.   that applications and information can be shared with other people at remote locations.

12. Teachers should, in relation to secondary mathematics and ages of pupils:

(a) know how to use ICT to find things out, including:
    i.   identifying sources of information and discriminating between them;
    ii. planning and putting together a search strategy, including framing useful questions, widening and narrowing down searches;
    iii. knowing how to search for information, including using key words and

strings and logical operators such as AND, OR and NOT, indexes and
directories;

iv.   collecting and structuring data, and storing it for later retrieval,
   interpretation and correction;
v.   interpreting what is retrieved;
vi.   considering validity, reliability and reasonableness of outcomes;

(b)   know how to use ICT to try things out, make things happen and understand
how they happen, including:

i.   exploring alternatives;
ii.   modelling relationships;
iii.   considering cause and effect;
iv.   predicting patterns and rules recognizing patterns, and hypothesizing;
v.   knowing how to give instructions;
vi.   sequencing actions;
vii.   defining conditions, e.g. 'if this happens, do that . . .';
viii.   understanding how feedback works and the difference between things that
   do and do not rely on feedback;

(c)   know how to use ICT to communicate and exchange ideas:

i.   presenting ideas, including: identification of audience and purpose;
   deciding the best means with which to communicate;
ii.   exchanging ideas, including identifying the most appropriate medium, and
   information.

13. Teachers should know those features of ICT that can be used, separately or
together, to support teaching and learning in mathematics, including:

(a)   speed and automatic functions – the function of ICT that enables routine tasks
to be completed and repeated quickly, allowing the user to concentrate on
thinking and on tasks such as analysing and looking for patterns within data,
asking questions and looking for answers, and explaining and presenting
results, as appropriate to secondary mathematics, including how ICT can be
used to:

i.   measure events at long- or short-time intervals in order to compress or
   expand events that would normally take very short or long periods of time,
   and illustrate them to pupils at speeds appropriate to their pace of learning;
ii.   measure and record events that might otherwise be impossible to gather
   within a classroom environment;
iii.   explore sequences of actions and link the sensing of events with the
   control of actions;

(b)   capacity and range – the function of ICT, as appropriate to secondary
mathematics, to access and to handle large amounts of information; change
timescales, or remove barriers of distance; give teachers and pupils access to
and control over situations that would normally be outside their everyday
experience, including:

i.   the range of forms in which ICT can present information;
ii.   the range of possible appropriate ICT sources, including local sources
   such as CD-ROM, and remote databases;

iii. how to judge the accuracy of the information and the credibility of its source;

iv. how ICT can be used to gain access to expertise outside the classroom, the school and the local community through communications with experts;

(c) provisionality – the function of ICT that allows changes to be made easily and enables alternatives to be explored readily, and as appropriate to secondary mathematics:

i. how to make best use of the ability to make rapid changes, including how to create text, designs and models that may be explored and improved in the light of evaluation;

ii. how to judge when and when not to encourage exploration and change using ICT;

iii. how saving work at different stages enables a record to be kept of the development of ideas;

(d) interactivity – the function of ICT that enables rapid and dynamic feedback and response, as appropriate to secondary mathematics, including how to determine the most appropriate media to use.

14. Teachers should understand the potential of ICT to make the preparation and presentation of their teaching more effective, taking account of:

(a) the intended audience, including matching and adapting work to subject matter and objectives, pupils' prior attainment, reading ability or special educational needs; recognizing the efficiency with which such adaptations can be made using ICT;

(b) the most appropriate forms of presentation to meet teaching objectives.

15. Teachers should:

(a) in relation to secondary mathematics, understand the ICT requirements of the statutory curriculum for pupils and the application of ICT as a key skill;

(b) be familiar with the expectations of pupils' ICT capability, relevant to secondary mathematics, and know the level of ICT capability they should expect of pupils when applying ICT in mathematics.

16. Teachers should know how each of the following is relevant to secondary mathematics:

(a) generic procedures and tools, including:
    i. understanding the key features and functions used within mathematics;
    ii. using ICT to prepare material for pupil use;

(b) reference resources, including:
    i. how to search reference resources;
    ii. how to incorporate the use of reference resources into teaching;

(c) the ICT specific to mathematics;

(d) the contribution made by ICT to the professional, commercial and industrial applications of their subject;

(e) the major teaching programs or 'courseware' to ensure that material is matched to the pupils' capabilities:
  i.   where content and activities are presented in sequence to teach specific topics;
  ii.   where teaching activities are combined with assessment tasks and tests.

17. Teachers should be aware of:

(a) the current health and safety legislation relating to the use of computers, and be able to identify potential hazards and minimize risks;
(b) legal considerations including those related to:
  i.   keeping personal information on computers, as set out in the Data Protection Act;
  ii.   copyright legislation relating to text, images and sounds and that relating to copying software;
  iii. material which is illegal in this country;
(c) ethical issues including:
  i.   access to illegal and/or unsuitable material through the internet;
  ii.   acknowledging sources; confidentiality of personal data;
  iii. the ways in which users of information sources can be (and are) monitored;
  iv.   material which may be socially or morally unacceptable.

18. Teachers should know how to use ICT to improve their own professional efficiency and to reduce administrative and bureaucratic burdens, including:

(a) using ICT to aid administration, record-keeping, reporting and transfer of information;

(b) knowing about current classroom-focused research and inspection evidence about the application of ICT to teaching mathematics, and where it can be found;
(c) knowing how to use ICT to join in professional discussions and to locate and access teaching plans, material and other sources of help and support;
(d) knowing how ICT can support them in their continuing professional development.

4.3 ANALYSING EFFECTIVE USE OF ICT: CASE-STUDIES

In this section we will consider a number of case-studies and examples in which ICT has been used to enhance the teaching and learning of mathematics. We will analyse each example/case-study to judge the extent to which they address the outcomes in parts A and B section 2, of the TTA document *Use of ICT in Secondary Mathematics (Identification of Training Needs)*. The level of detail of this analysis diminishes throughout the chapter, as we hope that you will be getting more confident and expert in deciding professional issues for yourself. In order to indicate relative coverage of the expected outcomes we have summarized the analysis in a table.

TTA expected outcomes

Case-study	A1	A2	A3	A4	A5	A6	A7	A8	B10	B11	B12	B13	B14	B15	B16	B17	B18
4.3(a) & 4.3(b)	d	b	a, b, f					a			b						
4.3(c) & 4.3(d)	c	f	c	b, e				b		a		d	a				
4.3(e) & 4.3(f)	b	a, c, g	a	c, e	SEN				b	b	a, b	b	a				
4.3(g)		a	e		c		b	a	c		b	a, b, c	b	b	a		
4.3(h)			d					b			a		c		b		
4.3(i)		b	a, c, g	b				a	a			b	c, d			b	

We will keep in mind the three key aspects of ICT use outlined earlier:

- *Pedagogical*: can it be used to help teach content, to develop concepts, to increase knowledge, to improve understanding, to practise and reinforce skills?
- *Mathematical*: can it be used to compute results, to produce tables, to draw graphs, to solve problems, to manipulate expressions, to compute statistics?
- *Organizational*: can it help me more efficiently to produce materials, to keep records, to manage time, to communicate with others, to find resources?

A useful checklist from a student's perspective at Key Stages 3 and 4 is provided by the BECTa document on students' entitlement.

The six categories are:

1. *Learning from feedback*: The computer often provides fast and reliable feedback which is non-judgemental and impartial. This can encourage students to make their own conjectures and to test out and modify their ideas.
2. *Observing patterns*: The speed of computers and calculators enables students to produce many examples when exploring mathematical problems. This supports their observations of patterns and the making and justifying of generalizations.
3. *Seeing connections*: The computer enables formulas, tables of numbers and graphs to be linked readily. Changing one representation and seeing changes in the others helps students to understand the connections between them.
4. *Working with dynamic images*: Students can use computers to manipulate diagrams dynamically. This encourages them to visualize the geometry as they generate their own mental images.
5. *Exploring data*: Computers enable students to work with real data which can be represented in a variety of ways. This supports interpretation and analysis.
6. *'Teaching' the computer*: When students design an algorithm (a set of instructions) to make a computer achieve a particular result, they are compelled to express their commands unambiguously and in the correct order; they make their thinking explicit as they refine their ideas.

4.3(a) Not just building a fence

How many posts? How many rails?

Background

The following case-study was written by a newly qualified teacher. This activity arose from the mathematics department's desire to develop students' reasoning and idea of proof/justification. Currently most students are able to organize data and tabulate it in ways that enable them to spot patterns and describe simple inductive rules and/or formulate simple generalizations. However, they would rarely give reasons as to why their rule or formula worked. The department also wanted to increase their confidence in using algebra to model situations and their knowledge of algebraic conventions and techniques. The following is an account of the work done with a mixed-ability set of Year 9 students to help them make progress in these aspects of the mathematics curriculum. The school is an inner-city all-girls comprehensive. However, it has been tried with both lower-ability Year 7 and higher-ability Year 8 students using slightly different starting-points and extensions. Students had access to various grid papers, matchsticks and graphing calculators (originally TI-80, now replaced by the TI-83 Plus). In the following, GC is shorthand for graphing calculator.

Lesson-plan

Teaching/learning objectives

Students should be able to:

- formulate linear rules based on geometric patterns;
- explain why their rules work in terms of the way they see the patterns grow;
- collaborate with other students to pool and compare results;
- present their findings clearly and concisely to a group/whole class.

Methodology and organization

1. Introduction to whole class using context of 'growing matchstick triangles' to establish students' understanding of number patterns and rules (use OHP). Ask for next pattern, ten triangles how many match. Initially students to work in pairs explaining and justifying answers.

2. Tabulate results with whole class and ask for 'rule'. Demonstrate how this data can be entered and the 'rule' can be checked on the GC {A3a}.
3. Students to work in pairs on a range of problems (some similar so that different 'equivalent' forms can be compared) and combine to form a group of four to share findings and prepare poster/OHT for rest of class. They will have GCs to help them establish and/or check their rules {A4b}.
4. Check on progress and question or challenge students (such as looking for the inverse): have a range of different growth patterns of increasing difficulty including some leading to quadratic formulas {A3b}.
5. Overall time on topic, two or three 50-minute lessons including students' presentations and feedback.

Differentiation

Having a range of different growing patterns of increasing difficulty, including some involving quadratics, will ensure all students are appropriately challenged. Also, ask them to generate some of their own patterns.

Assessment opportunities/criteria

The initial interaction and discussion with students will help to establish students' knowledge and understanding.

- Observe and question individual students and groups while they are carrying out the work.
- Listen to the presentations and look at their work, including the posters summarizing their findings.

   Students should be able to do the following:
- find and write down their generalizations in conventional algebraic form, some progressing to inverses and quadratic forms;
- carry out simple algebraic manipulations to check for equivalent expressions;
- give reasons, explain and justify their rules in terms of the spatial patterns/ arrangements.

Resources

- matchsticks, range of different grid papers such as square and isometric dotty paper
- variety of diagrams of growing patterns
- 16 GCs, sufficient for one between two
- teacher's graphing calculator and view screen for whole-class display on OHP.

   The whiteboard display will be useful for writing the students' rules as well as showing the GC display and will be helpful for linking the form and notation used by the GC compared with the students' own notation.

Other points

This is the first time most students have used the data-handling/spreadsheet facilities of the GC. Students working in pairs should help alleviate the difficulties about 'which keys to press' {A3f}. The large poster of the GC indicating the menus 'under each key' will also act as a reminder. Also, the GCs can be easily used in the maths classroom so there is no need to book the computer suite. At a later stage we can plot the table of results and look at the links between the graphs and their formulas.

The starting-point – 'tricky triangles'

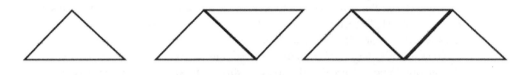

Ten triangles, how many match? Why?

The activity was introduced by looking at 'tricky triangles'. The first few diagrams were formed on the OHP using matchsticks, and students were asked to work out the number of matches for ten triangles. In the first instance they worked in pairs and were asked to explain and justify their answers. All could continue the pattern 'by adding two matches each time'. It was then decided that a rule was needed to speed up the process, and enable prediction of the number of matches for greater numbers of triangles. The students offered several different suggestions. In order to familiarize students with the TI-80 for use with further work and, to display the results for all to see, the data was entered into an OHP version of the GC.

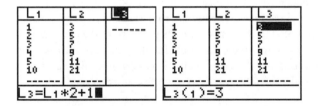

The students were able to draw up the tables of results in lists L1 and L2 using the calculator STAT function. They then tried out their rules in L3 and checked the results against those entered in L2 {A2d}. This initially encouraged a trial-and-improvement method for getting the solution. It was interesting to note that, in later presentations to the class, students used this phrase naturally when describing their work.

The calculator accepts the conventional algebraic hierarchy and will allow L1 × 3 + 1, 3L1+1 or even L1 3+1. This has the advantage that students are not forced to write their rules according to some 'textbook' convention and allows for development and discussion about acceptable forms. Students had little problem converting their own formula, which might have been written in terms of say a symbol t or n, into one using L1, etc. The main advantage of the calculator is the rapid feedback students receive. Lack of, or misuse of brackets, for example, is soon picked up.

Students were given a variety of different spatial sequences, ranging in difficulty, to work on. They quickly devised their own methods for finding rules. A number used the difference method and recognized that the number you add on to get the pattern must have some bearing on the formula. Others relied on the spatial arrangements and began grouping dots or lines to help find a rule. While some discontinued using the calculator to check results, others, less confident, continued to use it for trial and improvement. Also, those concerned with presentation found it quicker to enter their results into the 'calculator tables' than to spend time drawing one in their books.

For some of the harder problems the students again returned to the calculator. They only used the technology when it was relevant and helpful rather than for the sake of it {A2b}{A4e}. The more able students were challenged to find the inverse rules or to move on to more difficult arrangements.

The same idea was used with three classes but with spatial arrangements and rules (linear, quadratic . . .) appropriate to the ability of the students. As a means of sharing their findings one class went on to produce posters. Another class (slightly lower ability) used the OHP to present their findings. This encouraged them to explain their thinking and justify their results. Students expressed their rules in several different ways; $2 \times n$ was written as $n \times 2$, $2n$, or even $n2$ all of which were accepted by the calculator. Some students had discovered this for themselves and took great delight in explaining this to the rest of the class, especially when they were told that this also demonstrated the commutative law.

In her presentation one girl wrote her 'linear' rule as n^3. When asked whether this looked confusing, students were quick to point out that this 'looks like n to the power 3, Miss, which means $n \times n \times n$, not $n \times 3$'. This led to the class deciding that the shorthand form of $n \times 3$ was best written $3n$ (the 'textbook' convention). Other points that came up in the various presentations were that one student had expressed her rule as $3a + a$, while the same sequence was expressed by another student as $4a$ – are these the same I asked? A rule was written $3n + 3$ by one group and $(n + 1) \times 3$ by another, are these the same? These presented further opportunities to return to the calculator to explore 'different' equivalent forms. Algebraic manipulation had been given ownership and the students were eager to find out if someone else's version of a rule really does work. Wanting to try out more algebra – that really is a worthwhile outcome!

Review and evaluation – activity review
The following is an analysis {A8a} of the lesson(s) using the activity review sheet. The purpose of this sheet is to provide some prompts to guide your analysis of the activity.

1. What did you expect to get from the task, i.e. purpose and learning intentions?
    These are defined in the Teaching/learning objectives in the lesson-plan.

2. What additional knowledge and skills did **you** need:
    about the technology?
    Using the data-handling facilities associated with the 'stat' key and the calculator's ability to manipulate 'lists'. For the follow-up lesson, how to plot data and superimpose functions.

about the mathematics?
Fairly confident with the mathematics, but talked to mentor about the expectations and level of challenge appropriate for this Year 9 group.

about teaching strategies and approaches?
How to engage all students in the whole-class interaction, use of the growing design and matchsticks as an initial task accessible to all students. The use of more open-ended questioning at the start of the lesson to establish what students already know. Getting the students to discuss in pairs to ensure everyone is involved was a good idea. I like collaborative work and often use this approach in my lessons. Students learn so much when they have to explain their thinking to others. It also improves their listening skills.

3. What additional knowledge and skills did the *students* need:
   about the technology?
   How to enter, edit and manipulate data in lists.

   about the mathematics?
   An ability to analyse growing patterns and convert observations in words into conventional mathematical symbols.

   about learning strategies and approaches?
   Be prepared to explore, {B12b} look for patterns and try things out, develop their use of visual imagery to explain their thinking. Work and cooperate with other students in their group. Explain and communicate ideas to other students in the class.

4. Was the focus of your teaching on developing skills or understanding?
   Both; I wanted students to develop students' reasoning and communication skills through an accessible context. I also wanted to develop students' understanding of equivalent algebraic expressions and introduce them to algebraic manipulation and give purpose for further work on this topic. Although I think it is much more important that students can use algebra to formulate/model situations.

5. Did the students focus on understanding or pressing buttons?
   At the beginning of the first lesson some time was spent getting used to the data-handling facilities on the GC. However, students were quick to come to terms with these and after an initial hiatus were able to use the GC with confidence to explore, check and validate their algebraic rules.

6. In what ways were your answers to questions 4 and 5 affected by the use of the technology for the topic?

   The technology acted as an extra 'teacher'. Students were able to try out their ideas on the calculator and it provided them with instant feedback on the validity of their conjectures and formulas.

7. Would the use of the technology for this topic change the order in which concepts were taught?

   Might try to introduce simple modelling and formal algebraic conventions earlier. Students coped well with the symbolism in the context of growing geometric patterns and had little difficulty using the GC.

8. What were the benefits/disadvantages of using the technology?

   Benefits; see 5,6 and 7. Disadvantages; some initial problems getting to know the GC. I had considered using 'mouseplotter' and/or a spreadsheet in the school's computer room but chose the GC because of its easy use in the classroom and the similarity of the GC's notation with the standard algebraic convention.

9. What would you do differently next time?

   As students become familiar with the GC I will get the students to plot the results and link the graphs to the rules such as the kind of rule that produces a straight line and the connection with the gradient and the intercept.

4.3(b) Modelling skeleton towers

We have included here another example of a teacher using a practical context to help Year 10 students develop their algebraic modelling skills. As you read through the following account, try to identify which of the 'Individual Training Needs' apply to this activity.

 In which do you feel confident already?

 Which would you identify as your priority?

You might like to use the activity review sheet (available on the accompanying website and summarized on p. 159) to help you with this process.

Background
Following the purchase of our TI-82 graphing calculators, I was very keen to develop activities that related to Ma3 (Algebra) and in particular, modelling sequences. I had in mind an activity that used the STAT Plot facility to scattergraph a sequence and then 'fit' this data to an equation using the function graphing facility.

I was aiming this activity at a set 1, Year 10 class.

If I was to develop this activity, I needed to accomplish two things:

- Spend some time investigating numbers generated from a series of linear, quadratic, cubic, quartic . . . functions and then investigate the differences. This was a prerequisite as I wanted students to discover that this could be a key to the type of function that they were dealing with.
- Generate the sequence that the students were going to fit from a practical situation, as I wanted students to be able to prove their function both geometrically and algebraically.

The following task sheet summarizes the two activities:

Exploring sequences using the TI-82

Make a growing pattern using multi-link cubes.

Record the cumulative number of cubes needed for each layer.

Enter the layer number in List 1 and the cumulative number of cubes in List 2.

Select a suitable window and plot the data as a scattergraph.

Explore the differences in your sequence to try to determine the type of function that it could be, i.e. linear, quadratic, cubic, quartic, etc. Try to determine the exact function by superimposing your guess using the Y = button.

Check for accuracy using zoom.

Once you have found your equation, can you 'prove' it geometrically by remaking your shape?

Why does your equation work?

Activity 1
This was a mammoth task in itself, as I was asking students to investigate $y = mx + c$, $y = ax^2 + bx + c$ and $y = ax^3 + bx^2 + cx + d$ in about three 50-minute lessons, so I used a teaching method that is very successful when you wish students to discover things through investigation in a short timescale. I delegated each table of three or four students a function to investigate, and within the group each student would change one variable at a time. This also meant that I could differentiate, with more able students investigating the most challenging equation. Each student set up a master spreadsheet that allowed them to put in a sequence of numbers and watch the differences pan across. I gave the students two options for generating their sequence. Having chosen an equation, they took x values from 1 to 7 and either typed the equation into the spreadsheet to generate the sequence or used the TI-82s to define L2 as a function of L1.

Each group collated their results and presented their findings to the rest of the class. I then coordinated the whole-class collection of results into a table for future reference.

Activity 2
The next part of the task was to generate a sequence from a practical activity, and I decided that an extension of the 'growing patterns' work in Year 8 was in order.

Students had previously investigated linear growing patterns, graphed their results and come up with some rules. We discussed these models and how we could 'put them together' to make something more interesting. We talked about counting the number of cubes cumulatively and looking for patterns. The students expected there to be a 'rule' for any pattern that was building up in an orderly way and I did not put restrictions on the type of pattern they chose. The group discussion seemed to throw out any dodgy models!

The class was already familiar with putting sequences into STAT memory and I then showed them how to do a STAT plot, plotting the data as a scattergram. We discussed the idea of modelling the curve by choosing a function in the Y= graphing mode and trying to make it go through the points. Very quickly it became obvious that there were an infinite number of equations to try, so students looked at the differences in their sequences to get some clues as to the type of function they were looking for.

This is where the table of results in Activity 1 became invaluable.

Having found their function, students used the zoom function to check for accuracy. Some interesting points came out . . .

If each layer of the model was constructed from a linear growing pattern they were looking for a quadratic function. (These I called the skeleton models as they built up in two dimensions.) If each layer of their model was built up from a quadratic growing pattern (i.e. a space-filling one) the function was a cubic one. This gave my most able students something to bite on as they were thinking how they could generate a quartic function. Other ideas that we discussed were:

- taking a step back to the original Year 8 growing-pattern graphs and investigating the areas beneath the lines (or curves) and looking for connections;
- investigating the gradients of the modelled curves at different x-values;
- some of the students were looking for an equation for the sum of the square numbers, so they were directed to A level text for research.

The final part of the project was to prove the shape geometrically by rebuilding the model from the equation and there was immense satisfaction from the students if they were successful.

Extension

It would be an ideal opportunity to introduce some calculus. Initially, students would need to explore the linear function of their growing pattern by looking at each layer separately. They could explore the area under the line between zero and different values of x. These could be related back to the x-values of the linear function.

Evaluation

This is definitely an activity that is firmly on our Year 10 scheme of work. It enabled students to make great progress in their understanding of the nature of functions both graphically and algebraically. The multi-link skeleton towers gave a practical context that was easy for students to explain and justify their algebraic models. It has also been used as a short task for GCSE coursework with linear models for foundation-level students. This has produced some coursework of a high standard.

4.3(c)   Polygons and stars

The following worksheet is a summary of the task given to Year 10 students studying for the intermediate and higher tiers of GCSE.

POLYGONS/STARS

Figure 1 was created using parametric (Par), degree (Degree) and connected (Connected) mode and the following functions:

$$X_{1T} = 5\cos T$$
$$Y_{1T} = 5\sin T$$

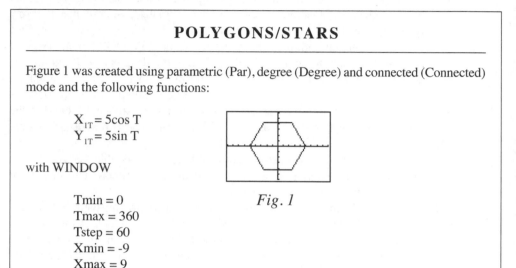

with WINDOW

Tmin = 0
Tmax = 360
Tstep = 60
Xmin = -9
Xmax = 9
Xscl = 1
Ymin = -6
Ymax = 6
Yscl = 1

Fig. 1

Experiment with the values in WINDOW. Make a note of your observations and try to explain them. What effect does changing the number **5** in X_{1T} and Y_{1T} have on the appearance of the polygon?

Try $X_{1T} = 5\cos (T+30)$, $Y_{1T} = 5\sin (T+30)$

Sketch the result. Explore values other than **30**.

CHALLENGE – FIVE-POINTED STAR

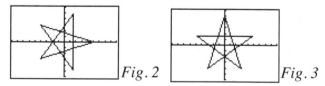

Fig. 2   *Fig. 3*

Figs 2 and 3 were produced by changing values in the WINDOW and small alterations to X_{1T} and Y_{1T}. Try to find out what these were.

Create your own pointed stars. How many different pointed stars can you make?

Background
This activity has been used with a wide range of students at both Key Stages 3 and 4 for different purposes. In one particular class it was used as a means of revising trigonometry and extending the trigonometric functions beyond the normal range of 0° to 90° {A4a}. It was also used to motivate students and help them see how mathematics can be used to model images and pictures. More able students extended their use of trigonometry to model and explore variations of the 'Tea-cup ride' (see case-study 4.3.4).

The lesson(s)
I first showed the whole class octagonal and pentagonal ATM mats and asked them what other designs or logos they were familiar with. Some mentioned the logos used by car manufacturers and those of the different TV channels. I said we could use the graphing calculator to create pictures such as these using trig. functions. I drew a 30°, 60° right-angled triangle, with hypotenuse 5, on the blackboard and asked them how they could calculate the lengths of the other sides. The students had done some work on bearings and rectangular grid references and I then showed them how these calculations could also be used to calculate the coordinates of a point.

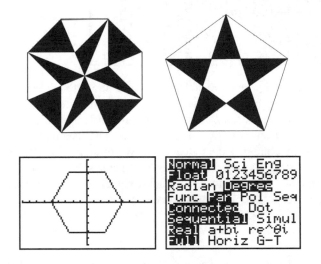

I showed them the picture of the hexagon using the viewscreen and OHP {A4a} and how I had created it using the Degree, Par mode. Also, the trig. functions I had used and the WINDOW settings.

This was quite difficult for a large portion of the class but they were undaunted and I set them the task of trying to draw a pentagon. I challenged the more able students to draw the pentagonal star and gave out the Polygons/Stars worksheet {B11a} as a reminder for the calculator settings and to prompt their thinking about how they might reorientate their polygons/stars. Some students worked in pairs while others worked in threes and fours. By the second lesson, students were setting themselves their own challenges, some creating nested polygons in different orientations {A1c} {B13d}.

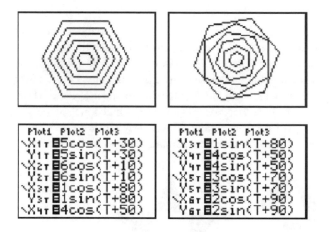

I asked the students who produced the diagrams above to tell me which hexagons matched which functions. They were able to explain quite clearly how they had arrived at their 'family' of hexagons, which numbers affected the size and which affected the orientation. A number of other students noticed that they could change the orientation by changing the value Tmin. We then discussed why this was so. Other groups of students generated circles (small step size) and families of ellipses. We discussed how the calculator draws 'approximate' circles. One particular group decided to produce a 'poster' of their work.

To ensure that students gained as much from the activity as possible I got different groups to explain what they had been doing and how they had created their particular designs {A2f}. At different stages throughout the lesson I would ask the students to explain their designs in terms of the trig. functions {A2f}.

Of course this activity is suitable for exploration with any type of graphing software which plots parametric functions, such as Autograph.

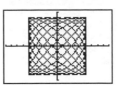

, Circles and ovals

First we drew a circle on the graph:

$$x_{1T} = 5\cos(t+20)$$
$$y_{1T} = 5\sin(t+20)$$

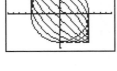

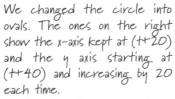

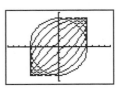

We changed the circle into ovals. The ones on the right show the x-axis kept at (t+20) and the y axis starting at (t+40) and increasing by 20 each time.

This made the shape narrower.
On the left we kept the y axis constant at (t+20) and changed the x axis by 20 each time starting at (t+40).

For each set we loaded them on top of each other to make an envelope of shapes. As we were able to store the pictures in the calculator we printed the pictures out so it was possible to see how the 'family of lines' was made up. Finally we put the envelopes of both sets together and made a picture which made up a square even though the shape was not actually drawn as a square.

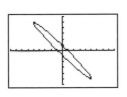

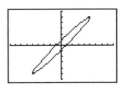

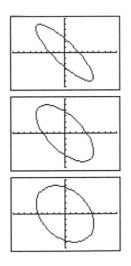

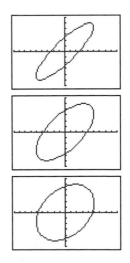

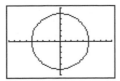

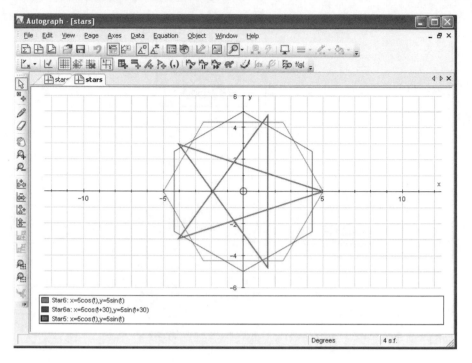

What were the learning outcomes from this lesson?

4.3(d) The 'Tea-cup ride'

The lesson(s)
I introduced this task by asking students how many had been to the local theme park
and which rides they had been on. Several of them knew the 'Tea-cup ride' and I
asked one of them to describe it to the others.

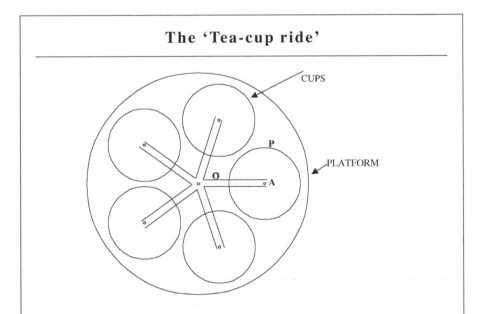

The diagram shows a view of a fairground ride. The ride consists of a rotating
platform upon which sit five 'cups'. Each 'cup' in turn rotates about its own
axis. The platform rotates about the centre '**O**', while each cup rotates about
the end of an arm (e.g. '**A**').

   Explore the loci of a person sitting at the perimeter of a cup (e.g. '**P**') for
different radii and rates of rotation.

I showed them a movie clip of the ride that I had taken at a fairground and the plan view of the ride (prepared using a word-processing and dynamic geometry package) {B11a} on the IWB. I then asked them to imagine looking down on the ride and to visualize the path (locus) of a person sitting in one of the cups as both the platform and cup rotated. I told them that for a single revolution of the platform (about O) the cup travelled through two revolutions (about A). Also, that the radius of the cup (AP) was half the length of the arm (OA). I asked them to sketch their ideas in their exercise books and compare them with their neighbour's drawings. There was a great deal of discussion about the number of loops and whether they would be inside or outside a larger 'circle', whether the starting position of the person (P) made any difference. I asked them how they could check. Several said that they could make some accurate drawings. I said that in addition to their compasses, protractors and rules they could use geostrips, paper-fasteners and card. I also made available some A3 paper {B13d}. Some of the students decided to construct part of the ride, i.e. a single arm with an attached circle, marked every ten degrees. They were then able to produce quite a rapid locus.

This took most of the lesson, but as students arrived at their solutions to the particular problem I told them that for the remainder of the lesson and the next, I now wanted them to explore the ride for different radii and rates of rotation. They had to decide on the particular values. I said it would be sensible for them to divide up the tasks in their groups.

There is a small group of very able students in this class, and I set them the task of trying to model the ride using trig. functions. They could then use *Omnigraph* or the graphing calculator to produce several different loci quickly {B13d} {B14a}. They had coped well with the 'Polygons/Stars' using the graphing calculator and this was a natural extension to see if they could apply their knowledge of trig. functions to this new problem. To start with they modelled the first problem, with the cup revolving twice about A for every revolution of the platform about O, incorrectly with the coordinates of P being:

$$X = 2\cos(T) + \cos(2T)$$
$$Y = 2\sin(T) + \sin(2T)$$

They had actually produced a cardioid instead of the figure which they had produced from their compass-and-ruler drawings.

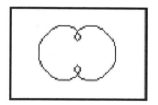

They soon realized their mistake {A8a}. They had forgotten to take into account that the cup was rotating *relative* to the platform and therefore at three times the rate, not two, from the observer's point of view.

```
Plot1 Plot2 Plot3
\X1T■2cos(T)+cos
(3T)█
 Y1T■2sin(T)+sin
(3T)
\X2T=
 Y2T=
\X3T=
```

They were then able to produce a wide range of loci to model and explain the effect of different starting-points for *P*. For example, the following locus was produced with *P* starting at 90 degrees to the arm.

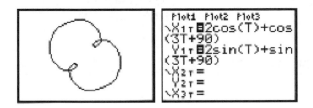

```
Plot1 Plot2 Plot3
\X1T■2cos(T)+cos
(3T+90)
 Y1T■2sin(T)+sin
(3T+90)
\X2T=
 Y2T=
\X3T=
```

They also explored what would happen if the cup rotated in the opposite direction, e.g.

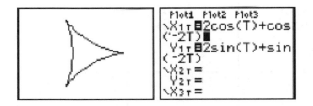

```
Plot1 Plot2 Plot3
\X1T■2cos(T)+cos
(-2T)█
 Y1T■2sin(T)+sin
(-2T)
\X2T=
 Y2T=
\X3T=
```

and the impact this would have on a person sitting in the ride.

A number of these students continued to work on this activity and submitted it for their GCSE coursework {A3c}. They also generalized their formula to increase the efficiency and speed of producing loci:

$$X = A\cos(T) + B\cos(RT)$$
$$Y = A\sin(T) + B\sin(RT)$$

where *A* and *B* are the radii of the platform and cup respectively, and *R* depends on the comparative rates of revolution of cup and platform. Other students, although unable to model the locus using trig. functions, were able to insert values into the given model to check their own loci {A8b}. I also set the class the task of finding out the names of the curves that they produced. This introduced them to new words to describe curves that crossed and touched (double points and cusps) and ways in which they might classify their loci.

Extensions in the sixth form

I have used this and other fairground rides to add interest and context to the mechanics section of the A level course. I added the following extension task:

> The central point can be driven up to about 20 rpm and it is recommended that 'a force of no more than 2g be exerted on the human frame' (NASA).
>   Design a suitable ride.

Of course this activity is also suitable for exploration with any type of graphing software which plots parametric functions, such as TI-Nspire™.

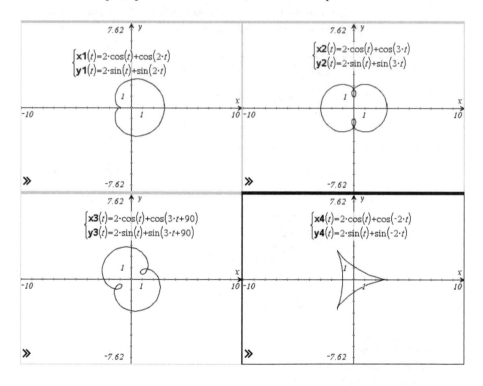

✎ *You might like to tackle this problem yourself.*

4.3(e) Distance–time match

Background

The following classroom studies are taken from a cross-curricular research project supported by the Teacher Training Agency (TTA) and the project report *Data-capture and Modelling in Mathematics and Science*, (Oldknow and Taylor, eds, 1998). It was written for the Mathematics Curriculum IT Support group, which was funded by the Department for Education and Employment to help promote the use of ICT to enhance the teaching and learning of mathematics.

Each school used the CBR motion-detector, in both science and maths lessons, attached to a teacher's TI-82 or 83 graphing calculator, projecting via the 'Viewscreen' LCD pad on top of a standard OHP. The CBR contains a program in its own memory called 'Ranger' which can be easily downloaded to any compatible graphing calculator. This enables easy control of the CBR and allows a variety of styles of use. In the first classroom study, a mathematics teacher from one of the Portsmouth schools (a girls' school) describes some of the approaches he has used. They illustrate nicely how he managed his lessons around a minimum provision of technology, and also how he built progression into the different activities he planned.

We have also included summary reports from other schools in other studies to indicate the different approaches and methods of organization that can be used with this technology.

Classroom study

At my school, distance–time graphs are introduced in Years 8/9 depending on the abilities of the groups, and so the following work was developed mainly for use at KS3. My main aims for the CBR activities were to try to address some of the issues concerning understanding of graphical interpretation using activities that promoted discussion and provided time for reflection {A2a, c}. Brian Hudson (*Micromath*, **13**(2), 1997) describes this as a 'cycle' of: 'observation, reflection, recording, discussion feedback (test)'. The first set of activities are using the 'Distance Match' option from the 'Applications Menu'. I found that this was suitable for intermediate and higher groups in Year 8. With a higher Year 9 group the second set of activities are using the distance–time graphs from the plot menu and the third set involved using the functions of the graphing calculator to fit equations of lines to parts of the distance–time graphs {A2a, c} {B14b}.

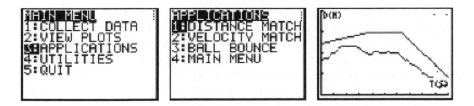

The lesson(s)

This activity was started by showing on the OHP one of the graphs from the 'Ranger' program that fitted the constraints of the room. There was then classroom discussion about what the graph could mean and what it represents. We examined the axes and looked to see if we could work out the coordinates of what were considered by the students to be the key points of the graph. The class was then split up into groups and given 15 minutes to try to work out a journey that would correspond to the graph shown. They were each given an A3 piece of squared paper so that they could, if they wished, sketch the graph. They put a diagram of the journey onto a piece of sugar paper. At the end of the 15 minutes, one of the groups volunteered to show their conclusions and to map out the journey in the classroom. The CBR was then used so that one of the members of the group could walk through the journey to see how close their match was. There was then a class discussion about how successful the attempt had been and how the journey could be changed in order more closely to match the graph on the OHP {A1b}. The class was then given another five or so minutes to review their ideas in the light of what they had seen and then another group volunteered. After two or three attempts quite a successful match was made {B11b}. The students were then encouraged to write about their experiences: how their ideas had changed throughout the lesson, and how they had changed their initial ideas to get a closer match.

For the second set of activities the 'Plot' menu was used. Working in groups of five, the students started by devising a journey which they mapped out on the floor of the classroom, taking measurements as necessary. Then, on a piece of A3 graph paper using the same axes as in the 'Plot' menu, they sketched as accurately as they could the graph of what the journey would look like on a distance–time graph. They needed to consider not only the distances involved but also the time needed to travel each part of the graph. When their graphs were ready, after about 30 minutes, the groups took it in turns to explain about their journeys, show their graphs and then, after some rehearsal, to plot their journeys using the CBR {A1b}. There was then some classroom discussion about how close the OHP graph was to the sketch that the group had produced, and the good points of the sketch were picked out by the students and ideas were offered about how the sketch could be improved. This activity ran over three lessons and during that time the groups were increasingly more able to recreate their journeys on the OHP.

The third activity again used the 'Dist Match' application. One of the graphs was chosen and shown on the OHP. Each student then wrote a report about the graph, describing it as a journey as accurately as they could. Meanwhile I copied the distance–time data stored in the two lists L1, L2 from the OHP calculator onto eight other graphing calculators, using the cables and the transfer function. There followed a classroom discussion about the graph on the OHP and the key features were agreed on by the class. They were then split up into groups of four so that they could work on a copy of the graph that I had loaded into their calculators. I showed them on the OHP how to do a graph fit using the 'Y =' functions and set them the task of finding the equation for the first part of the graph. They were given about five minutes to get as close as they could and then volunteers put their ideas onto the OHP. There was classroom discussion about how close each attempt was to the original graph and a consensus was reached about the 'correct' equation {B12b}{B13b}. Similarly the equations of the other parts of the graphs were worked out. During the next lesson, the activity was repeated using a different 'Dist Match', and the equations of the lines were compared. The students then set out to find out how they could set up a system so that they could describe lines, i.e. how steep they were, etc. Once the students had written a journey in the form of a set of equations, they were encouraged to devise a journey which they mapped out in the classroom and to work out the journey in the form of equations only. Each group then set the rest of the class the task of sketching the graphs from the equations that they gave them and then of translating the graphs into a journey. Whilst the rest of the class were engaged upon this task, the group setting the problem were using the 'Plot' menu to produce their own graph using the CBR, and then were encouraged to see how closely their equations-based graph matched the one produced by the CBR.

Other studies

Other teachers preferred to prepare an OHP foil with examples of, say, five possible distance–time graphs and to get the students to try to match each one using a CBR and a graphing calculator in groups. Using say five CBRs and graphing calculators, it was possible to organize groups of six to perform the movements on the playground or in the corridor.

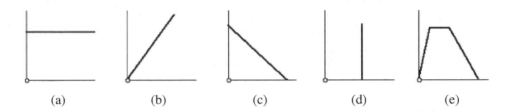

(a)　　　　　(b)　　　　　(c)　　　　　(d)　　　　　(e)

For example, in a Year 10 science lesson the students were given a variety of different shapes of (piecewise-) linear distance–time graph to try to reproduce: (a) horizontal, (b) diagonal upward, (c) diagonal downward, (d) vertical and (e) a mixture of diagonal upward, followed by horizontal, followed by diagonal downward. Groups of seven or eight shared a TI-82 and a CBR, and were let out into the playground to try to 'walk' appropriate journeys, and to keep notes. Subsequently they were asked to write up their observations back in the laboratory, and to describe the velocity at different points on each distance–time graph. The vertical line generated a great deal of discussion, and some very creative thinking {B14b}!

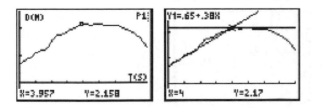

Meanwhile, in a Year 11 maths class, the students had also spent a lesson on data-collection and qualitative fitting. This was followed by a lesson on quantitative work in trying to decide suitable linear equations to 'fit' the distance–time graphs. Then they were asked to think of other shapes of mathematical curves they knew, and to try to 'walk' the appropriate trip. The following right-hand screen shows one group's attempt to 'walk a parabola'. The noisy data-points in the middle are due to the limitations on the CBR's operating range between a maximum of about 6 m and a minimum of about 0.5 m. With this data projected, the teacher then got the class to work at finding a quadratic function which gave a good fit to the data-points. At first they tried fitting a quadratic in the form: $y = ax^2 + bx + c$, but then it was suggested that, since its minimum was around (4,0) a curve of the form $y = k(x - 4)^2$ might be easier to work with.

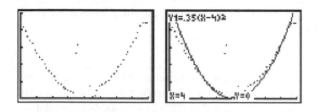

4.3(f) Modelling a bouncing ball

The CBR can also be used easily in other situations. For example, the 'Ball Bounce' application in the 'Ranger' program allows you to capture the distance from a bouncing ball to the ground against time as on p. 245–246. The CBR can be detached from the calculator while performing the experiment. Person A stands, perhaps on a chair, holding the CBR pointing towards the ground, while person B holds a ball (such as a basket ball) at least 0.5 m below the CBR. On the word 'go', A presses the CBR's trigger button and B releases the ball. It may take two or three attempts to get the ball bouncing more or less vertically. Then the CBR can be reconnected to the calculator for the captured data to be downloaded and displayed. The data has been transformed so that measurements are taken from the lowest point reached (i.e. the floor), rather than the distance from the CBR.

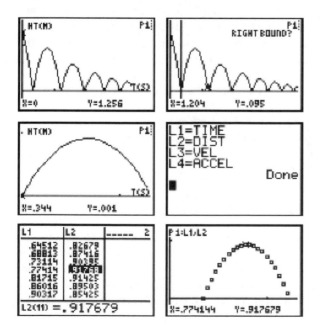

A cross-curricular project

The following account was written by a maths and a science teacher who were working together. They were keen to forge links between the two subjects and draw upon the relevant and *natural* opportunities in science lessons involving data-handling to carry out mathematical analysis and modelling.

Although the language used in mathematics and science is similar, the words used can often have different meanings, for example the word 'modelling' can be used qualitatively or quantitatively. When the pressure of a gas is measured as it is compressed in a cylinder at various volumes, a phrase such as 'the smaller the volume, the greater the pressure' expresses one model of the relationship between the volume V and the pressure P. The expression $PV=$ constant is a stronger quantitative model which allows you to predict the pressure P at any volume V. In science lessons we tended to place greater emphasis on the less precise qualitative form of modelling. For the most part, students are given scientific formulas such as $d = v \times t$ (distance = speed × time), and these are then rearranged and used to solve straightforward problems. We wanted our students to formulate their own models and be able to form links between the two subjects. We decided that a piece of coursework that able Year 10/11 students could use for both mathematics and science would be an effective and efficient way of forging these links for both students and teachers. It would need to satisfy both the science and the mathematics criteria, and encourage an investigative approach using research, planning, collection of data, analysis of results and evaluation. We felt that exploring the bounce of a ball would satisfy these criteria {A2a, c, g}.

We decided that we should do the practical ourselves so that we not only had first-hand experience of it but we could also help the students identify and iron out any technical difficulties. We also wanted to explore the potential scientific and mathematical content. This is what we came up with:

- *Science*: we would expect the students to research the science behind the bounce. They could predict the height of bounce based on previous experience and identify the equation (research for level 8 planning) {A3c}. Once they had identified the equation they would be able to apply it to their real data and explore the effect of different variables on the bounce of the ball. They could also look at energy changes that have taken place and try to explain them {A2g}.
- *Mathematics*: they would need to research the equation for the bounce of a ball and then establish how closely this model fitted the real data they would collect in their experiments. (See Chapter 5, section 5.5(e) for ways in which students tackled this problem.)

We were surprised at the ease with which data could be collected and the speed at which the students could analyse and fit different functions/models to this data. Our own scientific and mathematical knowledge was being stretched, and we both felt that we were working *with* the students, doing real maths and science. The students suggested several lines of enquiry on how the size, temperature and material affected the path and height of the bounce. They also dealt well with the practicalities of how to get fair and consistent real data.

Following is a list of hints and tips that we and the students found useful for carrying out this experiment:

- It is best to have the CBR clamped to a surface and to let the ball drop from a predetermined, labelled height.
- The surface that the ball bounces on should be smooth and hard. An upturned table can be used for carpeted areas.
- Large balls are better than small ones, with a smooth rather than rough surface. A tennis ball causes problems because the vibrations are absorbed and there is a fuzzy picture, similarly with a golf ball.
- The drop of the ball should be between 0.85 and 1.5 m.
- Remember the ball must be at least 0.5 m from the CBR.

Evaluation: students' and teachers' reactions
Here are some students' comments from one school on how they found using the CBR for practical work in the classroom had helped their learning.

Sebastian Day   **Maths Lesson**

The main thing about the lesson wasn't what I learnt but what I will remember.

Because of the lesson I doubt that I will ever forget the equation for a line.

$$y = mx + c$$

Nor will I forget what each of the letters stand for.

Thinking about the lesson, having some one walk up and down the classroom made it easier to understand the graph and decode the information that was given to you.

But now, because of this, whenever I see a complicated graph all I have to do is imagine myself walking the same as the graph lines and then I can understand exactly what's happening.

Another thing that I learnt that I'm sure I'll find useful is that the gradient for a line on a distance–time graph is the same as the speed.

Russell Labibi   Maths Homework

The lesson worked well and it was a good way of teaching something which otherwise could have been boring. I learnt a lot about distance-time graphs. I learnt about accelaration and velocity. The equation y = m x + c is used to draw lines on graphs. y stands for the y axis, m for the gradient, and c for the intercept.

The intercept can easily be read off of the graph. To work out the gradient you do the distance travelled divided by the time travelled. The graphing calculators were also good, keeping the class interested. It was also a good way of teaching us how to find gradients and intercepts.

Terry Ward 10 HW

In maths leat week we were doing work with a graphing calculator. In the first lesson we were using sensors to learn how a graphing calculator plots a distance-time graph. We had to move forward or backwards to try and match a graph on a wall. The sensors detected how far backwards or forwards we travelled and plotted it against the graph displayed on the whiteboard, e.g.

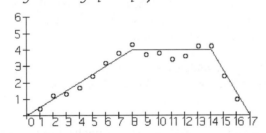

In the second lesson, sir displayed a graph on the whiteboard and then handed out some graphing calculators. The graph was displayed on each calculator and our job was to enter the coordinates to match the graph. After a while we found out the equation by trial and improvement. Sir told us how to find the intercept without an intercept point and we also re-learned the equation for a straight line.

All the teachers in the project found the equipment extremely reliable and easy to use. Obviously the sensitivity of the CBR, and its range of 0.5–6 m, restricted some of the ideas that they discussed for practical work. For example, it wasn't really possible to measure speeds of cars on a road, or easy to pick up a rolling object on the ground. But clearly a good range of practical activities was possible, which previously would have been impracticable to carry out, either in science or mathematics. The teachers were clearly encouraged by the way that the students responded to this kind of work.

The teacher from the Portsmouth Girls' School summed up his reactions:

> The use of the CBR and the graphing calculators was very popular with the girls. By monitoring the discussions and the interactions during the activities I observed many cycles of 'observation, reflection, recording, discussion feedback (test)'. The technology used in this way, supporting collaborative learning, empowered the girls to develop their levels of understanding as they tried to fulfil the aims of the activities. I believe that by developing more activities within the framework that I have set out above, using the CBR actively encourages students to make the very important links between graphs and algebraic relationships.

He went on to quote from Paul Ernest's chapter 'Social constuctivism and the psychology of mathematics education', which was published in a book he edited titled *Constructing, Mathematical Knowledge: Epistemology and mathematics education* (1996):

> First of all there is the active construction of knowledge, typically concepts and hypotheses, on the basis of experience and previous knowledge. These provide a basis for understanding and serve the purpose of guiding future actions. Secondly there is the essential role played by experience and interaction with physical and social worlds, in both the physical action and speech modes. This experience constitutes the intended use of the knowledge, but it provides the conflicts between intended and perceived outcomes which lead to the restructuring of knowledge, to improve its fit with experience.

It is interesting to contrast the students' positive responses with those problems observed by Kath Hart in *Children's Understanding of Mathematics: 11–16* (John Murray, 1989)

> . . . several students found difficulty with travel graphs, even though they appeared to be able to give the correct answer. It was clear that several of those interviewed had incorrect perceptual interpretations of the graph. Some thought of the graph as a journey that was up and down hill, or as directional on the ground, and found it difficult to deal with the abstract notion of distance from the origin . . . Many had no idea what was intended, while others had very vague ideas about graphs . . . While many children will be able to read information from a graph or to plot given data, it seems only a few will be able to understand the connection between an equation and a graph.

Other teachers reported on the remarkable progress of less able students, such as a bottom set Year 9, in their understanding and interpretation of such graphs, even with access to a single CBR {A5}.

4.3(g) Wrists and necks – designing a long-sleeved shirt/blouse

How do manufacturers decide on the sizes of collars and cuffs? What advice can we give?

Background

This starting-point has been used with GCSE mathematics and statistics classes as a means of introducing them to a range of statistical measures and forms of representation such as box and whisker plots, histograms, scattergraphs, etc. It is also a useful way of showing students how ICT can be used to support their statistical surveys in increasing the speed and efficiency of processing their data. In the study that follows, the teacher used the TI-83 graphing calculator because of its range of statistics features and the fact that it could be used in the normal mathematics classroom. She also used the opportunity to cover the topics of ratio and proportion, place value, degrees of accuracy and rounding to two decimal places. The students were reasonably familiar with the graphing calculators, having used them for everyday calculations and for plotting graphs.

The lesson(s)

Clothes play an increasingly important part in students' lives and I thought this task would make an interesting starting-point for the mathematics, in particular data-handling skills, that I wanted to teach. I asked them if they were aware of the kind of decisions that clothes manufactures have to make when designing and making, say, shirts and blouses. How do manufacturers decide on the size of collars and cuffs? A number of students suggested that this would depend on the design of the shirt or blouse, whether it was loose- or tight-fitting. I agreed, but asked them whether they thought there was a connection between wrist and neck measurements. Several said that they thought that there might be, and suggested that the neck was probably about three times the wrist. I then said we would collect some measurements from them and that I would show them how to use the statistics functions on the calculator to find answers to this, as well as look at the different ways we could display the data. Later they could use the graphing calculator to explore questions of their own.

I didn't have sufficient numbers of tape measures, so I handed out strips of A3 paper for them to take measurements. I said that it would be interesting to see if there were a gender difference and that it would be useful to enter these separately. I entered their results directly into the 'teacher's' graphing calculator using the viewscreen and OHP for the whole class to see. I inserted four headings: FW, FN, MW, MN (female wrist size, female neck size, etc.).

FW	FN	MW	1
15	32	16	
17	35	20	
20	41	19	
15.5	35	19	
17.5	36	17	
16	33	18	
15	35	17	

FW ={15,17,20,15...

FN	MW	MN
32	16	36
35	20	39
41	19	42
35	19	41
36	17	38
33	18	38
35	17	39

MN ={36,39,42,41

The full set of results is as follows:

FW	15	17	20	15.5	17.5	16	15	15	15	17	17	16	15.5	16
FN	32	35	41	35	36	33	35	34	34	37	35	35	36	34
MW	16	20	19	19	17	18	17	15.8	17.6	16.5	17.8	19.5	17.5	
MN	36	39	42	41	38	38	39	38	40.1	37	37	40	36	

Some of the students wanted to enter the data into their calculators, while others wrote them down in their exercise books. At this stage I did not want students to be distracted by questions about 'which keys to press'.

I then asked them how we could check out their conjecture that the neck was three times the wrist. Some suggested that we just divided **FN** by **FW** and **MN** by **MW** and compared several answers, others suggested finding the average size neck and wrist.

I asked them to do this in any way they chose. Most students used the graphing calculators in the normal home-screen mode. I showed them how we could calculate the ratio male wrist : male neck very quickly using the list commands (much like a spreadsheet).

MW	MN	L_1	↓ 5
16	36	2.25	
20	39	1.95	
19	42	2.2105	
19	41	2.1579	
17	38	2.2353	
18	38	2.1111	
17	39	2.2941	

L1 =" LMN/ LMW"

I then showed them how we could calculate the average ratio for boys in two ways:

```
sum(L₂)/13
        2.178609011
```

```
EDIT CALC TESTS
1⃝1-Var Stats
2:2-Var Stats
3:Med-Med
4:LinReg(ax+b)
5:QuadReg
6:CubicReg
7↓QuartReg
```

```
1-Var Stats
x̄=2.178609011
Σx=28.32191715
Σx²=61.8885735
Sx=.1245624309
σx=.1196757126
↓n=13
```

I said they could choose whichever they found easier. We discussed the 'funny' symbols on the right-hand screen above, including standard deviation, and I said that this was a way of measuring the variation. We also discussed what would be a suitable degree of accuracy.

I then asked the students to look at the female data and compare it with the male data.

I encouraged students to help each other, and most worked in pairs or threes. This makes it a lot easier when working on new skills with computers or graphing calculators. As a memory aid I also have a large display of the calculator pinned to the notice-board at the front of the class with some of the key menus such as WINDOW, STAT and MATH highlighted.

I asked them what else they could do to check the relationship, and several suggested a scattergraph. I said they could plot the data (boys and girls) onto graph paper or use the calculator. They would need to think about scales and starting-points on the axes. I showed them how to plot the points on the GC and for them to find a line of best fit. They could plot the data (boys and girls) separately and/or together.

I asked them for suitable sets of values for the axes. Wrist is on the *x* axis and neck the *y* axis. We superimposed both sets of data, squares for females and crosses for males.

They were familiar with plotting functions, so I asked them to select better values in the WINDOW and experiment with lines of best fit for both sets of data. One group produced the following for the combined data-sets:

Later, students established that $Y = 2X + 3$ gives a better fit (by eye).

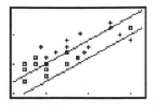

In the following lessons we discussed how we might try more 'mathematical' ways of getting a line to fit, through, for example, finding the 'average' wrist, neck point on the graph and looking at the lines that passed through this point. I also suggested that they could split the data in half (say, sorting on wrists) and find two averages, or use the line that passed through the lower and upper quartiles. (They noticed that they could get the quartiles, along with the mean, in the 1-Var Stats option.) I told them that the graphing calculator will work out a 'best fit' and showed them how this was done for the female data.

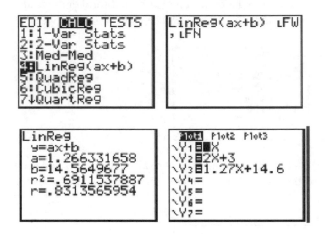

I then asked them to round the 'calculator equation' to a suitable degree of accuracy and compare this with their own. Some were curious to know how the calculator did this and I said that 'basically it minimizes the distance between the line and the points'. The plot below shows the female data.

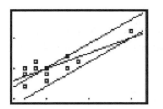

Later on, with the more able students, I showed them how they could manipulate the lists to look at the difference between their observed data (O) and the expected data (E) predicted by their model. We found the 'average difference' in two ways; using ABS(O-E) and $(O-E)^2$.

By the second and third lessons they were quite familiar with plotting scattergraphs manipulating the lists, including transferring data between calculators. I also showed them how to use the box and whisker plots and histogram options. The box and whisker plots are a really useful and accessible way of comparing data-sets.

I highlighted different parts of the box and whisker and asked them to interpret the diagram for the female and male wrist measurements. After showing them how to plot a histogram for the female neck sizes, I asked them to experiment with the scales (group size) and to compare male and female results.

In the third lesson I asked them to think of other data, and relationships, that might be important to manufactures in the clothing industry. Some students continued this topic and presented it for their coursework. One student found a reference to Leonardo da Vinci's 'Vitruvian Man' and the Golden Section/ratio on the Microsoft Encarta™ CD-ROM, and explored relationships between different sections of the body.

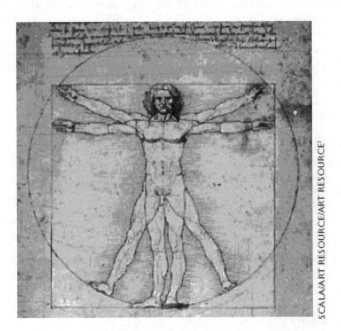

This drawing from the notebooks of Leonardo da Vinci, known as 'Vitruvian Man' after the architect Vitruvius, demonstrates the proportions of the Golden Section: the sections of the body from head to waist and from waist to feet are to each other what the section from waist to feet is to the length of the whole body.The fact that the 'divine proportion' was to be found in the human body was seen as highly significant in the Renaissance, the age of humanism.

He also got a great deal of satisfaction in understanding the following explanation (provided by Microsoft Encarta™).

Golden Section, in art and mathematics, a geometric proportion based on a specific ratio in which the greater part is to the lesser what the whole is to the greater. It is most clearly expressed as a line intersected in such a way (see diagram below) that the ratio of AC to CB is the same as that of AB to AC.

This ratio has the numerical value 0.618 . . . , which can be derived as follows: If AB = 1, and the length of AC = x, then AC/CB = AB/AC becomes $x/(1 - x) = 1/x$. Multiplying both sides of this equation by $x(1 - x)$ gives $x^2 = 1 - x$; therefore, $x^2 + x - 1 = 0$. This equation can be solved by using the quadratic formula, which yields the equation $x = (-1 + \pi)/2 = 0.6180339$ . . . Recognized as an aesthetically pleasing ratio, the Golden Section has been used as the basis on which the elements in a painting, or in an architectural scheme, are arranged. Plato is generally credited with establishing the study of the Golden Section, and the Greek mathematician Euclid, writing in the 4th century BC, defined this proportion in his chief work, *Elements*. The Golden Section was of great interest to artists and mathematicians of the Renaissance, when it was known as the Divine Proportion and was regarded as the almost mystical key to harmony in art and science. *Divina Proportione*, a treatise on the subject written by the great Renaissance mathematician Luca Pacioli and illustrated with 60 drawings by Leonardo da Vinci, was published in 1509, and influenced artists and architects of the age, among them Leonardo, Piero Della Francesca, and Leon Battista Alberti.

The Golden Section has also been used by later artists. Experiments suggest that human perception exhibits an innate preference for proportions that accord with the Golden Section. This in turn implies that artists may almost subconsciously arrange the elements of a picture according to those ratios.

Much of the data-handling can be done using hand-held devices, particularly GCs such as the TI-84s and TI-Nspire™. The report writing will need to be done on PCs – but data and images can be easily exported from GCs and other portable devices using Link software.

Of course the analysis and reporting could be carried out using data-handling software such as TI-Nspire™.

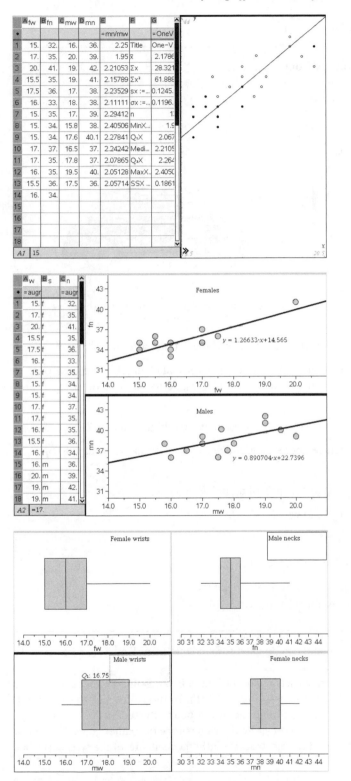

4.3(h)   A garage door

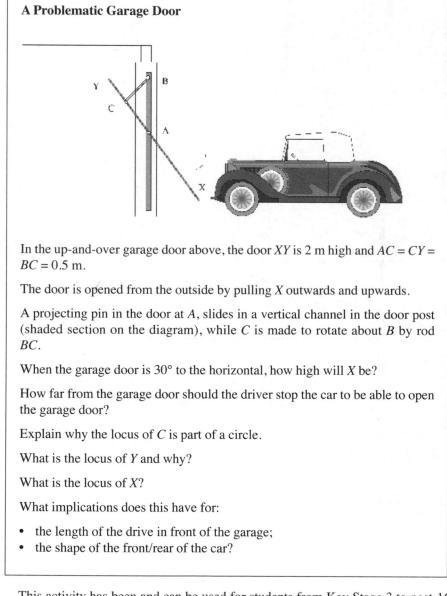

A Problematic Garage Door

In the up-and-over garage door above, the door *XY* is 2 m high and *AC* = *CY* = *BC* = 0.5 m.

The door is opened from the outside by pulling *X* outwards and upwards.

A projecting pin in the door at *A*, slides in a vertical channel in the door post (shaded section on the diagram), while *C* is made to rotate about *B* by rod *BC*.

When the garage door is 30° to the horizontal, how high will *X* be?

How far from the garage door should the driver stop the car to be able to open the garage door?

Explain why the locus of *C* is part of a circle.

What is the locus of *Y* and why?

What is the locus of *X*?

What implications does this have for:

• the length of the drive in front of the garage;
• the shape of the front/rear of the car?

This activity has been and can be used for students from Key Stage 3 to post-16 years.

It has been adapted from an activity described in Brian Bolt's Mathematics Meets Technology (Cambridge University Press, 1991). In the following study we will attempt to indicate how this task might be developed with students of different age and ability. I hope this will also illustrate the rich source of mathematics that can be found in the study of everyday objects, especially mechanisms of the type described in Brian Bolt's book. The brief reports below give a flavour of the kind of mathematical activity that can derive from this starting-point.

 We leave it to you to flesh out the details using your own choice of ICT tool.

The lessons

Key Stage 3 The whole of this task can be done practically using geo-strips, drawing-pins and/or paper fasteners. The loci of *C* and *Y* could be drawn practically which will help students in their explanations and reasons for their loci. The locus of *X* can be constructed using the above practical resources, but a proof is probably beyond students at this key stage.

Key Stage 4 (higher) and post-16 The problem can be modelled using coordinates and parametric equations involving trigonometric functions. Graphs can be drawn using ICT. Additionally, or alternatively, the problem can be modelled using dynamic geometry software.

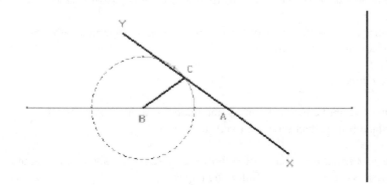

4.3(i) A collaborative project between a mathematics and a science teacher

Real life applications of the parabola and other conic sections

Background

Sharing a lift with colleagues from other subjects can lead to some very positive spin-offs. The benefits and outcomes for learners and the two teachers involved, one from mathematics and the other from science (physics), has encouraged two teachers to pursue other joint initiatives. This case-study refers to the work of a Year 10 class of high-attaining students, but sections of the work have also been carried out with a group of low-attaining students.

Aims of the project:

- to improve students' motivation and engagement through links between mathematics and science;
- to develop a deeper understanding of the formation and uses of parabolas in the real world;
- to increase familiarity with ICT software and tools including, video-analysis software, graphing packages/calculators and dynamic geometry;
- to utilize their prior knowledge of constructions, loci and transformations of graphs;
- to generalize and link the focus-directrix definition and properties with the Cartesian equation of the parabola.

Specific linked aims:

- to recognize parabolic paths of comets and understand they have a focal point;
- to understand how reflection in a curved surface works.

The students carried out a range of activities to address the above aims. A brief outline of these is described on the following pages.

✎ *How many different applications of the parabola can you think of?*

✎ *When and in what way were parabolas first considered?*

Modelling a suspension bridge

Although this series of lessons was about the properties of the parabola and its applications {A2g}, it was also felt that students should be aware that there was a range of other functions suitable for modelling the 'real world' and that, for example, a suspension bridge was not the same as a 'free' hanging chain (catenary), but that a catenary could be approximated or adjusted to form a parabola.

In this lesson the students were provided with a large picture of a pre-drawn parabola, retort stands, Blu-tack, string and paper-clips. They had to hang the string from the retort stands or Blu-tack but found that it would not hang as a parabola. They then added paper-clips to the string to achieve a match with the parabola. Students found that the paper-clips needed to be attached at equal intervals (horizontally) to achieve this. The application of this to suspension bridges was then considered.

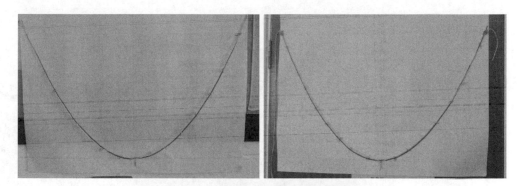

Modelling the projectile path of a 'siege' machine (catapult)

The particular catapult used for this activity can be adjusted for launch angle, speed of projection (adjusted by two variables: number of elastic bands and distance/arc of backward pull). In the first instance students were required to assess the effect of each of these variables on the distance covered by the ball and produce a suitable table of values that would predict its landing position.

They soon realized that changing too many variables at once prevented close analysis, took more time and meant that results could not be predicted with a good degree of accuracy. With a more systematic approach they were beginning to make reasonably accurate predictions within 15 minutes. Their understanding of the effect of the different variables was assessed by challenging them to catapult a ball into a bin, either sitting upright or lying down at a given distance.

A series of video-clips was also taken and imported into free video-analysis software Tracker.

This allowed for a more in-depth analysis of the path, for example the pull back angle and equation of the parabola {A2a}.

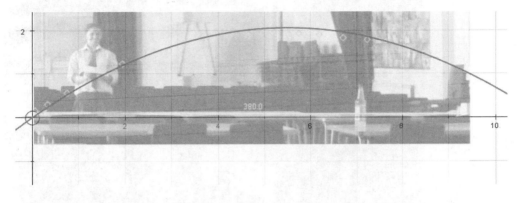

This image was then inserted into Autograph upon which a parabola was superimposed. In the above example the student forgot to adjust the scales to match the known distance (380 cm). Some students were more familiar with GSP and did the necessary adjustments to the *x–y* axes (see figure below).

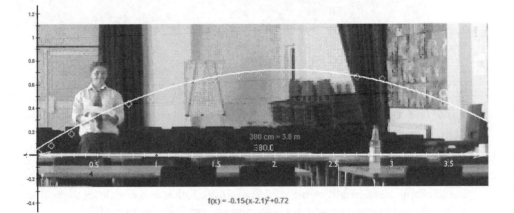

A number of the students used Tracker to analyse the graphs of x and y against time and the horizontal and vertical speeds of the ball. Being able to view simultaneously the video-clip, tracked markings and the resulting graphs and tables gave students insights in to the motion of the ball that would have been difficult, if not impossible, without this kind of software {B13d}.

Understanding the parabola as a locus and linking to the Cartesian equation

The line   *Me*

Here we see the students forming a 'human parabola' based on two fundamental loci; i.e. the set of points at a given distance from a *fixed point* and the set of points from a *fixed line*. The meaning of this latter locus led to good deal of discussion and after some debate students agreed that this was the shortest distance measured perpendicular to the line. They were then asked to stand equally distant from their teacher and the line. It took some time to appreciate the different positions that they could stand in, but once this was understood they then looked at how their location would change dynamically as their teacher moved further away or closer to the line. They then had to come up with ways they could construct this using ICT.

✎ *How would you construct a parabola from the focus-directrix definition using dynamic geometry software?*

The whole class managed to construct the locus, and over three-quarters of the class by the end of the lesson had also linked the focus-directrix distance to the Cartesian equation for the parabola. To simplify their investigation, all students placed the focus on the y axis but the position of the directrix varied. They produced two general forms for the parabola viz: $y = x^2/(2d)$ for focus $(0, d/2)$ and directrix $y = -d/2$ or $y = x^2/(2d) + d/2$ with focus $(0, d)$ and directrix on the x axis.

Modelling parabolic reflectors

In this lesson the main aims were to help students understand how lines reflect in parabolic curves, for them to recognize the practical implications of this, and to apply this knowledge to find the focal point of a given parabola.

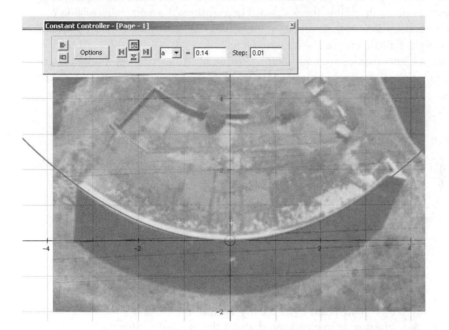

The lesson started by using Flash Earth to zoom in to the south-east coast of England and find the sound mirror in the Dungeness area {A1b}. This prompted some discussion about what it was for and whether it was parabolic. To review and consolidate earlier work the image was then rotated and inserted into Autograph. The class then gave instructions on the most 'efficient' positioning and modelled its equation, using the 'Constant Controller' to obtain its equation (i.e. modelling the picture rather than the actual object).

We then discussed {B16b} and what it was used for: a forerunner of radar, the sound-mirrors were intended to provide early warning of enemy aeroplanes (or airships) approaching Britain. They did work, but the development of faster aircraft made them less useful, as an incoming aircraft would be within sight by the time it had been located. Increasing ambient noise made the mirrors harder to use successfully, and then radar rendered acoustic detection redundant.

Suggest some topics that students could research prior to this lesson.

The class considered how the 'parallel' sound-waves would reflect off this curved surface. Quickly the students realized that these waves would essentially reflect off the tangent at the point of contact and they used their prior physics understanding that the 'angle of incidence equals angle of reflection'. Before we could actually 'reflect' these waves, they needed to realize that the mirror line was perpendicular to this tangent and so the concept of a Normal was introduced. They guessed that these waves reflected back to the focal point (which was to form the basis for their ICT investigation in the following lesson). There followed a wider discussion on the various applications of this property of parabolas – headlights and careful placement of the light-bulb, telescopes, solar ovens, etc.

The students then used graph-plotting software (Autograph) to model the above (i.e. the path of the incident rays parallel to the axis of symmetry and reflected rays).

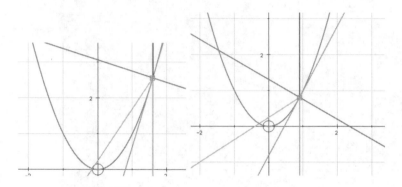

As they pulled their point dynamically around the parabola they were able to validate this amazing geometrical property of the parabola – that the reflected rays maintain a constant y-intercept – the focal point {B12b}.

Synthesizing learning – applying skills and knowledge to a new problem
The students were given the task of creating their own parabolic mirror. To create their template they could use any of the methods that had been taught and explored in previous lessons. They were also required to mark the focal point prior to testing. This was a way of assessing just what the students had learned and whether they could apply this to a new, and practical, real problem.

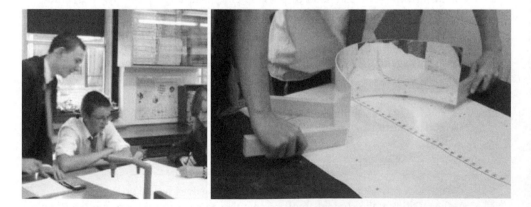

They had a range of practical materials: large sheets of flip-chart paper, mirrored plastic with blocks of wood attached and clamps to help secure the mirror in place. Once created, the accuracy and quality of their mirrors would be checked. This was done using a laser and smoke, generated by an artificial smoke machine, so that the entire length of the beam could be seen. For a true parabola, all rays parallel to the axis of symmetry and incident on the parabolic mirror should reflect and pass through their focal point.

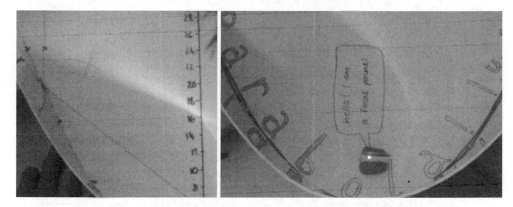

It was revealing {A8a}, and somewhat surprising, to see just how many students were unsure of how to draw a parabola with a reasonably wide curvature on the unfamiliar-sized flip-chart paper. There were basic practical considerations for students to think about, such as the scaling of the *x* and *y* axes. The methods used to draw the parabola and focal point were varied. Some used examples written in their books; some used their generalized focus-directrix formula to come up with an equation and the vertical distance from the turning-point, and others constructed tangents and normals to reflect a vertical line {A3b}.

Evaluation: student and teacher reactions

The following is the teachers' and students' own account:

> The depth of understanding the students gained was achieved because of the variety of activities and range of different approaches. Despite students having plotted quadratic equations and studied transformations of graphs, including those of parabolas, for their GCSE, there were still students in the first few lessons telling me they 'didn't know what parabolas were' {A7a}!
>
> Using ICT allowed the students to verify the parabolic nature of shapes, paths and loci generated by the different methods {A2c}. Loci, Cartesian equations and their graphs could be changed dynamically, and verified accurately and easily. Once the graph/locus had been constructed, being able to 'drag' it around to view the overall effect of an 'infinite' number of constructions was something that could not have been done by hand. Nor would it have been feasible for students to have created sufficient examples to generalize the connection between the equation and distance between the focal point and the directrix without the use of ICT {B12b, 13c}. I asked the

students how ICT use had added to their understanding and what ICT had enabled them to do. Here is a summary of their responses:

- It made things much quicker, so I made more progress.
- We couldn't possibly do this on paper.
- You can move things around and see how that affects things.
- You can see a range of results rather than just a single construction.
- ICT is very precise and it means that I can't make silly mistakes.
- It helps when I can see it happening in front of me – for example the trace to create a parabola.
- It has enabled me to do things a lot quicker rather than having to draw it on paper.
- It made our work very accurate.

However, the use of ICT would have been less effective, if not futile, without the preceding physical and written activities. The initial introduction via Human Loci was necessary to give students a concrete understanding of the focus directrix definition of the parabola and possible construction methods. Working through the constructions on paper further helped their understanding before they modelled the parabola using ICT.

I thought that the different approaches to creating the parabola were very effective, for example working from the focal point to find the parabola and vice versa significantly increased the depth of the students' understanding and the range of mathematical opportunities. This was most obvious in the final lesson where students were required to make their own parabolic mirror. The quality of discussion as groups considered the various options for drawing their parabola and its focal point was impressive. Their high degree of knowledge and understanding was also apparent when we discussed real-life examples – sound mirrors, shapes of headlight reflectors and the effect of varying the position of the bulb, solar ovens, etc.

These cross-curricular/real life applications added to their motivation by providing further relevance and purpose to their studies; however, the variety of intrinsically interesting activities and the beauty of maths was all that was necessary for many of them.

Next steps
Early next year these students will have opportunities to apply this knowledge when studying the paths of comets and reflection in curved mirrors in physics. If we have the time and resources, next year I would like the students to take what they have learned into 3D and design-nets that can be folded up to form a solar oven which we can use for a barbeque. This will help to form a bridge between our current work, other conic sections and 3D geometry.

This concludes the case-study aspect of this chapter. We have already shown the use of a completed activity review sheet at the end of case-study 4.3(a) 'Not just building a fence'. We have also prepared the following simple planning tool with a list of the activity review questions.

Planning a lesson

Some points to consider when planning a lesson incorporating ICT:

- The main learning objectives/intentions for the lesson.
- How will you cater for students of differing ability?
  This might be through, e.g.
  - a common starting-point accessible to all, with differentiation through questioning, extension tasks;
  - differentiated tasks.
- To what extent will the use of ICT enhance teaching and learning?
  ICT may support students' learning through, for example, enabling them to explore many cases rapidly (increased efficiency) and learning from feedback (see 'The pupil's entitlement to ICT in mathematics' on the accompanying website).
- Classroom organization and resources:
  - The kind of task(s) you will use, adapt or design yourself including ICT support/prompt sheets, prepared files (e.g. spreadsheet template, data file, etc.), extension tasks.
  - Will the class be working together, in collaborative groups or in pairs?
  - Encouraging students to help each other is particularly important when students are using a particular ICT tool for the first time.
- How will you judge the extent to which learning objectives have been addressed?
- Review and evaluation. You might also include an evaluation of the task itself, whether it was appropriate for the learning objectives, any adaptations you might make in future, etc. In addition you should evaluate the contribution that ICT made to students' knowledge and understanding. The activity review sheet should help here.

Activity Review

The purpose of this sheet is to provide you with some prompts to guide your analysis of the activity.

1. What did you expect from the task: i.e. purpose and learning intentions?
2. What additional knowledge and skills did you need:
   - about the technology
   - about the mathematics
   - about teaching strategies and approaches?
3. What additional knowledge and skills did the students need:
   - about the technology
   - about the mathematics
   - about learning strategies and approaches?
4. What was the focus of your teaching on developing skills or understanding?
5. Did the students focus on understanding or pressing buttons?
6. In what ways were your answers to questions 4 and 5 affected by the use of the technology for the topic?
7. Would the use of the technology for this topic change the order in which concepts were taught?
8. What were the benefits/disadvantages of using the technology?
9. What would you do differently next time?

At this point we hope you have read, and tried, enough to feel enthused to want to try using some ICT in your classroom (if you haven't already done so!) As with almost every other aspect of teaching, you should find it gets easier as you practise more. If possible it is best to have someone else you can compare notes with, seek advice from, plan jointly with, talk through your successes and disasters (yes – we have all had them!), etc.

 You should now re-read the TDA's Expected Outcomes to see just how far you think you match up to them at this point.

It would be a miracle if you could say that you have already met all the Expected Outcomes! But you should be able to see just how much progress you have made towards them already.

Before leaving this practical section of the book you should now start to draw up a personal action plan for your intended development over, say, the next three or four years. Think which activities and ICT tools you are going to concentrate on to begin with, and plan to get confident and competent in their use. Prioritize your 'gaps', and plan to meet some of them next year, some the year after, and so on. Keep an eye on what forms of further CPD may be open to you.

Look out particularly for activities mounted via subject professional associations, such as the ATM and MA in the UK. There is also a worldwide training organization called T-cubed, for Teachers Teaching with Technology, which exists in most countries around the world to support teachers using hand-held, and other, technology particularly in mathematics and science.

Obviously we hope that you will enjoy reading the rest of this book, but we will take the opportunity to wish you *bon voyage* in applying ICT in making your teaching, and your students' learning, of mathematics more effective. Good luck.

Chapter 5

How to choose appropriate ICT for your curriculum

5.1 INTRODUCTION

In this chapter we break the curriculum down into bite-size chunks and look for ways in which ICT tools can support teaching and learning of specific pieces of mathematics content, such as number or algebra. However, there are many dangers in creating false divisions between parts of mathematics and in treating mathematics apart from other subjects, so we also try to inject examples of more synthetic, and cross-subject, approaches. By the end of this chapter you should be in a strong position to identify *which* aspects of school mathematics are amenable to its use.

You have had an opportunity to learn about and, we hope, explore a wide range of different ICT tools (hardware and software) which are potentially of interest to mathematics teachers. Now we take a look at the mathematical content of the school curriculum and start to identify a selection of material and approaches where ICT can be an integral part of the teaching and learning process. Of course there is variety in both the content and style of presentation in the mathematics curriculum between different countries. For example, within the UK there are different curricula for England, Scotland, Wales and Northern Ireland, as well as differences between the amount of mandatory ICT use which teachers are obliged to provide for their students.

Our style here is one of 'theme and variations', where we take an aspect, such as place value in arithmetic, and suggest a number of different ways in which it can be supported, depending on the ICT available. We also provide references to relevant examples of teachers writing about their own experiences. Our aim is to stimulate your imagination (and, we hope, whet your appetite) so that you will come up with ideas of your own to fit in with your personal teaching style and strategies. We also aim that, by working at applications which are realistic to you in the context of mathematics teaching, to enable you to become more aware of the capabilities of suitable ICT tools and proficient in their use.

Of course there is more to the curriculum than just a content list. The current version of the English mathematics curriculum 11–16 includes the following passage on the importance of mathematics:

> Mathematical thinking is important for all members of a modern society as a habit of mind for its use in the workplace, business and finance; and for personal decision-making. Mathematics is fundamental to national prosperity in providing tools for understanding science, engineering, technology and economics. It is essential in public decision-making and for participation in the knowledge economy.
>
> Mathematics equips students with uniquely powerful ways to describe, analyse and change the world. It can stimulate moments of pleasure and wonder for all students when they solve a problem for the first time, discover a more elegant solution, or notice hidden connections. Students who are functional in mathematics and financially capable are able to think independently in applied and abstract ways, and can reason, solve problems and assess risk.
>
> Mathematics is a creative discipline. The language of mathematics is international. The subject transcends cultural boundaries and its importance is universally recognized. Mathematics has developed over time as a means of solving problems and also for its own sake.

It also places key concepts and key processes at the heart of the curriculum, e.g.:

1. Key concepts
There are a number of key concepts that underpin the study of mathematics. Pupils need to understand these concepts in order to deepen and broaden their knowledge, skills and understanding.

1.1 Competence
a. Applying suitable mathematics accurately within the classroom and beyond.
b. Communicating mathematics effectively.
c. Selecting appropriate mathematical tools and methods, including ICT.

1.2 Creativity
a. Combining understanding, experiences, imagination and reasoning
b. to construct new knowledge.
c. Using existing mathematical knowledge to create solutions to unfamiliar problems.
d. Posing questions and developing convincing arguments.

1.3 Applications and implications of mathematics
a. Knowing that mathematics is a rigorous, coherent discipline.
b. Understanding that mathematics is used as a tool in a wide range of contexts.
c. Recognizing the rich historical and cultural roots of mathematics.
d. Engaging in mathematics as an interesting and worthwhile activity.

1.4 Critical understanding
a. Knowing that mathematics is essentially abstract and can be used to
b. model, interpret or represent situations.
c. Recognising the limitations and scope of a model or representation.

2. Key processes
These are the essential skills and processes in mathematics that pupils need to learn to make progress.

2.1 Representing
Pupils should be able to:
a. identify the mathematical aspects of a situation or problem
b. choose between representations
c. simplify the situation or problem in order to represent it mathematically, using appropriate variables, symbols, diagrams and models
d. select mathematical information, methods and tools to use.

2.2 Analysing
Use mathematical reasoning
Pupils should be able to:
1. make connections within mathematics
b. use knowledge of related problems
c. visualize and work with dynamic images
d. identify and classify patterns
e. make and begin to justify conjectures and generalizations, considering special cases and counter-examples
f. explore the effects of varying values and look for invariance and covariance
g. take account of feedback and learn from mistakes
h. work logically towards results and solutions, Recognizing the impact of constraints and assumptions
i. appreciate that there are a number of different techniques that can be used to analyse a situation
j. reason inductively and deduce.

Use appropriate mathematical procedures
Pupils should be able to:
k. make accurate mathematical diagrams, graphs and constructions on paper and on screen
l. calculate accurately, selecting mental methods or calculating devices as appropriate
m. manipulate numbers, algebraic expressions and equations and apply routine algorithms
n. use accurate notation, including correct syntax when using ICT
o. record methods, solutions and conclusions
p. estimate, approximate and check working.

2.3 Interpreting and evaluating
Pupils should be able to:
a. form convincing arguments based on findings and make general statements
b. consider the assumptions made and the appropriateness and accuracy of results and conclusions
c. be aware of the strength of empirical evidence and appreciate the difference between evidence and proof
d. look at data to find patterns and exceptions
e. relate findings to the original context, identifying whether they support or refute conjectures
f. engage with someone else's mathematical reasoning in the context of a problem or particular situation
g. consider the effectiveness of alternative strategies.

2.4 Communicating and reflecting

Pupils should be able to:

a. communicate findings effectively
b. engage in mathematical discussion of results
c. consider the elegance and efficiency of alternative solutions
d. look for equivalence in relation to both the different approaches to the problem and different problems with similar structures
e. make connections between the current situation and outcomes, and situations and outcomes they have already encountered.

The Explanatory notes also include some specific references to ICT such as the following.

Select mathematical information, methods and tools: This involves using systematic methods to explore a situation, beginning to identify ways in which it is possible to break a problem down into more manageable tasks, and identifying and using existing mathematical knowledge that might be needed. In statistical investigations it includes planning to minimise sources of bias when conducting experiments and surveys, and using a variety of methods for collecting primary and secondary data. ICT tools can be used for mathematical applications, including iteration and algorithms.

Varying values: This involves changing values to explore a situation, including the use of ICT (e.g. to explore statistical situations with underlying random or systematic variation).

Evidence: This includes evidence gathered when using ICT to explore cases.

Alternative solutions: These include solutions using ICT.

There is also guidance on the opportunities which should be provided to students:

4. Curriculum opportunities

During the key stage students should be offered the following opportunities that are integral to their learning and enhance their engagement with the concepts, processes and content of the subject.

The curriculum should provide opportunities for pupils to:

1. develop confidence in an increasing range of methods and techniques
2. work on sequences of tasks that involve using the same mathematics in increasingly difficult or unfamiliar contexts, or increasingly demanding mathematics in similar contexts
3. work on open and closed tasks in a variety of real and abstract contexts that allow them to select the mathematics to use
4. work on problems that arise in other subjects and in contexts beyond the school
5. work on tasks that bring together different aspects of concepts, processes and mathematical content
6. work collaboratively as well as independently in a range of contexts
7. become familiar with a range of resources, including ICT, so that they can select appropriately.

In considering the content we can identify some different roles for the ICT, for instance, as:

1. a generator of problems, e.g. using random numbers;
2. a checker of results, e.g. in comparing a student's input with computed results;
3. a provider of context, e.g. in the form of a game.

We can also think of different ways the ICT may be deployed by:

4. the teacher using ICT with whole-class display, e.g. to stimulate discussion;
5. students working in pairs or small groups using ICT in a task or investigation;
6. the teacher using ICT to prepare material for the class;
7. students using ICT to communicate results.

Beware! There are very many ideas contained in this chapter so you will probably just want to select a few at first reading, and maybe come back for more when those have been digested.

5.2   NUMBER

5.2 (a)   Place value

If we start with the idea of rounding an integer to a given power of 10 then we can consider illustrating some of the different approaches in the points 1–7 above. For example, a very simple way of combining 1 and 4 is to use a graphing calculator to generate a random integer with, e.g., five digits, and to display it using an LCD panel for the overhead projector. An alternative is to use 'emulator' software such as TI-SmartView™ projected onto an interactive whiteboard, or to use mathematical software such as TI-Nspire™.

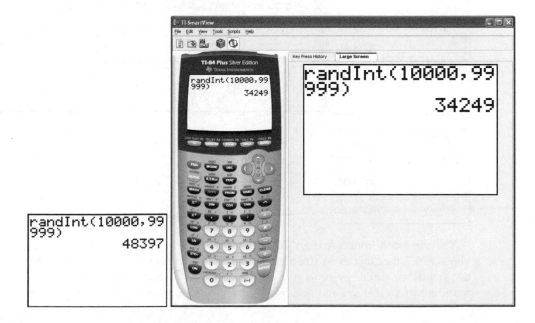

	A	B	
1	91748	randint(10000,99999)	
2	23201		
3	56323		
4	46522		
5			
6			

A1	=randint(10000,99999)

Then the class can be asked to write down what they think the answer is to the nearest 10, 100, 1,000 and 10,000. The advantage here is that the teacher is just as unprepared for the actual problem as the students. So, psychologically, it may appear to be the class and teacher working together to crack the problems posed by the machine. Of course, we can get the calculator and/or computer to display the set of answers.

	A	B	C	D	E
1	91748	91750.	91700.	92000.	
2	23201	23200.	23200.	23000.	
3	56323	56320.	56300.	56000.	
4	46522	46520.	46500.	47000.	
5					

B1	$=\text{round}\left(\dfrac{a1}{10},0\right)\cdot 10$

```
round(A/100,0)*1
00
               48400
round(A/1000,0)*
1000
               48000
```

```
Ans→A
               48397
round(A/10,0)*10
               48400
■
```

The command 'round(A/10,0)*10' first divides the number stored in A by 10 to give 4,839.7, then rounds it to 0 decimal places (i.e. the nearest integer) giving 4,840, and finally multiplies by 10 to give 48,400. Dividing by successive powers of 10, rounding to an integer, and multiplying by the same power of 10 produces the required results. The layout of a spreadsheet, such as that provided in TI-Nspire™ might be more attractive, and it can help show informative intermediate steps.

Pedagogical point: Why is place value important? What are the main difficulties learners have with it?

5.2(b) A ready-made number line

The Skoool area of the London Grid for Learning contains software for mathematics and science. You can download the BETT award winning Mathematical Toolkit, or run it online. One component is called the Interactive Number Line. Here a single number line has been set between 0 and 100 with marks every five units. The 'balloon' labelled n can slide along the line, and its current position is shown to the nearest decimal in the box marked '$n =$'. Two variables a and b are calculated from n, using the 'Options' button. a is defined by the function 'round(n)' using the 'int' button on the pop-up keypad, and b is defined as 'round ($n/10$)*10'. The value of b is currently hidden. As you slide the independent variable n, so the dependent variables a and b change position, and their values also change. By dragging n students can see dynamically when b is behind and when it is in front of n.

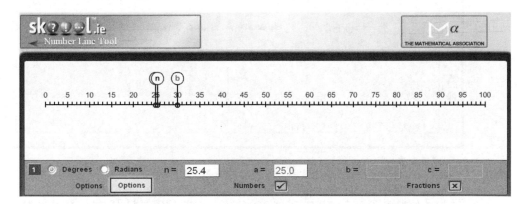

5.2(c) Directed numbers

Now we turn to negative numbers. The English national curriculum suggests using a geometric model. So we can make good use of a tool such as the Interactive Number Line, or dynamic geometry (Cabri or Sketchpad). In the screen-shot overleaf we have defined variables a, b and c depending on n by the following formulas:

$a = n - 10 \quad b = n/5 \quad c = -2*n.$

Now we have a dynamic impression of how the positive and negative quantities combine.

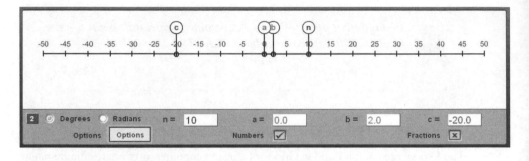

✎ *Can you construct a number line in dynamic geometry software such as Cabri or Sketchpad ?*

One possible result is shown below.

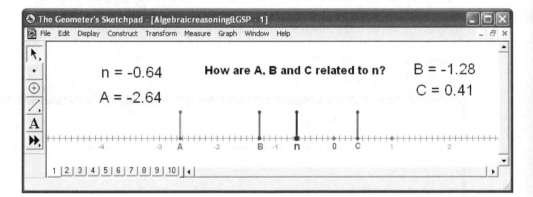

You can see a case-study, with lesson-plan and video-clips, of a teacher using dynamic geometry in a related fashion on The Practical Support Pack website at `http://www.dcsf.gov.uk/psp/case.aspx?cs=812&p=i`. That work was part of a wider project on Algebra and Geometry undertaken for the QCA (see `http://www.qca.org.uk/libraryAssets/media/7421_dev_reason_thro_algebra_geometry.pdf`).

✎ *1/7 = 0.142857 142857 . . . has a block of six recurring digits . . .*

✎ *Can you suggest which ICT tools might help you to set up an exploration into the number of digits in the block for recurring decimals?*

You can read more about ideas for such activities in Malcolm Swan *et al.*'s, *The Purposes of Mathematical Activities and Pupils' Perceptions of them* (http://www.manchesteruniversitypress.co.uk/uploads/docs/630011.pdf).

5.2(d) Standard form

A simple starting-point for work on standard form is provided by carrying out an iterative process on a graphing calculator and seeing when it changes the output. First we start with 1 on the display, and then continually use: ANS * 2 to make a doubling pattern. You can also divide by 2 to generate negative exponents.

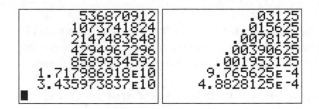

A good opportunity for developing students' knowledge and understanding of place value, including standard form, is provided by access to data-sets where the units of measurement are very large or very small – such as for measurements of the planets in our solar system, or for molecules of chemical elements.

5.2(e) Factors

Now we can turn to ideas such as: 'use the concepts and vocabulary of factor (divisor), multiple, common factor, highest common factor, least common multiple, prime number and prime factor decomposition'.

Obviously we can use a calculator to help split an integer into its prime factors. For example, the following screens show how we can use a blend of machine and mental calculation in finding the prime factors of 2009.

```
2009/2                    401.8
           1004.5 2009/7
2009/3                      287
       669.6666667 287/7
2009/5                       41
           401.8 7*7*41
■                         2009
```

With TI-Nspire™ you can open up a Calculator window and then, from the Number menu you can choose 'factor'.

$$\text{factor}\left(2009\right) \qquad\qquad 7^2 \cdot 41$$

The IT Maths Pack was published by the National Council for Educational Technology (NCET) in 1994 and was distributed via the Association of Teachers of Mathematics (ATM), and the Mathematical Association (MA). One of the four books is called *Number and Algebra with Computers and Calculators*. This refers to a number of interesting articles and resources. Accompanying it are various activity sheets, one of these is called 'A database of numbers'. Here the suggestion is that students should build up their own computer database of properties of numbers such as:

Is it even?
Is it a square number?
Is it prime?
Is it a triangle number?
What are its divisors?

So here we have an example of the seventh kind of ICT use, where students use ICT to gather, store and communicate results. For an interesting collection of number facts see David Wells, *The Penguin Dictionary of Curious and Interesting Numbers* (Penguin, 1986).

A popular way of displaying patterns in multiples is to set up a grid and to highlight, for example, all multiples of a given number. This is quite easy to set up in a spreadsheet, such as Excel™.

✎ *Can you think which formulas could be used to generate, e.g. a 10 × 10 number grid?*

	A14			f_x	=IF(A3/$A$1=INT(A3/$A$1),A3,"*")				
	A	B	C	D	E	F	G	H	I	J
1	3									
2										
3	1	2	3	4	5	6	7	8	9	10
4	11	12	13	14	15	16	17	18	19	20
5	21	22	23	24	25	26	27	28	29	30
6	31	32	33	34	35	36	37	38	39	40
7	41	42	43	44	45	46	47	48	49	50
8	51	52	53	54	55	56	57	58	59	60
9	61	62	63	64	65	66	67	68	69	70
10	71	72	73	74	75	76	77	78	79	80
11	81	82	83	84	85	86	87	88	89	90
12	91	92	93	94	95	96	97	98	99	100
13										
14	*	*	3	*	*	6	*	*	9	*
15	*	12	*	*	15	*	*	18	*	*
16	21	*	*	24	*	*	27	*	*	30
17	*	*	33	*	*	36	*	*	39	*
18	*	42	*	*	45	*	*	48	*	*
19	51	*	*	54	*	*	57	*	*	60
20	*	*	63	*	*	66	*	*	69	*
21	*	72	*	*	75	*	*	78	*	*
22	81	*	*	84	*	*	87	*	*	90
23	*	*	93	*	*	96	*	*	99	*

Now we can enter a particular integer into, e.g., cell A1. Then we can produce a replica of the grid with only the multiples of A1 being shown. The formula in A14 is = IF(A3/$A$1=INT(A3/$A$1),A3,'*').

If you copy this to the block of cells A14:J23 then the pattern will be shown. There is a variety of number games based upon this sort of grid. For example you could edit the formula above so that multiples of A1 are shown by one symbol, e.g. an asterisk, and others are shown by a dot. Now you could copy a subset of the grid, e.g. B15:H21, and paste it into a new sheet and print it out. In this way you could use a spreadsheet to produce resource materials, illustrating the sixth of our examples of ICT use. Students then have to work out which multiples are being shown by the asterisks and suggest possible numbers for them, depending upon where they think the grid was taken from.

A set of grids generated this way could also be stored on a school's network for access by students and/or teachers as required.

A simple way to generate powers is using the ANS key on a graphing calculator. For example, to produce powers of 3, just type '1' and 'ENTER' and then repeatedly use '3*ANS', where 'ANS' is found from '2nd' and '(-)'.

A different approach to this little foray into integers is to look at different ways of implementing Euclid's algorithm for the highest common factor of two integers. This is based on the result that if a positive integer p is a divisor of two positive integers a and b, then it is also a divisor of their difference $c = |a-b|$. Here is a rather inefficient way of coding the algorithm in TI-Nspire™.

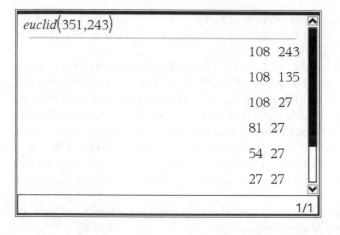

✎ *Can you adapt the program to produce the least common multiple?*

We conclude this section on factors with an idea for an extended task, or coursework project, on prime factorization. The starting-point is to find numbers with exactly, say, four divisors, such as 15 which has the four divisors: {1,3,5,15}; or 343 which has the four divisors: {1,7,49,343}.

✎ *Can you find the smallest integer with exactly four divisors?*

✎ *Can you make up a table of the smallest number with exactly n divisors for, e.g. n = 1,2,3,4,5,6 ... ?*

✎ *Can you devise a way of finding the smallest number with any given number of divisors?*

✎ *Would you advise using ICT tools to help pose the problem, to help with the data-gathering, to check results, to communicate results ... ? If so, which tools would you think are most appropriate?*

Of course there are many examples of small software available to provide contexts and games to engage students in using numeric reasoning. One example is in the professional development section on questioning on the Bowland Mathematics DVD – it's called Multiplication Grids. The player(s) have to arrange the numbers 1–9 or 0–8 on a 3 × 3 grid so that each set of three digits in each of the rows and columns multiply together to give the totals shown.

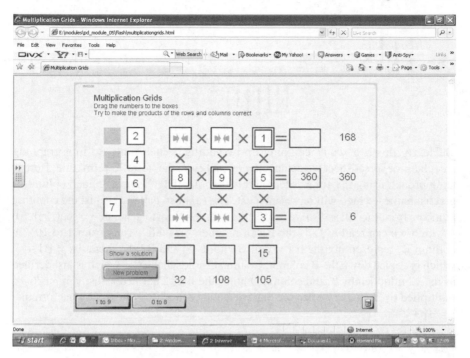

5.3 ALGEBRA

Now we turn to some ideas to do with sequences of numbers and their relationships with functions and, later, with graphs.

5.3(a) Sequences

Students should be taught to:
- generate common integer sequences (including sequences of odd or even integers, squared integers, powers of 2, powers of 10, triangular numbers);
- generate terms of a sequence using term-to-term and position-to-term definitions of the sequence;
- use linear expressions to describe the nth term of an arithmetic sequence, justifying its form by reference to the activity or context from which it was generated.

Suppose we have a sequence such as 5, 8, 11, 14, 17 . . . It is a common task to try to continue the pattern, and maybe to predict the tenth term, etc. As a first step it might be helpful to visualize the pattern in terms of pins in the number line. Current versions of software for interactive whiteboards include many tools to help with just this sort of visualization. For example the SMART Math software has a graph tool which includes number lines. You can then draw an arrowhead, copy-and-paste many examples of it and then get students to drag an arrowhead to represent each element of the sequence.

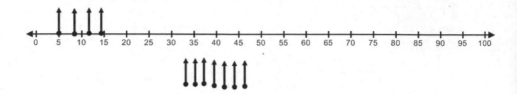

Clearly this is a sequence going up by adding 3 each time. So in a graphing calculator or spreadsheet we could enter the data and the 'term-to-term' rule. Here is an approach using the spreadsheet and lists tools of TI-Nspire™. Each column is given a name – which will represent a list. The first list, called x, is just the counting numbers from 1 to 10, and so we use the list function 'seq' to generate $x = \text{seq}(r,r,1,10)$ – which we can read as 'x is the list of numbers r where r runs from 1 to 10'. In column B, representing the list y, cell B1 holds 5, and B2 the formula: $= B1 + 3$, which is copied down the B column. Column C holds the list $x1$ which is just defined as list x multiplied by 3, and column D holds the list $x2$ defined as list y minus list x multiplied by 2. Hence we can see that we could define list y directly by the formula: $y = 3x + 2$.

A x	B y	C $x1$	D $x2$	E $y1$	F
=seq(r,r,1,10)		=3*x	='y–3*x	=3*x+2	
1	5	3	2	5	
2	8	6	2	8	
3	11	9	2	11	
4	14	12	2	14	
5	17	15	2	17	
6	20	18	2	20	
7	23	21	2	23	
8	26	24	2	26	
9	29	27	2	29	
10	32	30	2	32	

On graphing calculators, such as the TI-83 and TI-84, there is a Sequence mode – which is also available in TI-Nspire™. Use 'MODE' and select 'Seq'. When you press 'Y =' you get a rather unusual form of editor. You have three sequences available, called u, v and w. The nth term of the u sequence is denoted by $u(n)$ so the rule which says that it is three more than the previous term becomes: $u(n) = u(n\ 1) + 3$, which you enter into the editor. Note that u is '2nd' '7' and n is 'X,T,θ,n'. We also need to specify the starting value as 5.

```
NORMAL   SCI  ENG
FLOAT  0123456789
RADIAN  DEGREE
FUNC  PAR  POL  SEQ
CONNECTED  DOT
SEQUENTIAL  SIMUL
REAL  a+bi  re^θi
FULL  HORIZ  G-T
SET CLOCK 07/19/09 1:07PM
```

```
Plot1  Plot2  Plot3
nMin=1
\u(n)Bu(n−1)+3
 u(nMin)B{5}
\v(n)=
 v(nMin)=
\w(n)=
 w(nMin)=
```

In order to see the numeric output as a table we first use '2nd' 'WINDOW' for 'TBLSET' to set up the starting value and step for the sequence. Then press '2nd' 'GRAPH' for 'TABLE'.

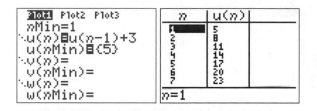

When a student has a suggestion for an equivalent function in terms of *n* alone to try, it is a simple matter to put the potentially equivalent expression into the *v* sequence and to re-compute the table.

So now there is plenty of scope for a 'guess my rule' kind of task-sheet. Students can then work at producing their own suggestions for 'position–term' definitions, and check their conjectures using ICT, such as a spreadsheet or graphing calculator. We show a couple of variants on this idea, still with the TI-83/4. First we use MODE to return to ordinary 'Func' graphing. In the '2nd' 'STAT' menu are a number of operations on lists. Choose '5:seq('. We will enter our rule as:

Seq(3X+2,X,1,10)→L1

So you can see the list on the screen, or by using 'STAT' 'Edit'. Item 7 on the LIST OPS menu is a useful one. We can use it to make list L2, say, hold the differences of the numbers in list L1.

If we change the MODE back to FUNC then we can use Y= to enter the function Y1 = 3X + 2 and view its table.

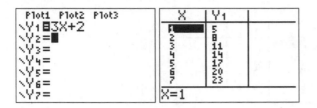

Through exercises such as this we can use ICT to make a firm relationship between the *symbolic* representation as a function (or, informally, as an 'equation') and its *numeric* representation as a table or list of its values.

Once this is established we also have the tools at hand to make the links with a third, *graphical*, representation. We already have the function in Y1, so just choose a suitable WINDOW and press GRAPH. You can use TRACE to read off data from the cursor position on the graph. Finally, from MODE, you opt to have the screen split between a graph and a table with 'G↔T'.

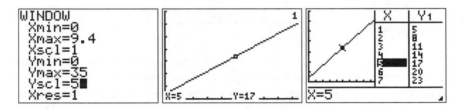

The screen above right shows all three representations on the same screen.

Note:
- We have to be careful about values for Xmin and Xmax to make sure (Xmax-Xmin) is a round multiple of the number of pixels across the screen, otherwise when you use TRACE the X values show an unhelpful number of decimals!
- We really ought to be careful about distinguishing between the discrete data from which we started, where the function $u(n)$ was only defined on the natural numbers, and the continuous function Y1(X) defined for all real X.
- Unless the WINDOW is chosen to match the aspect ratio of the display screen then the gradient of our linear function cannot be interpreted geometrically. For example Y = X will not be at 45° to the *x* axis.
- The low resolution of the calculator's display screen gives rise to a rather stepladder graph in the last screen-shot. Any graph shown on a computer display, or on paper, is only an approximation to our ideal mental image of the graph – after all the line drawing the graph should have no thickness!

5.3(b) Linear functions and their graphs

We now show the similar approach taken in TI-Nspire™. We can define a function in a Graphs and Geometry window, and compute its table in a Lists and Spreadsheet window.

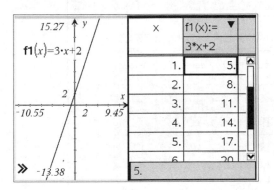

The last of the group of screens above shows all three representations of the function $Y = 3X+2$, i.e.

- symbolic
- numeric
- graphic.

Similar output can be arranged in a spreadsheet such as Excel™. Once the formulas have been evaluated in columns A and B, you can highlight the block of numbers to be graphed as (x,y) coordinates. The trick is to select Scattergram for the graph type, and then choose the format which joins the data-points with line-segments. You can then edit the title, axes, labels, etc., until you have a representation with which you are happy.

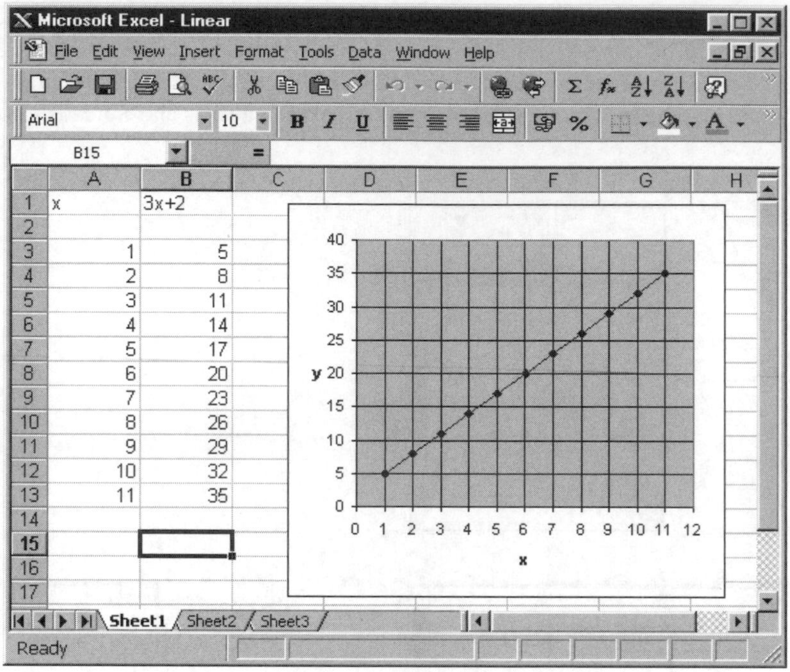

One major problem with using ICT tools with students to investigate sequences, functions, tables, graphs, etc., is that they can explore many cases very easily, without keeping any records of what they have been doing, what they have discovered, what problems they have encountered, etc. So another useful application of ICT could be for a teacher to produce a pro-forma on which students can record what they have been doing.

My equations   Name: Class: Date:

My sketch

Y1 =
Y2 =
Y3 =

My table

X	Y1	Y2	Y3

Comments:

In summary, we have reviewed some of the ways you can reinforce the links between different representations of linear functions:

- as a table of numbers with constant first differences;
- as a straight line graph with constant gradient;
- as an algebraic expression of the form $mx + c$.

In the case of linear sequences, which are discrete sets of numbers, they can be defined by

- a term-to-term rule such as $u_{n+1} = a.u_n + b$; and
- a position-to-term rule such as $u_n = p.n + q$.

✎ *Investigate the cumulative sums of linear sequences, e.g. if* u = {1, 3, 5, 7, 9 ...) *then its sums are* S = {1, 4, 9, 16, 25, ... } – *what sort of function generates this sequence?*

✎ *Investigate the differences of quadratic, cubic and other polynomial sequences.*

✎ *We leave it to you as an exercise first to develop some ICT approaches to the conventional interpretation of the* m *and* c *in* y = mx + c, *and then, using numeric and graphic representations, for the solution of simultaneous linear equations.*

5.3(c) Simultaneous linear equations

A different approach to simultaneous linear equations is afforded by the symbolic manipulation functions of CAS such as TI-Nspire™. The following screen shows a step-by-step approach to the algorithm for solution by elimination and back-substitution. Step 5 involved substituting the value 1 for x. Can you adapt the approach to one where the equations are first reduced to the form $y = f(x)$ and $y = g(x)$?

$e1 := 2 \cdot x - y = -1$	$2 \cdot x - y = -1$
$e2 := x + 2 \cdot y = 7$	$x + 2 \cdot y = 7$
$e3 := e2 + 2 \cdot e1$	$5 \cdot x = 5$
$e4 := \dfrac{e3}{5}$	$x = 1$
$e5 := e1 \mid e4$	$2 - y = -1$
$e6 := 2 - e5$	$y = 3$

6/99

5.3(d) Quadratic functions

Now we look at an approach to move from linear functions into quadratic functions.

The basic idea is to have a pair of simple linear functions defined in a graph plotter or graphing calculator as, say, $Y1(x)$ and $Y2(x)$ with their graphs drawn in a suitable window. The investigation is one on the 'arithmetic of lines'. For example, can you predict the shape of the graph of the function $Y3(x) = Y1(x) + Y2(x)$? If it is a linear function, how are its gradient and y-intercept related to those of Y1 and Y2?

The surprise should come when we change to: $Y3(x) = Y1(x) * Y2(x)$!

We illustrate this with the TI-83, but again you can use other ICT tools similarly by now (we hope).

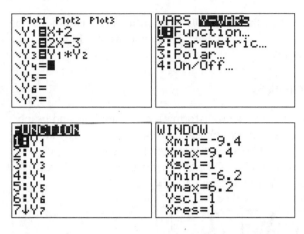

In order to enter the variables Y1 and Y2 you need to use the VARS menu and select Y-VARS and Function, then you can select, e.g. Y1 to paste into the equation for Y3.

Again you will need a judicious choice of WINDOW, depending on how important you judge maintaining the aspect ratio to be. By tracing, you should be able to relate the zeros of Y3 to those of Y1 and Y2, and the sign of Y3 to the signs of Y1 and Y2.

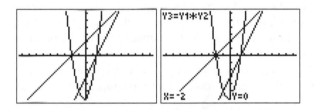

You can also change the screen representation. By moving the cursor over the '=' sign in Y1 and pressing 'ENTER' you can stop the graph of Y1 being displayed, and similarly for Y2. By moving to the left-hand edge of the screen on the Y3 line and continually pressing 'ENTER' you can cycle through a range of possible graph types for Y3. We have chosen a dotted one. Now you could try to write an expanded version of Y3 as a quadratic function without brackets (or parentheses). If you can't distinguish whether the graphs are equivalent or not you might have to adjust the WINDOW.

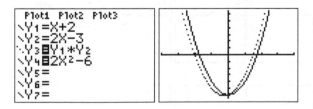

So in this example we are close, but not close enough!

Here we have an example of using ICT effectively to reverse a conventional teaching order. Instead of splitting a quadratic function into linear factors we have used a converse approach of arriving at a quadratic function by the product of two linear functions. Of course it is true that all products of linears are quadratic. Is the converse true? How would you demonstrate it? Of course we could extend the product of lines to produce cubics!

5.3(e) Transformations of functions

Another approach to quadratics is via the transformation of functions and graphs, which is usually only attempted with more able students in the 11–16 age range. Yet with ICT tools this becomes accessible to a wider range of students.

Suppose we start with the function $Y1(X) = X^2$. Then we can easily investigate transformations such as $Y2(X) = Y1(X) + 2$, or $Y3(X) = Y1(X+2)$.

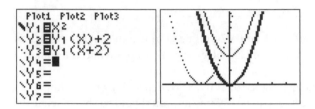

You can use TRACE to sort out which graph is which.

Of course Y1 can be any function, so the same technique can be used for older students, say, to explore the transformations of graphs of trigonometric functions, where terminology such as amplitude, phase shift, frequency, etc. take on both graphical and symbolic meanings.

If we build up the general quadratic in terms of transformations then we arrive at the expression $y(x) = a + b(x + c)^2$ as a much more informative representation than the conventional $ax^2 + bx + c$.

A popular activity to do with guessing functions, and their transforms, is to have a set of screen-shots taken from the graphing calculator's screen and re-scaled so that they are the physical size of the calculator's display. These images can then be printed, and photocopied onto overhead transparencies. These can be cut up with scissors and used for a 'match my graph' game. We provide here a set of 15 such images that you are welcome to use, but you may prefer to make up your own set.

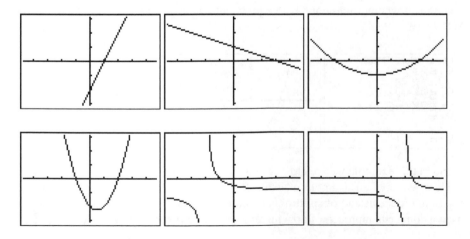

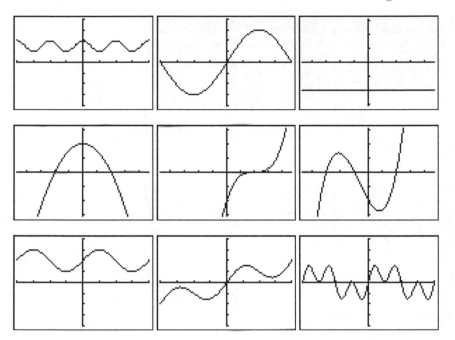

Note: we must stress that in this section we are being guided by the way that algebraic content is usually described in formal syllabuses and curricula. We have not chosen to give practical examples and contexts from which, say, linear, quadratic, polynomial, trigonometric or inverse functions might be derived. Instead we introduce these in a later section of this chapter about statistics and modelling.

5.3(f) Differences

We conclude this exploration on functions with an interesting way of looking at the differences of linear, quadratic and other polynomial functions. Here we have chosen a spreadsheet, using Excel™ as our example. Here the three values in the F column correspond to the coefficients in the conventional representation of the quadratic polynomial as $y = ax^2 + bx + c$. A set of consecutive integers are generated in the A column. The formula for the quadratic is entered in cell B4 in terms of cell A4 using either the absolute references, such as $F$1, or the facility in Excel™ to define names for cells – which produces something more like conventional algebraic notation. This is copied down the B column. In column C we find the differences of the values in column B, and similarly column D has the differences from column C. Now we can enter different values for a, b, and/or c in cells F1:F3. We should find that D always has a constant value.

	A	B	C	D	E	F
1	Differences				a =	3
2					b =	2
3					c =	-1
4	1	4				
5	2	15	11			
6	3	32	17	6		
7	4	55	23	6		
8	5	84	29	6		
9	6	119	35	6		
10	7	160	41	6		
11	8	207	47	6		
12	9	260	53	6		
13	10	319	59	6		
14	11	384	65	6		

✎ *Can this be zero? How is it related to the value of* a, b *or* c?

✎ *Investigate changing the step-size* d *of the* x-*values in the A column, e.g. for* 1, 3, 5, 7 . . . *or for* 1, 1.5, 2, 2.5 . . .

✎ *Can you make a general rule for quadratics?*

✎ *Can you extend the idea to cubics? To higher-order polynomials?*

5.3(g) Iteration and convergence

There is an interesting activity to be found in the NCET *IT Maths Pack* about iteration and convergence. This is described on pp. 8 and 9 of its booklet: *Secondary Mathematics with a Graphic Calculator*.

In words and symbols the process is:

1. choose two numbers A and B (with B > 1)
2. think of a number X
3. add A to X to get Y
4. divide the result by B to get Z
5. If Z is different from X, replace X by Z
    and go back to step 3.
6. Otherwise write down Z as the result.

We could investigate this using a spreadsheet, or TI-Nspire™, or a graphing calculator such as the TI-83/4. We can convert rules 3 and 4 into the single rule $(Ans + A)/B$.

The following screen shows the start of a sequence which after a number of repeated presses of the 'ENTER' key produces 2 as the output:

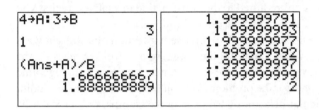

✎ *Can you write programs in Logo, for TI-Nspire™ or for the TI-83/4 to implement the algorithm?*

Results can be entered in a table:

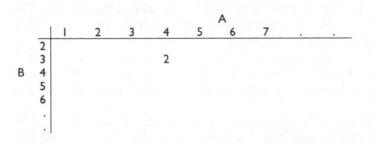

With A = 1 and B = 8 we get a result like 0.1428571429, so we also have an investigation which can lead into patterns in recurring decimals.

Of course this problem can be solved analytically by seeing if we can find a value X such that $(X + A)/B = X$ which we could illustrate graphically for any given values of A and B as the intersection of two straight lines. Solving algebraically we have $X = A/(B - 1)$, so we can see why the restriction that $B \neq 1$ was needed. Graphically we see that we would then have a pair of parallel lines, with no intersection.

> *Have a good look through your own number and algebra schemes*
> *of work for classes which you teach and see where these and other*
> *ICT approaches might be integrated.*

We conclude this section on number and algebra with an unusual application of dynamic geometry software. Here we will use Sketchpad to try to find the isosceles triangle of side 5 with the greatest area. This is the problem described in section 3 of the TTA's book, *ICT Needs Identification in Secondary Mathematics*, and also one of the case-studies on its CD-ROM.

5.3(h) Algebraic modelling with dynamic geometry

Here we shall try to give the steps required in the construction in such a way that you can carry them out in either Cabri or Sketchpad, or both!

First we construct a segment, labelled *VW* to represent a section of a straight wall. Then create another segment *FG* to represent the length of a fence. We measure the length of *FG*, and drag *G*, say, until it is as close to 5 cm as we can get. In algebraic terms this length is a *parameter* for the problem. We can now construct the midpoint *M* of *VW*, and the perpendicular bisector of *VW*. Using the Compass tool (or Circle By Center + Radius) from the Construction menu we can describe a circle centre *M* whose radius is the segment *FG*. We must drag *V* and *W* sufficiently far apart for the circle to intersect the segment *VW* in *B* and *C*. It also intersects the perpendicular bisector in *A*. Now we have made the perpendicular bisector and the circle appears in dotted format. The top vertex of the triangle can slide on the perpendicular bisector, but cannot leave the circle. So we construct the segment *MA* and choose a point *P* on it as the vertex. In algebraic language, *MA* is the *domain* of the *independent variable* *P*. Now we use the Compass tool again to draw a circle centre *P* with *FG* as radius. It intersects *VW* in points *Q* and *R*. Next we define the triangle interior *PQR*. This has been filled with colour, and its area has been measured. We now draw the segment *MP* and measure its length, i.e. the height of the triangle. As *P* slides on *MA* the height and area both change. So we can fairly easily find the geometric configuration that maximizes the area (i.e. when angle *QPR* is a right-angle) – and we could illustrate this by reflecting the triangle in *VW* as a mirror line to get a rhombus *PQP'R*.

We can also construct the graph of area against height geometrically. First we Show Axes, and drag the origin *O* to a suitable position. Then we can drag the Unit Point on the *x* axis to choose suitable scales to fit the screen. In Cabri we do not have a direct way of plotting a point from a pair of numbers as its coordinates. From the Construction menu choose Measurement Transfer and point first at the height measurement, and then the *x*-axis to define point *X*. Repeat with the area measurement and the *y* axis to define point *Y*. Now we just have to turn these two points into point *Z*. You could do this by drawing perpendiculars to each axis through *X* and *Y* and finding their intersection *Z*. Another approach is to define the vectors *OX* and *OY* and then construct their Vector Sum *OZ* starting from *O*. In Sketchpad just highlight the two measurements in order as the (x,y) coordinates, and select Plot As (x,y) from the Graph menu to create Z.

So now Z is a variable point *dependent* on P. As you drag P the point Z appears to describe a curve – try selecting 'Trace On' for the point Z so that it leaves a trace as you drag P. If you construct the locus of Z with P then you get the desired *graph* of the area as a function of the height. So here is a way of constructing graphs of functions without using the conventional symbolism of algebra. Using the Calculator tool in the Measurement menu, we can actually compute all sorts of functions based on variable measurements – so we now have another analytical tool in our armoury (Sketchpad actually allows direct algebraic definitions of functions to be plotted). The power of this representation is as soon as the parameter FG is altered, by sliding either of the points F or G, the whole locus deforms dynamically.

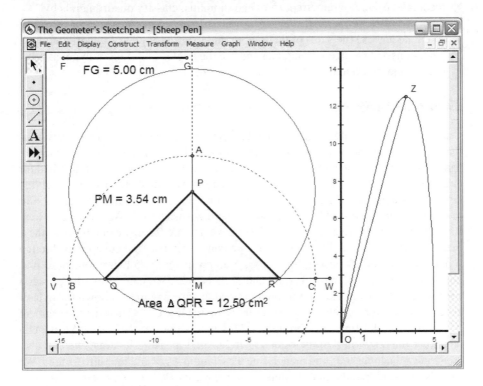

5.4 GEOMETRY

Following the Royal Society report on the Teaching and Learning of Geometry 11–19, the word 'geometry' has now been reinstated in the English National Curriculum, where the area of the curriculum known as Ma3 and headed 'Shape, Space and Measures' has now been replace by 'Geometry and Measures'. The geometric content includes applications of Pythagoras' theorem, circle properties, transformations, coordinates, construction, locus, etc. as well as work in 3D. There are also specific references to the use of ICT by students.

Obviously DGS (Cabri and Sketchpad, together with examples from GeoGebra and TI-Nspire™) will be our major ICT tools in this section, but we shall use Logo, TI-83/4, TI-Nspire™, spreadsheets and Autograph for work on coordinates, trigonometry, etc., as well as Cabri 3D for work in 3D.

Geometrical reasoning: properties of triangles and other rectilinear shapes
Students should be taught to:

- use their knowledge of rectangles, parallelograms and triangles to deduce formulas for the area of a parallelogram and a triangle from the formula for the area of a rectangle;
- recall the essential properties of special types of quadrilateral, including square, rectangle, parallelogram, trapezium and rhombus; classify quadrilaterals by their geometric properties;
- calculate and use the sums of the interior and exterior angles of quadrilaterals, pentagons and hexagons; calculate and use the angles of regular polygons;
- understand, recall and use Pythagoras' theorem.

5.4(a) Calculating area

One great advantage of the measurement tools within dynamic geometry software is that we now have the means of measuring areas of closed shapes such as rectangles, triangles, polygons and circles. So our first example is just a sort of DGS test-bed for carrying out investigations into areas. In this section we will alternate between giving details for Cabri and for Sketchpad, starting with Cabri. First we use Numerical Edit to enter the dimensions of a base rectangle: here we use 8 by 5. We construct a long line AX across the screen and also define the vector AX. Then we can transfer the 8 measurement to AX to define B. Similarly we construct a perpendicular to AX through A and a point Y on it. Define the vector AY and transfer the 5 measurement to it to define D. Perpendiculars through B and D meet at C. We can define the polygon (rectangle) $ABCD$ and measure its area to check it agrees with the known formula of area = base × height. Now define any point D' on the line CD. Construct the segment AD' and a parallel line to it through B. This meets the line DC in C'. So we can construct the polygon (parallelogram) $ABC'D'$ and measure its area. We can also construct a diagonal BD', and then define the triangle ABD' and measure its area. We can also drop perpendiculars to define the segments PC' and QD'. Hence we can define the (congruent) triangles $AD'D$ and BPC', and measure their area. Now, as D' slides on DC, we can see which areas change, which do not and which are equal. Then we can start to use visual imagery to find explanations for these phenomena.

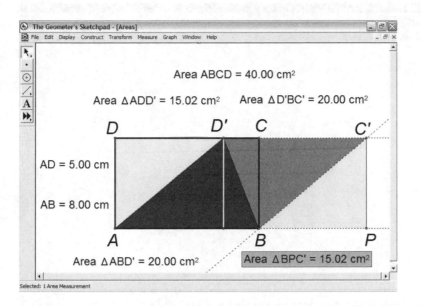

In the above diagram we have used a judicious mixture of line styles (thick, thin and dotted) and shades to try to bring out the features for attention. Of course our static picture is just a snapshot of what is now a dynamic image dependent on the position of *D'*. If you change either of the defining numbers (5 or 8) then the picture should change size without losing any of its essential properties.

5.4(b) Properties of shapes

A quite different use of dynamic geometry is by students themselves, starting with blank 'paper', to create the standard quadrilaterals in such a way that they are robust (i.e. you can't move any of the defining points or edges in such a way that the figure loses its essential shape). As an example, the diagram overleaf shows a construction for a rhombus of side 6 based on some of the known properties of a rhombus. Of course the way in which we construct such a figure gives us insight into its properties, and vice versa!

A good challenge for students at Key Stage 3 is to create a square using transformations of a line segment. This line segment could be defined as either one side of the square, or it could be one of the diagonals of the square.

✎ *Can you work out how the figure was constructed?*

✎ *Can you think of alternative ways to construct it using different properties?*

✎ *How about other common shapes?*

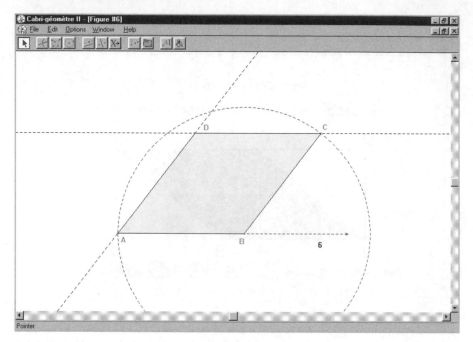

Below is another dynamic geometry test-bed. Here six random points $A, B, C, D, E,$ F have been joined using rays (half-lines). Points A', B', C', D', E', F' have been constructed on these rays so that external angles like $A'BC$ can be marked and measured. Using the Calculator tool in the Measurement menu you can find the sum of the six external angles. Now you deform the position of any of the defining points to see that, although some of the angles change, the sum remains an *invariant*. Of course such software cannot prove results such as this are always true. (Is it true if the hexagon is concave? Just what do we mean by a hexagon? Can it cross over itself?)

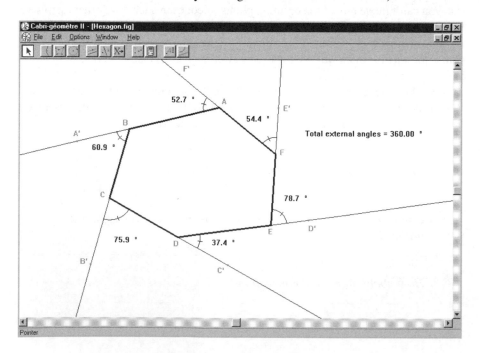

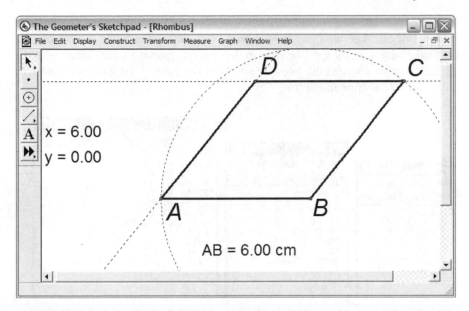

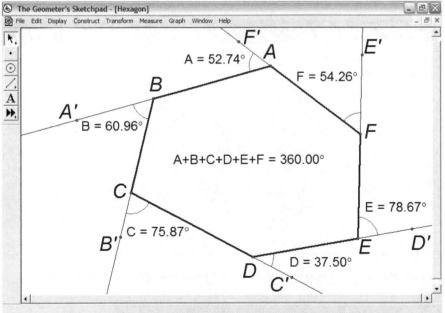

Now we consider how Logo handles polygons. First, can we draw a general hexagon? The procedure called Hex below shows a 'hit and hope' approach. It would have been a matter of pure chance if the sixth side had actually been exactly the right length and at exactly the right angle to close the polygon. Logo provides a very useful command called TOWARDS which returns the angle at which we need to head to be in the direction of a given point. So first we have to store the coordinates of the initial point, using POS to find them. The modified procedure, Modhex, uses this idea to close but overshoot the polygon. We have adjusted the angle, but not the length, of the final side. In our final version, Modmodhex, we use the DISTANCE function to calculate how far we need to move with the final side to return to the original position. If, though, we want to finish pointing in the same direction as we started then we can use the known fact about the sum of the external angles to calculate the last amount of turn.

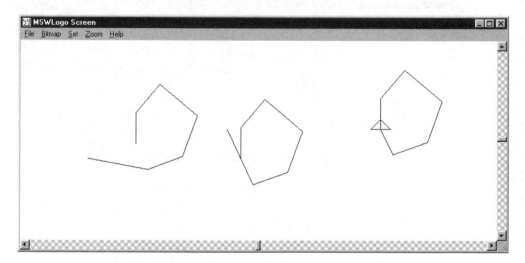

```
Editor
File  Edit  Search
Set  Test!  Help

To Hex
 FD 50 RT 40
 FD 60 RT 90
 FD 80 RT 70
 FD 70 RT 50
 FD 60 RT 30
 FD 100 RT 40
End
```

```
Editor
File  Edit  Search  Set
Test!  Help

To modhex
 MAKE "P POS
 FD 50 RT 40
 FD 60 RT 90
 FD 80 RT 70
 FD 70 RT 50
 FD 60 RT 30
 SETH TOWARDS :P
 FD 100
End
```

```
Editor
File  Edit  Search  Set  Test!  Help

To modmodhex
 MAKE "P POS
 FD 50 RT 40
 FD 60 RT 90
 FD 80 RT 70
 FD 70 RT 50
 FD 60 RT 30
 MAKE "A TOWARDS :P
 MAKE "B :A - HEADING
 SETH :A
 FD DISTANCE :P
 MAKE "C 40+90+70+50+30+:B
 RT 360-:C
End
```

A general form of Logo procedure for a regular polygon is given below.

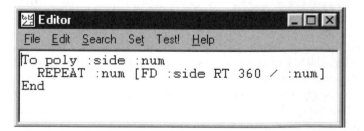

```
Editor
File  Edit  Search  Set  Test!  Help

To poly :side :num
 REPEAT :num [FD :side RT 360 / :num]
End
```

5.4(c) Reasoning, proof and ICT

One problem with teaching geometry, in the UK at least, is that it has been relegated to a very minor role for many years now, and so few teachers under 50, say, have met many of the key ideas being reintroduced through both the National Curriculum and the Key Stage 3 Strategy. The Royal Society's geometry report recognized this and underlined the need for a new pedagogy for teaching mathematics in a dynamic way using ICT tools. As an example, therefore, we will take the traditional geometric theorem 'the perpendicular bisectors of the sides of a triangle are concurrent' and see how it could be approached using either Sketchpad or Cabri.

First construct a triangle *ABC* – you might find it helpful to make the sides thick and in different colours, e.g. *AB* red, *BC* green and *CA* blue. Construct the midpoints of all three sides, and the perpendicular bisector of two of them, e.g. *BA* and *AC*. Construct their intersection and label it *P*. Now see if you can imagine the path of *P* as you drag *A* around the screen. Now set *P* to leave a Trace, and drag *A* about – what do you find?

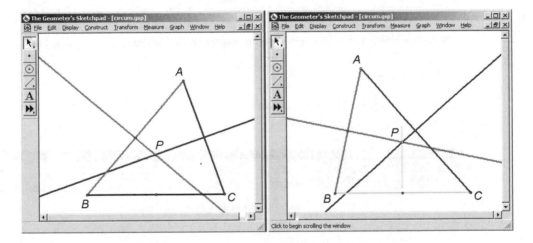

It certainly looks as if the path of *P* lies on the perpendicular bisector of *BC*, but that's not much of a proof – although it might be a surprise! We need to know what previous geometric results we can draw on. In this case we will presuppose that you have done some work on the locus of a point, like *P*, such that its distances from two fixed points, e.g. *A* and *B*, are always equal. You might think of this dynamically, as the path taken by a moving point, or statically, as the set of points that have this property. In either case we get the result that *P* lies on the perpendicular bisector of *AB* – and we can interpret this as 'the vertex of an isosceles triangle always lies on the perpendicular bisector of its base' – and also recognize that the converse is true: 'a triangle that has a vertex that lies on the perpendicular bisector of the opposite side must be isosceles'.

So now we can deduce that since *P* lies on the perpendicular bisector of *AB* then *PA = PB*.

What can you deduce about *PA* and *PC* – and why? What can you deduce about *PB* and *PC* – and why? So do you think this provides a proof that P always lies on the perpendicular bisector of *BC*? What happens if *P* lies on *BC*? Does the theorem still hold? Does the proof? What sort of triangle is *ABC* now? What path will *A* take if *P* is always at the midpoint of *BC*? Can *P* lie on the opposite side of *BC* to *A*? If so, for what kind of triangle *ABC*? What can you say about the circle centre *P* through *A*? Can you deduce a result about where the centre of a circle lies in relation to a chord?

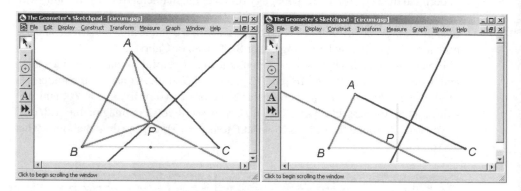

Now think how you might have tried to approach this without the use of ICT!

5.4(d) Pythagoras

And so to Pythagoras! Below is one example of another dynamic test-bed. We started by constructing the hypotenuse *BC*.

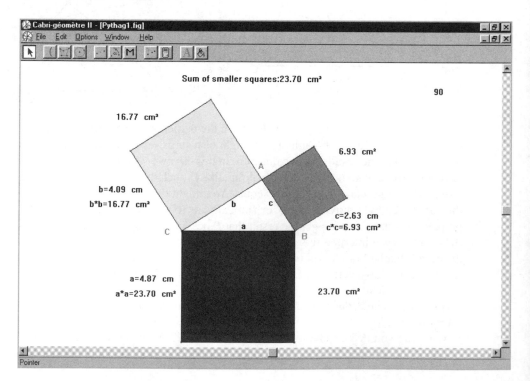

✎ *Can you think how* A *was constructed so that triangle* ABC *is always right-angled at* A?

In order to simplify the drawing of squares on the sides we used a powerful device, which Cabri calls a Macro and Sketchpad calls a Custom Tool (and which earlier versions called a Script). This is just like a little program or procedure to do something new using instructions already defined. This makes the software extensible. We will run over how to get the square drawn on side *AB*, and then how to turn it into a macro to use to get the square on *CA* and the square on side *BC*. First here is the technique with Cabri.

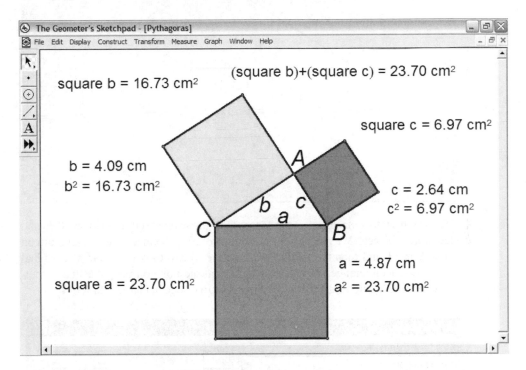

We use Numerical Edit to enter 90 as the angle for rotation. Select the Rotate tool from the Transformation menu and click in turn on point *B*, point *A* and the number 90. This rotates *B* anti-clockwise around *A* through 90° to *P*. Then repeat the process to rotate *A* around *P* to *Q*. Select the Polygon tool and click in turn on *A*, *B*, *Q*, *P*, *A*. Now we have constructed the square on side *AB*.

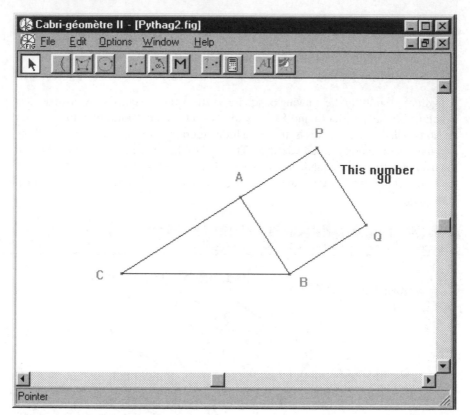

To turn this into a macro select the Macro tool (the seventh icon, shown as X→) and select Initial Objects. We need just three things to define the macro: so click in turn on points *A* and *B* and then the number 90. Use the Macro tool again and select Final Objects (the icon changes to →Y). Just click on the polygon *ABQP* as the output. Finally use the Macro tool and select Define Macro (the icon changes to X→Y).

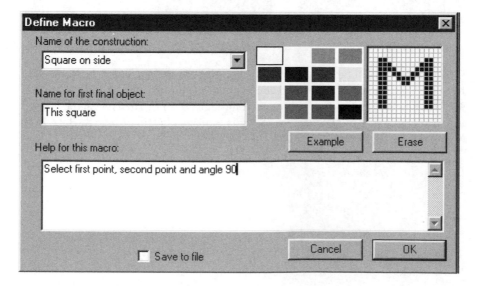

You need to give a name for the new macro, such as 'Square on side' and the message which Cabri will show when you point to the object created by the macro, e.g., 'This square'. You can also add some helpful comments in case you forget what the macro was supposed to do! It's a good idea also to tick the little 'Save to file' box, so that you keep your macros saved on your disk. Now when you use the Macro tool you will see 'Square on side' at the bottom of the list. Select this, and point in turn to C, A and 90. With luck you will now get the required square. What do you think would happen if you selected A, C and 90 instead? Then you can use the macro again with B, C and 90.

In Sketchpad we start as before from the right-angled triangle ABC, working to produce the square on side AB. To create segment AP we will rotate AB around A through 90°. First highlight just the point A, select the Transform menu and Mark Center. Then highlight just the segment AB and the point B, select the Transform menu and Rotate. The dialogue box will suggest using the Center A, and a Fixed Angle of 90°. It will also show you a faint of image of how AB will be rotated. Click on Rotate to perform this. Now mark B as the next centre, and then rotate A and AB about it through −90°. Construct the remaining side of the square, label the two new corners, define the square's interior and colour it (e.g. red). Now select all the objects that make up the square – its four vertices, its four sides and its interior. Sketchpad now has all the information it needs to work out which are the independent (input) and dependent (output) objects. Click on the Custom Tools symbol on the task bar (the bottom one with two arrowheads that looks like the fast-forward button on a cassette tape deck). Select Create New Tool, in the dialogue box enter a name, e.g. Square On Side, and click in the box for Show Script View. A new window appears with the rules of how to build a square starting from just two points. You can type in some explanation in the first line. Now click on the Custom Tool symbol again and drag out a point – click on C to define the first point for the next square, then drag open the construction so that you can click on A to define the second point. The square will take up its position on side CA. Similarly build a square on side BC.

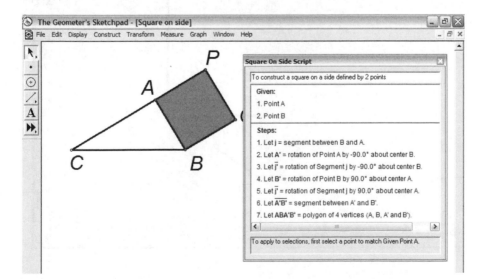

How many different proofs of Pythagoras' theorem can you find? Can you construct figures with Cabri and/or Sketchpad to illustrate them? You will find some interesting information in David Wells' *Penguin Book of Curious and Interesting Geometry* (Penguin, 1991). For example, there is a very nice figure attributed to Leonardo da Vinci. Another copy of triangle *ABC* is added to the bottom of the figure at *XWV* (how could you do this?). Segments *CV*, *UXY* and *TZ* are added to the figure. The quadrilateral *BXVC* is shown filled. Can you see three other identical ones in the figure? If you rotate it through 90° about *B* can you prove it will fit exactly over *BAUY*? How does this help you prove Pythagoras' theorem?

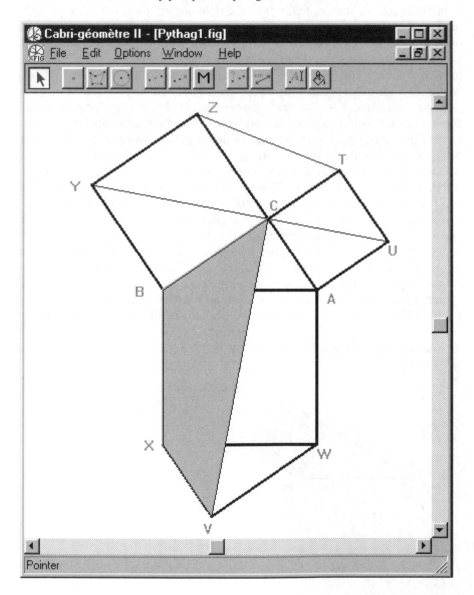

5.4(e) Further ideas

An interesting activity is to take a design with a certain amount of symmetry and try to construct it in Cabri and/or Sketchpad. Flags and logos are good starting-points.

✎ *Can you construct the European Union flag: 12 yellow pentagrams evenly spaced round a circle within a blue rectangle?*

As an example here is a Cabri version of the NatWest bank logo.

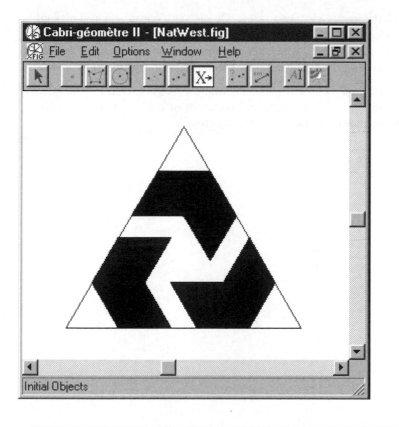

✎ *Can you work out how to construct it?*

Ideas such as these are regularly to be found in SYMmetry Plus, the Mathematical Association's magazine for young mathematicians.

An interesting investigation is concerned with golden ratio, equiangular spirals and constructions for the pentagon. Robert Dixon's *Mathographics* (Basil Blackwell, 1987) is another excellent source of geometric ideas such as these. Before we leave this kind of geometry we first mention some unusual theorems to explore (and explain?) and another interesting activity. Wells quotes the following theorems due to Aubel, Napoleon and Thébault.

✎ *See if you can construct Cabri and/or Sketchpad test-beds for them.*

Aubel's theorem: Draw any quadrilateral. On each side construct a square facing outwards. Join the neighbouring centres of these squares to form a quadrilateral, and show that its diagonals are always equal in length and are perpendicular.

Napoleon's theorem: Draw any triangle. On each side construct an equilateral triangle facing outwards. Join their centres to form a triangle, and show that it is always equilateral. (Note: this construction can also be used to find Fermat's point – can you find out what it is and why it is interesting?)

Thébault's theorem: Draw any parallelogram. On each side construct a square facing outwards. Join the neighbouring centres of these squares to form a quadrilateral, and show that it is always a square.

5.4(f) Circles and other loci

Now we will take a look at some ideas to do with circles. Here is a conventional diagram, shown in many textbooks, to establish the relationship between the angles subtended by a chord *AB* of a circle at its centre *O* and at a point *C* on the major arc *AB*. We can mark, and measure, appropriate angles, and also explore what happens as *C* is dragged round the circle.

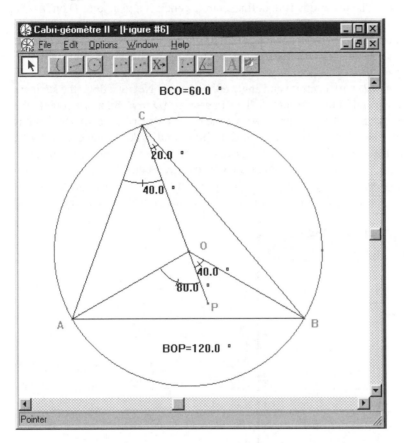

Of course we can use this to suggest the usual 'proof' that angle *BOP* is twice angle *BCO*. But what happens as *C* moves towards *B*, and *P* no longer lies inside triangle *AOB*? Can you adapt the proof to cope with this kind of case?

✎ *Can you extend the ideas to showing why angles in the same segment are equal, why the angle in a semicircle is a right-angle, and why opposite angles in a cyclic quadrilateral add up to 180°?*

As an alternative to reproducing dynamic versions of static diagrams, we can approach problems from unconventional directions. Suppose you are adrift in a small sailing boat with only a compass as an aid. You see two landmarks on the shore, maybe a church spire and a power station chimney. You take the bearings of each, and work out that they are 60° apart. If you use your mobile phone to tell the coastguard, what can he or she deduce about your position?

In balder terms we seek the locus of a point *P* which subtends a given angle from two fixed points *A* and *B*. We will try to talk through a general strategy for tackling such problems with dynamic geometry software such as Cabri.

First we construct the points *A* and *B* and use Numerical Edit to write the required angle, e.g. 60°. The technique is to define a circle centre *A* and a point *D* on it – we have used an arbitrary point *C* on *AB* as a radius point for the circle. The line *AD* is then like a bi-directional radar beam that we can use to scan over the plane. Our next problem is to be able to draw a line through *B* which makes the given angle with *AD*. This is easy.

We just rotate *D* with centre *A* and angle 60° to give *E*. Now we draw the segment *AE*, and a line parallel to it through *B*. This intersects *AD* in *P*. So as we 'crank' the handle *D* round the 'wheel' centre *A* we see the point *P* describe a path. But what is it? One way is to choose the Trace On/Off option and make *P* leave a trail as it moves. Another alternative is to use the Locus option in the Construction tool menu. Just choose the locus of *P* with *D* (on its domain, the circle centre *A* through *C*). Once again we have only really partially solved the problem. The internal angle *APB* is 60° when *P* is on the major arc *AB*, but flips to the external angle for the minor arc.

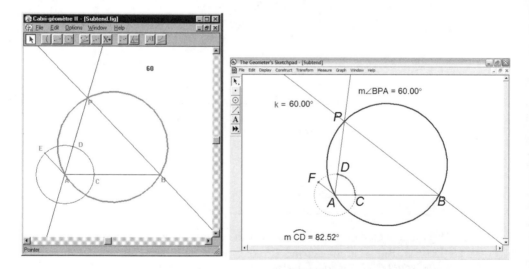

Often when tackling problems with dynamic geometry you will need to find a different approach from that which you might take when drawing. We have already seen how useful it can be to have a problem controlled by the position of a point moving along a straight object – a 'slider' – or round a circle – a 'handle'. Consider the problem of finding the locus of a point *Q* that moves so that its distance from a fixed point *F* is always the same as from a fixed line (not through *F*!) We need to know that the distance from a point to a line is the shortest distance – i.e. along the perpendicular through the point to the line. So we can set this up 'in reverse' by taking the line (or at least a segment of it) as the domain, and a point *P* on it as the 'slider'. Also construct the perpendicular to the line through *P*.

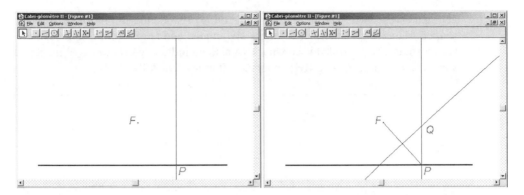

Now we know that if Q lies on this perpendicular then $FQ = PQ$, and we can use the same arguments about isosceles triangles that we met previously – so Q must be the point on the perpendicular that also lies on the perpendicular bisector of the 'base' FP. Construct this and mark its intersection with the perpendicular through P as the point Q.

Now you can slide P on the line and check that Q seems to be tracing a path. If you like you can Trace this, or just construct the locus of Q with P. We ought to join FQ as that was used in the definition. The great thing about such a locus is that it is redrawn dynamically as you change the position of F.

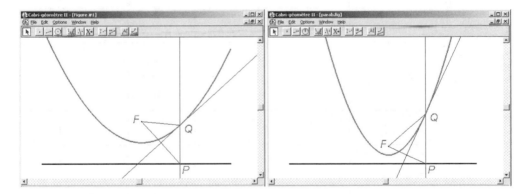

So now we have met our first conic (other than a circle!) – it's a 'parabola' with F as its 'focus' and the line as its 'directrix'. Of course the parabola is not on the 11–16 syllabus – but both locus and isosceles triangles are! What would be nice is to relate this geometric construction to the graph of the quadratic function in algebra – which is something we will return to later. For now we can also view the image as explaining how a reflecting telescope focuses parallel rays, and how the silver mirroring behind a car's headlamp produces a parallel beam of light.

5.4(g) Congruence and similarity

A standard piece of 'traditional' geometry is to 'understand and use SSS, SAS, ASA and RHS conditions to prove the congruence of triangles using formal arguments. . .'. Another way into this is to prepare a task-sheet for use together with dynamic geometry to see whether individuals, or groups of students, can produce different shaped triangles given any three of the six lengths and angles of a triangle. In this way it should be possible to see why ASA also includes SAA (because of the angle sum of a triangle) and why RHS is rather different from ASS.

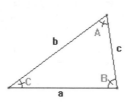

Construct a triangle from the following data, if possible. Measure and record the missing data. Make a sketch in your exercise book. If you think there are other triangles with different shapes using the same data then sketch them too.

a cm.	b cm.	c cm.	A°	B°	C°
3	6	5			
4	5				70
		4	60	50	
5	6		40		
3	4				90
		4	70		
			60	80	40

Another aspect is to 'establish the validity of standard ruler and compass constructions'. Obviously the key concept is that a circle is the locus of points in the plane equidistant from a given point. Another is that locus of points equidistant from two given points is their perpendicular bisector. Can you devise activities to establish and/or apply these ideas?

So now suppose we consider the standard ruler-and-compass construction for an angle bisector. A very powerful image here is the rhombus together with the properties of its diagonals (i.e. that they are perpendicular and bisect each other). So if we have an angle *ABC* defined by the half-lines *BA* and *BC* we just need to find a way of 'fitting a rhombus into the corner *ABC*'. So if you define a point *D* on *BA*, say, then you can construct a circle centre *B* through *D* to meet *BC* in *E*. So triangle *DBE* is isosceles. To complete a rhombus we need to construct another, congruent, isosceles triangle *DFE* on *DE* as base, so draw the circles' centre *D* through *B* and centre *E* through *B* to meet in a second point of intersection at *F*. Then *DBEF* is a suitable rhombus and hence its diagonal *BF* bisects the angle *DBE = ABC*. As you drag *D* on *BA* only the size of the rhombus alters, not the direction of its diagonals.

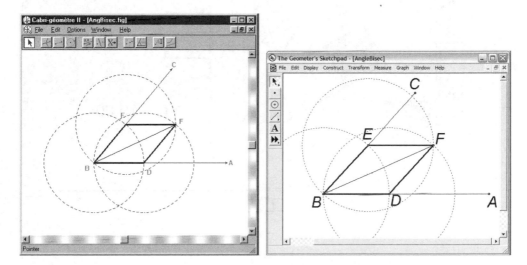

A good investigation for more able students is to use these constructions on the sides and angles of a triangle. For example, suppose the angle bisectors of angles *A* and *B* of a triangle meet in a point *P* – what can we say about *P*? Is it obvious that the angle bisector of *C* must pass through *P*? Is *P* the same distance away from corners (vertices) of the triangle? Is it the same distance away from the sides? How could you construct a circle to touch each of the sides? How is its radius related to the area and perimeter of the triangle? Repeat a similar exercise for the perpendicular bisectors of the sides. How about the medians of a triangle (e.g. the segment from vertex *A* to the midpoint *D* of the opposite side *BC*, etc.)? How about the altitudes of a triangle (e.g. the perpendiculars from the vertices to the opposite sides)? Can you construct a circle which passes through the midpoints *D, E, F* of the sides? Where is its centre? What happens to these various 'centres' as the triangle *ABC* is deformed? Are any lines concurrent, or any points collinear?

5.4(h) Transformation geometry

We turn from traditional geometry to studying geometric transformations. Most of the current dynamic geometry software packages, including Cabri and Sketchpad, provide tools for transformations. For example, we can show axes, and display a grid. On this we can define a polygon, such as a 'flagpole'. To define the angle of rotation in Cabri you use Numerical Edit, and in Sketchpad you can use Graph and New Parameter to define the name, the value and also the unit. Using the Rotation tool from the Transformation menu you can rotate your polygon through the given angle around a given centre. In the following figure we have taken an object polygon and shown three successive rotations around the origin through the given angle, currently 30°. As you edit this angle you can see the images deform dynamically.

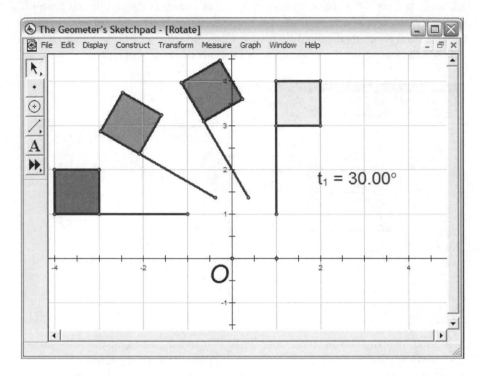

Similar approaches can be used by teachers or students to illustrate or explore properties of various transformations. In fact the new version of the English national curriculum draws specific attention to the ICT opportunities offered by the use of software to explore transformation geometry. For example, we can easily investigate the product of reflections in parallel and non-parallel lines.

In the next figure two mirror lines and an object polygon have been defined. The object *AEBCDE* is reflected in the first mirror (going from top left to bottom right) to give the first image. This is then reflected in the second mirror (going from bottom left to top right) to give the final image. What single transformation could map the initial object to the final image? If it was a rotation then corresponding points, such as *E* and *E"* would be the same distance away from the centre *P*. Hence *EE'* would be a chord of a circle centre *P*, and hence their perpendicular bisector passes through *P*. The same argument applies for each pair of corresponding points such as *AA"*, etc. Hence the perpendicular bisectors of *AA"*, etc. should all pass through *P*. Do they? If so, where is *P*? Does this *prove* that there is a rotation centre *X* which takes the object to the second image? If *X* is the centre, how can you find the angle of rotation?

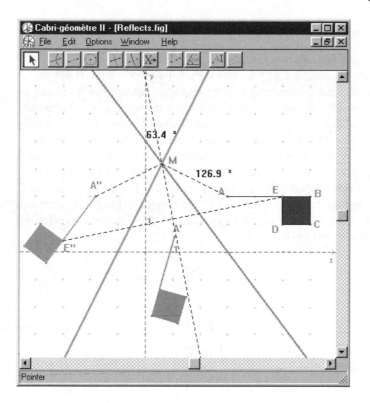

Another aspect to explore about combinations of transformations is whether or not the order matters (i.e. are they commutative?). For example, the following screen shows two different ways to reflect in lines *m* and *n*. Under what circumstances will the images marked *Rnm* and *Rmn* be identical? Will this stay true for any position of the object *R*?

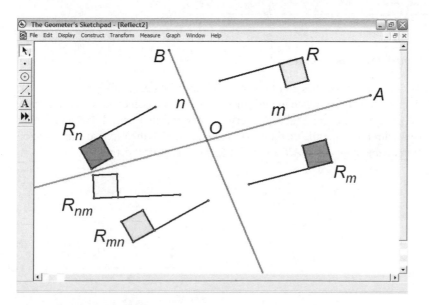

5.4(i) Interactive whiteboards

If the school has access to interactive whiteboard technology, then dynamic geometry is probably the area in mathematics which best exploits its potential. If not then a reasonable simulation can be made by projecting the computer's output onto an ordinary classroom whiteboard on which you can also write with, e.g., non-permanent dry-colour markers. Then, e.g., students can draw freehand suggestions which can be confirmed (or negated) by displaying computer-generated results. As an example, we could explore lines of symmetry of standard geometric objects, such as a parallelogram. Suppose we have the parallelogram *ABCD* projected together with the midpoints of its sides *P,Q,R,S*. A student might very well propose that, e.g., *PR* or *AC* is a line of symmetry and superimpose it on the projected image. The class can see whether they agree or not. If required then you can perform the reflections in the suggested mirror line to test the hypothesis.

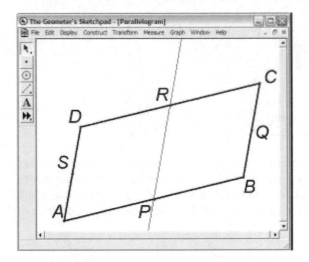

5.4(j) Coordinates and vectors

Naturally, similar approaches can be used with coordinates. For example, we can easily illustrate how to calculate the distance between two points whose coordinates we know. Here *A* and *B* are attached to grid-points, but they could just be floating points. Lines through *A* parallel to the *x* axis and *B* parallel to the *y* axis are constructed to meet in *C* (what happens if *AB* is parallel to the *y* axis, or the *x* axis?).

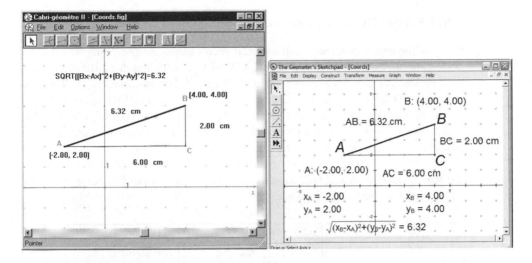

Similarly, higher-level students may use the same software to explore vectors. For example, we can look at various vector properties of the regular polygon. Here $AB =$ **a** and $AF =$ **b**. Can you define each of the other vectors in terms of **a** and **b**?

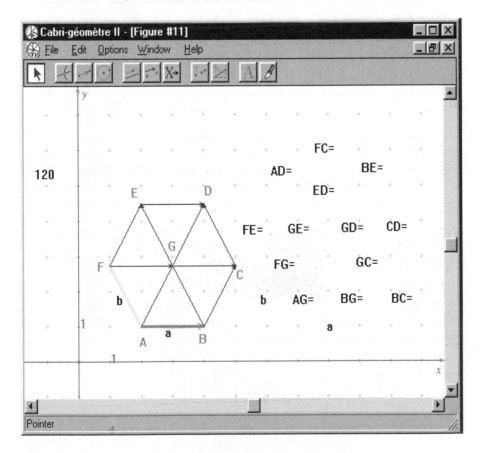

5.4(k) Further ideas: transformations, coordinates and Pythagoras

Many of the transformation, coordinate and vector ideas can also easily be explored with graphing calculators such as the TI-83/4 and versatile graph-plotting software, such as Autograph and that contained in TI-Nspire™. For example, we shall use the lists of the TI-83/4 to hold the coordinates of an object shape which we plot using a joined-up scattergram (called an *xy*-line). The idea is to use STAT PLOT to draw the object shape whose *x* coordinates are held in list L1 and *y* coordinates in list L2. The problem is to work out what combinations of L1 and L2 should go in list L3 and L4 if they are to hold the (*x,y*) coordinates of the image shape under different transformations, such as a reflection in the *y* axis. You will need to define a second STAT PLOT to display the image.

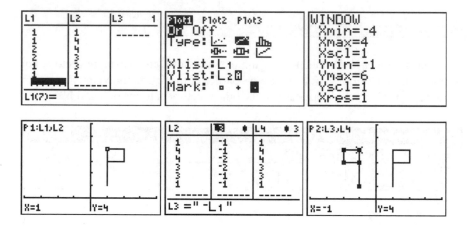

A different approach is to create a program to draw a shape using the Line(*x*1,*y*1,*x*2,*y*2) command. For example, the four-line program 'PYTHAG' draws a right-angled triangle. You will need to choose a suitable WINDOW and FORMAT for the screen and make sure that any function and statistics plotting is disabled. The problem is to extend the program to create the 'Pythagoras diagram' as shown.

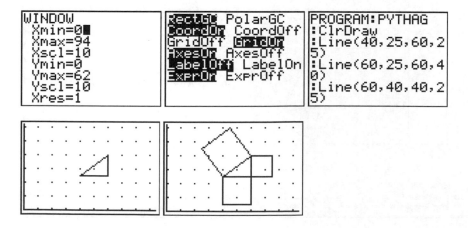

There are many variations on this theme, such as creating letters of the alphabet, symmetric shapes, etc., that appeal to students.

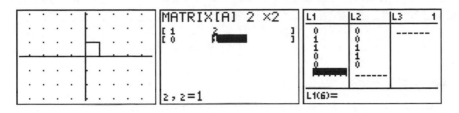

Although neither shears, nor the use of matrices, appears in the latest English national curriculum in mathematics for students aged 11–16, they are still in other nations' curricula. In any case the post-school literature in many subjects, such as physics, geography, statistics, etc. makes use of matrix notation, and students can be very disadvantaged if they have not encountered it at school. The NCET *IT Maths Pack* includes some geometry task cards. The one labelled 'Shears' was adapted from SMILE (No. 1957) and made reference to the MicroSMILE program Matrices. The activity can be undertaken using other ICT tools, such as graph-plotting software (Autograph, Omnigraph) or with spreadsheets (Excel™) or graphing calculators. It can also be carried out using dynamic geometry software. We just include a few screens to illustrate the idea and leave you to work out the fine detail. The first group of screens are taken using the lists and matrices of a TI-83 and Stat Plots for the object and image using first L1, L2 and then L3, L4.

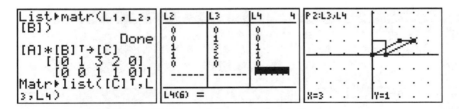

A similar approach can be taken in most spreadsheets. However, we have to make the rules of matrix multiplication explicit when entering the formulas (not strictly true, as some sheets do provide matrix multiplication as a function). We need to make use of the ideas of absolute reference to cells again. To produce the graph you need to start with a scattergram of columns C and D, and then insert the additional data for a second 'series' from columns E and F. It can take a bit of practice to get control over the layout of the axes, and you will need to drag the corners and sides of the chart window until the unit square appears square!

The next images show how the transformation can be illustrated using the graphing package Autograph and also a spreadsheet (Excel™).

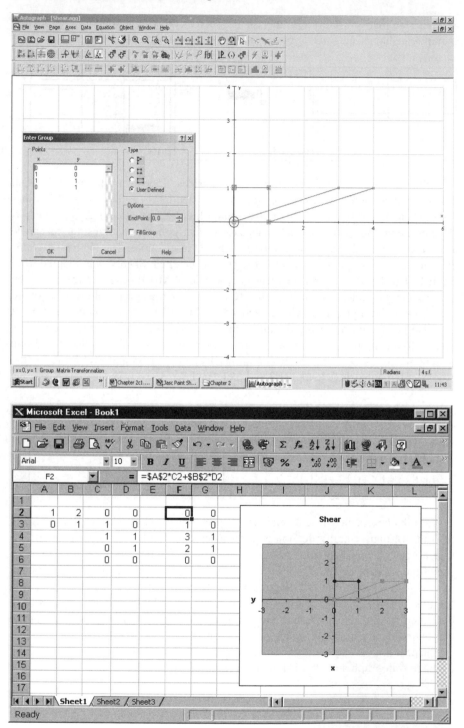

We can also use dynamic geometry to explore these situations. In Cabri we use a similar idea, using Numeric Edit to enter the four values of the matrix. Then you can define your object, and measure its coordinates. Using the built-in calculator you can 'teach' Cabri the rules of matrix multiplication to obtain the coordinates of the sheared image. Transferring these values to the axes you can draw the image. Of course now you can measure areas. A similar approach can be taken in Sketchpad using New Parameter and Plot As (x,y).

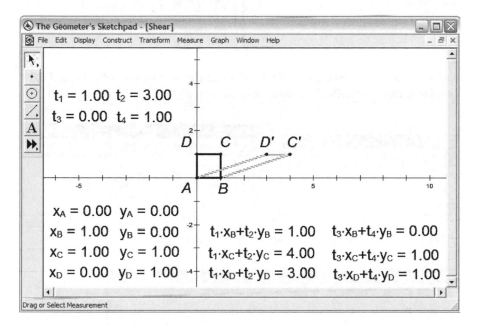

There are also plenty of applications for geometry in realistic situations and some of these will be included in further sections on modelling and on links with other subjects.

We conclude the part of this section on geometry by taking a look at some of the activities in the book *Geometry with Computers*, and accompanying Activity Sheets, included in the NCET *IT Maths Pack*. The book refers to some software which is available from Becta and other sources, but many of the ideas can be explored within Cabri, Sketchpad and MSW Logo™.

5.4(l) Further ideas: Locus

Chasing games

Chasing is an activity based on what are technically called 'curves of pursuit'. In MSW Logo™ we can have several turtles all performing on the same screen. Just use SETTURTLE followed by a number to give instructions to this turtle alone. So we will have turtle #0 to represent Jean who chases Jayne leaving a red trail. Turtle #1 represents Jayne who moves along some path leaving a blue trail. We define just four procedures for this Logo microworld. SETUP moves Jayne and Jean to their starting position. CHASE has two arguments. The first is the number of steps to take in the chase, and the second is the length of a step.

```
Editor
File  Edit  Search  Set  Test!  Help
to Chase :N :S
 SETUP
 REPEAT :N [Follow :S Evade :S]
end
```

```
Editor
File  Edit  Search  Set  Test!  Help
To SETUP
 CS
 MAKE "red [255 0 0]
 MAKE "blue [0 0 255]
 SETTURTLE 1
 PU FD 100 RT 90 PD
 SETTURTLE 0
 PU BK 100 PD
End
```

CHASE uses two procedures. FOLLOW makes Jayne turn towards Jean and move forward a distance S. EVADE makes Jean travel a distance S along some path.

```
Editor
File  Edit  Search  Set  Test!  Help
to Evade :S
 SETTURTLE 1
 SETPC :blue FD :S
end
```

```
Editor
File  Edit  Search  Set  Test!  Help
to Follow :S
 SETTURTLE 1 MAKE "Jayne POS
 SETTURTLE 0 SETH TOWARDS :Jayne
 SETPC :red FD :S
end
```

The command CHASE 50 5 results in the following output.

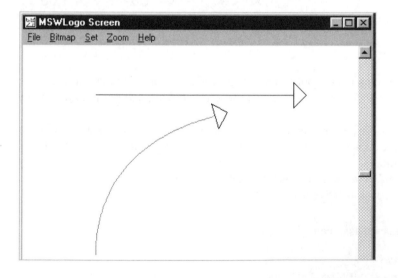

Equal areas

Take points *X* and *Y* on two different lines through *Z*. Choose any point *P* and construct the triangles *PXZ* and *PYZ*. Measure their areas. Drag *P* until they are roughly equal. Can you predict the set of points *P* for which the areas are exactly equal? Can you explain why?

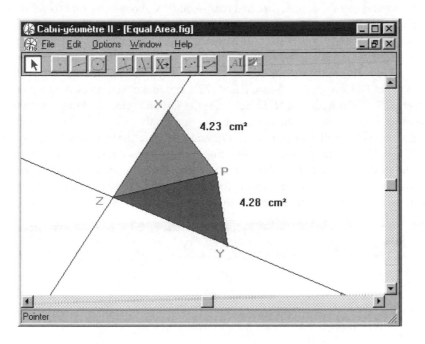

Imagine a clock

This consists of some activities to do with imagining loci and then confirming or amending your ideas when you use software to produce them. There is a piece of small software called Arms which was developed by members of the Association of Teachers of Mathematics and is contained in the NCET Locus software pack. However, the activity is equally one which can be carried out using the facilities of dynamic geometry such as Cabri. The essential idea is to have two circles of radii *r* and *r'*, say. Each has a radius vector (the 'arm of a clock') which starts from bearings *B* and *B'*, say. One radius vector rotates at a constant rate in a clockwise direction. The other rotates at a multiple *m* of this rate (possibly a negative multiple). The ends of the radii are joined by an 'elastic' segment *PP'*. The activity is to predict the locus of its midpoint *M*.

The task-sheet suggests you start with *OB* at 12 o'clock (or at a bearing of 000°), *O'B'* at 6 o'clock (180°) and take *m* = 1. Then try changing *O'B'* to 3 o'clock (090°). Now try changing both initial bearings to 000° but change *m* to 2.

We will run through a way to set up the test-bed for this activity and leave you to perform the 'thought experiments' and confirmation with the software. We start by giving detailed instructions for the Cabri approach. First construct the line *XX'* and points *O*, *O'* on it. Construct vectors *OX* and *OX'*. Use Numerical Edit to enter values, such as 3 and 3 for the radii of the circles, and add Comments as required. Use

Measurement Transfer to create points R, R' on OX and OX'. Construct the circles centre O through R, and centre O' through R'. Construct perpendiculars to XX' through O and O' to meet the circles in N and N'. Hide the lines XX', ON, ON' and vectors OX, OX'. Now use Numerical Edit to enter initial values of the bearings of B from N and B' from N', and annotate as required. Use the Calculator to multiply each bearing by -1 and call the results *rot1* and *rot2*. Rotate N about O by *rot1* to get B, and N' about O' by *rot2* to get B'.

Construct vectors OB and $O'B'$. Use Numerical Edit to enter a value for the multiplier m and the angle θ to turn OB through. Use the calculator to multiply θ by -1 to get *rot3*, and by $-m$ to get *rot4*. Rotate B about O by *rot3* to get P, and B' about O' by *rot4* to get P'. Construct vectors OP and $O'P'$, and make them thick. Construct the segment PP' and its midpoint M. Select Trace On/Off and select M. Finally select Animation, and select the turn angle θ, dragging out a rather short 'spring'. When you release this you should see the 'arms' OB and $O'B'$ rotating reasonably slowly on their 'clock faces', and the locus of M being traced out as a thick red line. Just click on the mouse button to stop the animation. To clear a locus just select Hide/Show and then click on the pointer icon. Now you can double-click on any of the numerical parameters to set another problem. Reset θ to 0, and use Animate again.

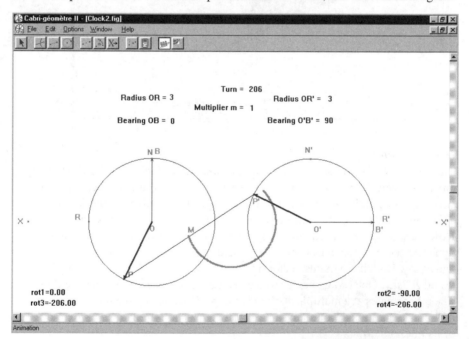

In Sketchpad use the Graph menu and select New Parameter to enter the value and unit for the 'turn', e.g. 220°.

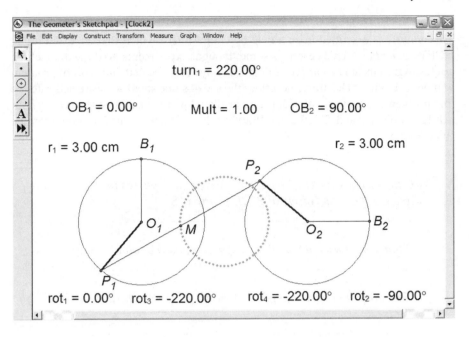

The tethered goat

A goat is tied to the corner of a shed measuring 4 m by 3 m. The rope tethering the goat is 5 m long. What is the shape of the grass that the goat can reach? What would happen if the goat was tethered to a different part of the shed?

Of course this is something that you can investigate with a variety of practical apparatus, starting with a pencil and ruler, before moving to ICT. It is a good problem, though, for testing your problem-solving strategies, e.g. using Cabri and/or Sketchpad.

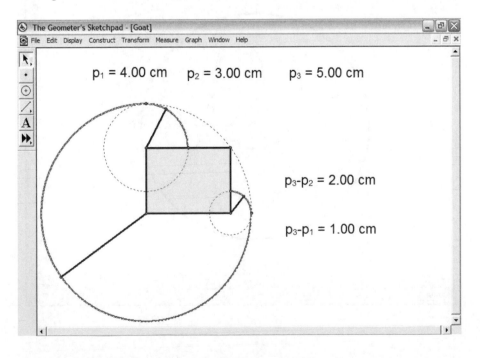

Circles

This activity is described in an article by Greg Morris, which first appeared in the NCET *Locus Pack*. This describes some 'thought experiments' to do with touching circles. Again there is a variety of practical ways to investigate this sort of problem without using ICT. The article describes the use of some small software dedicated to this problem. However with Cabri and/or Sketchpad we can again make a useful test-bed. Points *O* and *R* define the 'blue' circle. *Q* is any point. *P* is a point on the 'blue' circle.

✎ *Can you construct the 'magenta' circle which passes through* Q *and touches the 'blue' circle at* P? *Its centre is* S.

✎ *What is the locus of* S *as* P *is dragged round the 'blue' circle?*

✎ *How does the locus change as* Q *moves inside or outside the 'blue' circle?*

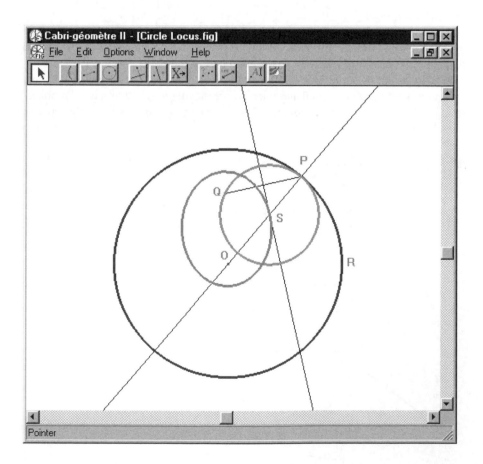

5.4(m) Trigonometry

We will start by building a useful tool – a dynamic set-square – based on a right-angled triangle. Here we have a little Cabri or Sketchpad test-bed with just two major variables. The point P can be moved on arc QR to define the angle $\angle A$, and the point A can slide horizontally in and out towards C to define the base AC. The sides of the triangle ABC can be measured, and their ratios calculated. Dragging the point A keeps the angles constant, so we have similar triangles ABC and OPS. We can see that ratios are invariants (and that ABC is an enlargement of OPS). Dragging the point P keeps the base constant, and changes the vertical and hypotenuse of the triangle, and hence the ratios.

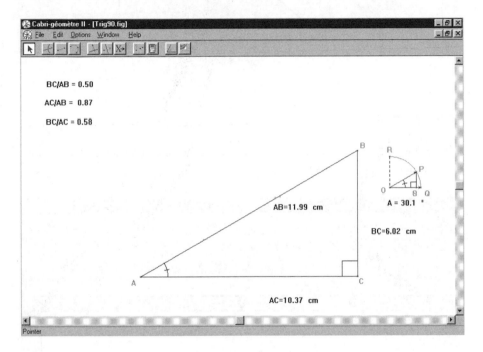

The ratios could be copied down and tabulated against $\angle A$ in a spreadsheet or graphing calculator. Needless to say both Cabri and Sketchpad include tools to tabulate measurement and calculations.

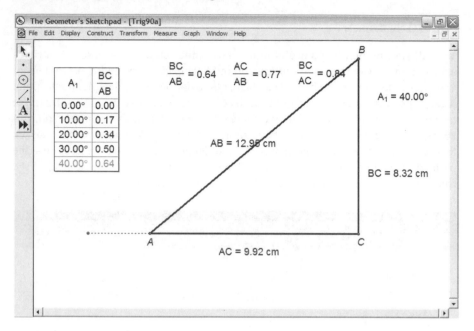

Once the table has been constructed it can be 'cut and pasted' to another application such as the Excel™ spreadsheet.

	A	B	C	D	E	F	G
1	**A**	**sin A**					
2	0	0					
3	10	0.17					
4	20.3	0.35					
5	30	0.5					
6	39.9	0.64					
7	50.1	0.77					
8	60	0.87					
9	69.9	0.94					
10	80	0.98					
11	89	1					

A similar idea can be used to illustrate the trigonometric functions for any angle. Here we start by showing axes and dragging the origin O to a suitable position. Now our x coordinates will be angles in degrees, so we need to reduce the x coordinate's unit length by dragging its unit point towards O. However, the y coordinates will be in the interval $[-1,1]$ so we need to increase the y coordinate's unit length by dragging its unit point away from O. With Numerical Edit we can transfer the measurement -1 to the y-axis and hence create a 'unit' circle (in the y-sense!). We can create the point of intersection E of the circle with the x-axis. Using Numerical Edit we can now enter a rotation angle, such as 397. Then we can rotate E about O by this angle to get P, and construct the triangle OPQ. For the sine function we just need to measure the y-coordinate of P. (We measured P's coordinates and then used the Calculator tool to extract just its y coordinate.) Now we transfer this measurement to y axis to obtain point Y and the rotation angle to the x axis to obtain point X. Using perpendiculars we can construct the graph point S. Now mark S as Trace On, edit the rotation angle to -100, say, and then Animate this number. As the 'rotor' P sweeps around the circle, so the point S traces out the graph of the sine function.

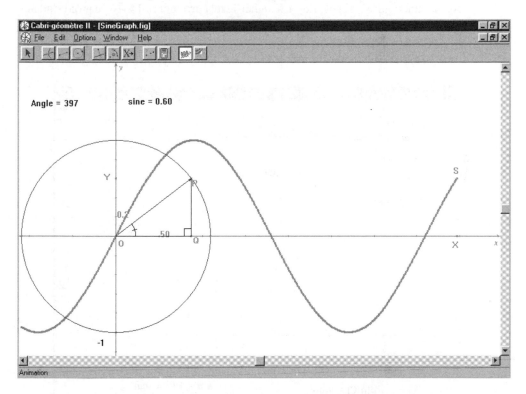

In Sketchpad we can again use the New Parameter command from the Graph menu to enter the angle used to control the animation. With two measurement or calculations selected in order, the convenient Graph command Plot As (x,y) allows you to create the point S whose path you can easily trace by highlighting the angle A and using the '+' or '−' keys to increment or decrement by preset amounts, e.g. in 5° steps.

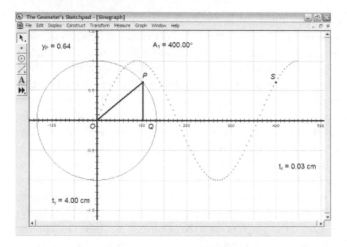

You will need to be just a bit more cunning to get the correct measurements for the cosine function! Within the English higher-level curriculum, 14–16 year old students are expected to meet the sine and cosine rules, and also know that area of a triangle is ½ *ab* sin *C*. The following Cabri screen suggests one possible useful visual aid for investigating both the cosine rule (as Pythagoras with an error term) and the area.

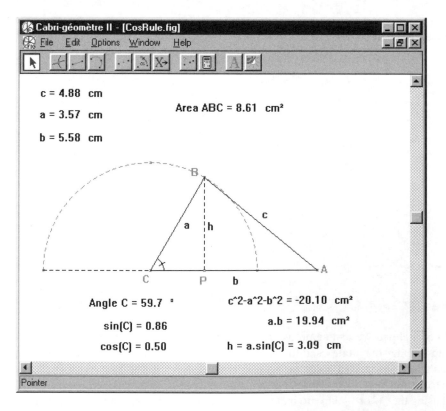

A useful application of trigonometric functions is in exploring parametric and polar curves. For example, using the parametric plotting mode of the TI-83/4 or

TI-Nspire™, you can explore graphs of the form $x = \cos^p(t)$, $y = \sin^q(t)$ for various values of p and q.

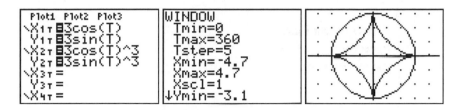

5.5   STATISTICS AND MODELLING

Section 3 of the current English secondary mathematics curriculum is described as 'Statistics' and starts with a description of what is known as the 'handling data cycle'.

The handling data cycle
This is closely linked to the mathematical key processes and consists of:

- specifying the problem and planning (representing)
- collecting data (representing and analysing)
- processing and presenting the data (analysing)
- interpreting and discussing the results (interpreting and evaluating).

The Explanatory notes make reference to ICT:

Presentation and analysis: This includes the use of ICT.
    Probabilities: This includes . . . simulations using ICT to represent a probability experiment, such as rolling two dice and adding the scores.

5.5(a) Handling data

The NCET *IT Maths Pack* contains a book entitled *Mathematics in Context*, subtitled *IT in Mathematics across the Curriculum*. An article entitled 'Why Data Handling?' describes the **PCAI** data-handling cycle, introduced by Alan Graham in *Investigating Statistics* (Hodder & Stoughton, 1990). That cycle forms the basis of the approach taken in the national curriculum.

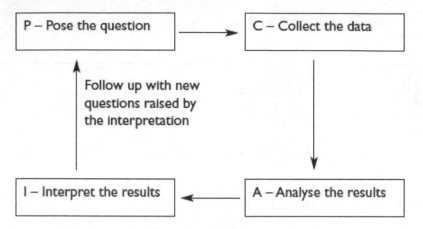

There is considerable scope for the use of ICT tools within the aspects **C**, **A** and **I**:

C: as sources of data and ICT tools for storing and retrieving data;
A: to compute statistics from data and to display data graphically;
I: to communicate results.

To start this section we will take a close look at how far the facilities in just one ICT tool, TI-Nspire™, can support work in data-handling and statistics. We will start with a data source which was included on a disk within the NCET *IT Maths Pack*. This contains versions of a file called *Cities*, which is described in the article 'City Life' in the *Mathematics in Context* book from that pack. This data file contains ten data-sets from 50 of the world's largest cities, and was published by the Population Crisis Committee in 1990. The article suggests providing opportunities for students to formulate their own questions in both whole-class and small-group discussion, and gives as examples:

'I wonder which city has the highest murder rate.'

'Which is the noisiest city?'

'. . . and the most congested?'

'Why don't you put in order all the data on murders and we'll do the data on noise?'

'Yes, then someone else can do traffic flow.'

Obviously we need to take care with this, and any other secondary sources of data, whether stored electronically or not. There may be errors, either in the way the data was collected or in the way the data were entered. The data may have been approximated, incomplete, too far out of date to be useful, etc.

Before you can pose and explore your own questions you need to know something about the data available to you. The data file is organized as a table with 51 rows and 12 columns. The first row contains the headings for the columns, which are known as the 'Field names'. They are as follows:

Field name	
CITY	Name of city
COUNTRY	Name of country
POPULATION	Population of city
MURDERS	Number of murders per year per 100,000 people
FOOD COSTS	Average per cent of income spent on food
LIVINGSPACE	Average number of people per room
WATER/ELEC.	per cent of homes with water and electricity
TELEPHONES	Number of telephones per 100 people
SEC. SCHOOL	Per cent of children (age 14–17) in secondary schools
INF. DEATH	Infant deaths (age 0–1) per 1,000 live births
NOISE	Level of background noise (1–10) (low–high)
TRAFFIC FLOW	Average miles per hour in rush hour

Unfortunately this is not a fully interactive book! So we will make some decisions about the questions we are going to use to illustrate an ICT-assisted data-handling approach. Of course you are quite at liberty to choose a completely different set of questions.

One question we often ask secondary school students, if we want to collect a quick data-set, is: 'How many telephones (mobile and conventional) do you have at home?' Clearly this number has escalated enormously in many countries over the past few years. So this data-file gives us some data about the spread of telephones 20 years or so ago. Our first problem then is to get a feel for just what that eighth column of data, headed TELEPHONES, actually tells us. We will start by opening the City Data file in the TI-Nspire™ spreadsheet. (We will abbreviate TI-Nspire™ to TIN from now on.) Here you can see a small extract of the file, and you can scroll across and down to see more of it. We will do the data analysis and displays using TIN's Lists. You can also do the same kind of things using the TI-83/4's STAT Editor. So our first task will be to highlight the data in column H ready to copy and paste it from the spreadsheet into the first column of a new Lists and Spreadsheet page.

	A	B	C	D	E	F	G	H
1	CITY	COUNTRY	POPULAT..	MURD...	FOOD.	LIVIN.	WATER.	TELE..
2	BAGHDAD	IRAQ	4400000	–	45	2.2	98	7
3	BANGALORE	INDIA	4100000	2.8	62	2.8	67	2
4	BANGKOK	THAILAND	7000000	7.6	36	3.2	76	12
5	BARCELONA	SPAIN	3975000	1.4	30	2.2	94	46
6	BEIJING	CHINA	7040000	2.5	52	1.2	89	2
7	BERLIN	GERMANY	3940000	6.7	23	0.6	100	51
8	BIRMINGHAM	UK	2655000	1.8	20	0.5	100	50
9	BOGOTA	COLUMBIA	4640000	21.1	22	1.5	89	18
10	BOMBAY	INDIA	12900000	3.2	57	4.2	85	5
11	BOSTON	USA	4085000	7.8	12	0.5	98	–
12	BUDAPEST	HUNGARY	2575000	4.1	27	1.2	99	31
13	BUENOS AIRES	ARGENTINA	12400000	7.6	40	1.3	86	14
14	CAIRO	EGYPT	11000000	56.4	47	1.5	94	3
15	CALCUTTA	INDIA	12800000	1.1	60	3.	57	2
16	CHICAGO	USA	7900000	10.6	13	0.5	97	53
17	DELHI – NEW DELHI	INDIA	9800000	4.1	40	2.4	66	5

The first problem is that two of the entries in column H are undefined (Boston and Tehran), and marked with a dash, and also the first entry is a name, not a number. Just highlight the whole of column H by clicking on the 'H' label, and do 'Edit' 'Copy'. Then move to a new Lists page, put the cursor in the cell A1 and do 'Edit' 'Paste'. Right click in turn on the cell A1 and the two cells containing the dashes, and, in each case, select 'Delete cell'. Alongside the label 'A' at the top of the first column enter the title 'phone' for the list's name.

We will now make a copy of this list in the B column, and then sort it into ascending order.

You can either copy and paste the A column, or give the 'B' column a name such as 'psort' and in the space below define 'psort := phone'. Now with column B already highlighted just click on the icon at the left above the table and select the last option: 'SORT'. From the dialogue box choose to sort B into ascending order.

	A phone	B psort	C
		=phone	
1	7	7	
2	2	2	
3	12	12	
4	46	46	
5	2	2	
6	51	51	
7	50	50	
8	18	18	
9	5	5	
10	31	31	
11	14	14	
12	3	3	
13	2	2	
14	53	53	
15	5	5	
16	2	2	
17	42	42	

B2 | =2

	A phone	B psort	C
1	7	1	
2	2	2	
3	12	2	
4	46	2	
5	2	2	
6	51	2	
7	50	2	
8	18	2	
9	5	3	
10	31	3	
11	14	3	
12	3	3	
13	2	4	
14	53	4	
15	5	5	
16	2	5	
17	42	6	

B | =2

Here we see that the minimum value is one phone per 100 people (corresponding to which city?). Of course we might have had some cities where the data recorded were 0 phones per 100 people – would that have meant that there were no phones at all in the city?

Now there is a whole lot of list operations that produce statistics from a given list. In the first cell of column C we typed 'mean(phone)' and in the second cell 'median(phone)'. If the results are given as fractions rather than decimals you can select 'File' and 'Settings' to change 'Document Settings' from 'Auto' to 'Approximate'.

	A phone	B psort	C	D	E	F	G	H
1	7.	1.	21.9792					
2	2.	2.	13.					
3	12.	2.	=max(**phone**)					
4	46.	2.						
5	2.	2.						
6	51.	2.						
7	50.	2.						
8	18.	2.						
9	5.	3.						
10	31.	3.						
11	14.	3.						
12	3.	3.						
13	2.	4.						
14	53.	4.						
15	5.	5.						
16	2.	5.						
17	42.	6.						

C3 | =max(**phone**)

Using this technique we find that:

min(phone)   =   1
max(phone)   =   75
mean(phone)   =   21.98
median(phone)   =   13
stdDev(phone)   =   20.66
variance(phone) = 426.96
dim(phone)   =   48.

The fourth icon above the screen has a menu which starts with 'Stat Calculations', and the first choice is 'One Variable Statistics'. You enter the column you want to use, i.e. 'phone' and the column where the results will appear, i.e. E.

	A phone	B psort	C	D	E	F	G
					=OneVar('phone,1): CopyV		
1	7.	1.	21.9792	Title	One–Variable Statistics		
2	2.	2.	13.	$\bar{x}$	21.9792		
3	12.	2.	75.	Σx	1055.		
4	46.	2.		Σx^2	43255.		
5	2.	2.		$sx := S_{n-1}x$	20.6629		
6	51.	2.		$\sigma x := \sigma_n x$	20.4466		
7	50.	2.		n	48.		
8	18.	2.		MinX	1.		
9	5.	3.		Q_1X	3.5		
10	31.	3.		MedianX	13.		
11	14.	3.		Q_3X	40.5		
12	3.	3.		MaxX	75.		
13	2.	4.		$SSX := \Sigma(x-\bar{x})^2$	20067.		
14	53.	4.					
15	5.	5.					
16	2.	5.					
17	42.	6.					

Here you now get a very full set of statistics for our data-set. These include the sum of the elements, and the sum of their squares, the population and sample standard deviations, and the quartiles.

As we all know, a picture is worth a thousand words, so next we look at some ways of displaying this data. The first is the histogram. Insert a 'Data and Statistics' page, and click on the bottom middle of the page to select 'phone' as the variable to display. Using the first icon, select 'Histogram'. From the second icon select 'Histogram Properties' and 'Bin settings', and from the fifth icon select 'Window Settings' to get the histogram to appear as you want.

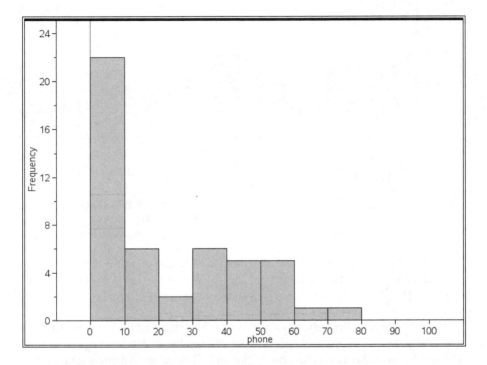

This confirms that the modal class is the half-open interval $(0,10)$ – or, for discrete data, 0–9, with a count of 22 (out of 48). Of course, both the shape of the histogram and the value of the mode change if you re-plot with different Bin Widths and/or Alignments. Another useful representation is the Box Plot (or box and whisker diagram). We cannot superimpose one over the histogram, but we can use a split screen and the same Window settings to make them align.

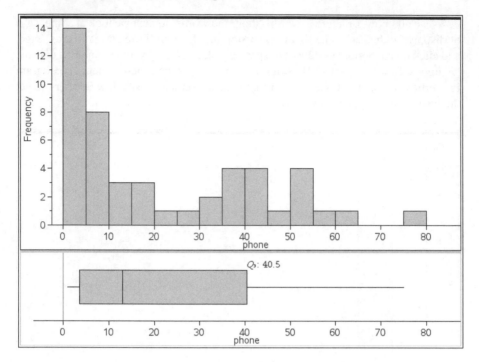

Tracing this you can read off the min, max, median and quartiles. Hence you can also calculate the range as max – min = 75 – 1 = 74, and also the inter-quartile range as Q3 – Q1 = 40.5 – 3.5 = 37. So now you have seen most of the tools of trade for working with a single data-set.

The box-plot is particularly useful for comparing data about the same aspect taken from different groups. For example we can split our list of data on telephones from 48 cities between three new lists corresponding to Europe, the Americas and the Rest of the World. An extra list has been created, called 'region' which contains categorical data: 'a', 'e' or 'r' for each city. The respective box-plots can be superimposed on the same axes. Only the scale on the horizontal axis is important. Can you guess which box-plot corresponds to which international grouping? Do you think a similar result would hold true if data was collected now?

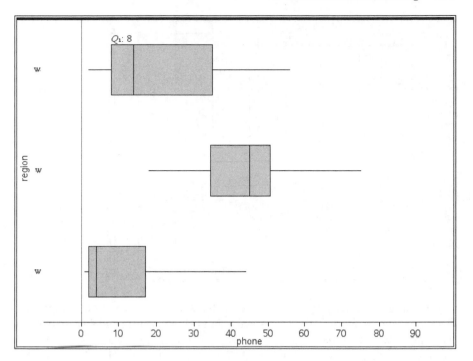

Another important aspect of data-handling is in looking for associations between data. For example, the data on telephones might be regarded as associated with the relative wealth of the people in the cities included in the data-set. But there is no data directly giving comparisons on e.g. income per capita. So we could choose another set of data which we also think might be related to wealth, such as LIVINGSPACE, i.e. the average number of people per room. Whereas the number of phones might be expected to increase with wealth, the number of people per room might be expected to decrease. So we might make the hypothesis that there is an inverse association between TELEPHONES and LIVINGSPACE, i.e. that the more phones there are per 100 people, the less people there are per room, on average.

So we will now look first at producing a scattergram, and then at fitting some models, both 'by eye', and using the TIN's built-in regression models. Before we rush into copying and pasting the LIVINGSPACE data into the List editor we must not forget Boston and Tehran! Remember that we did not have any TELEPHONE data for these two cities, so they must be struck off our list of comparisons. So before we go on to the next stage can you find the values of the min, max, mean and median for the LIVINGSPACE data from our remaining 48 cities?

	A city	B phone	C region	D living	E	F	G	H
1	BAGHDAD	7.	r	2.2				
2	BANGALORE	2.	r	2.8				
3	BANGKOK	12.	r	3.2				
4	BARCELONA	46.	e	2.2				
5	BEIJING	2.	r	1.2				
6	BERLIN	51.	e	0.6				
7	BIRMINGHAM	50.	e	0.5				
8	BOGOTA	18.	a	1.5				
9	BOMBAY	5.	r	4.2				
10	BUDAPEST	31.	e	1.2				
11	BUENOS AIRES	14.	a	1.3				
12	CAIRO	3.	r	1.5				
13	CALCUTTA	2.	r	3.				
14	CHICAGO	53.	a	0.5				
15	DELHI – NEW DELHI	5.	r	2.4				
16	DHAKA	2.	r	3.1				
17	HONG KONG	42.	r	1.6				

We can produce scattergrams in either a 'Data and Statistics' or a 'Graphs and Geometry' window. The following screen-shots show first a page split between a 'Data and Statistics' window on the left and a 'Lists and Spreadsheets' window on the right, and then one with 'Graphs and Geometry' on the left. Here Barcelona has been highlighted as the point (46,2.2).

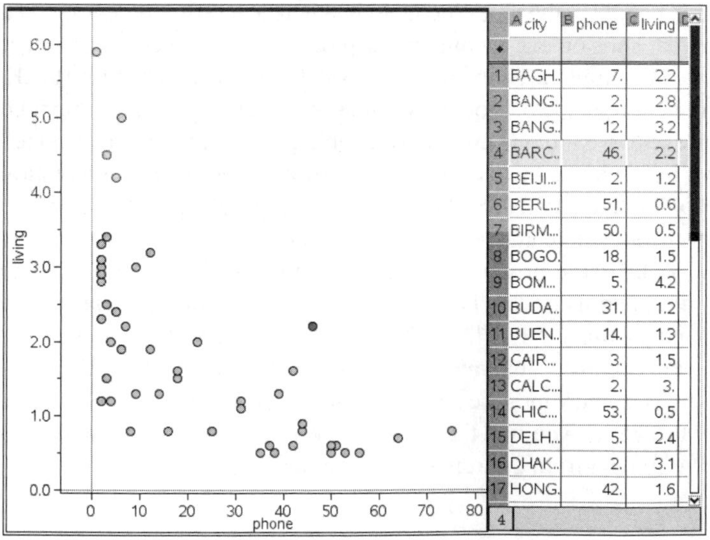

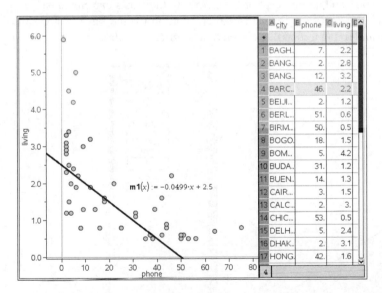

The data does seem to show an inverse relationship, although not necessarily a linear one! In the 'Data and Statistics' window you can use the fourth icon to 'Add Movable Line' which you can drag and twist to make a 'by eye' fit. As you manipulate the line so its slope and intercept values change.

If you think that an inverse function, such as $y = k/x$, would be a better fit, then you can compute values of xy by forming a list **xy** as the product **phone*living** of the lists. Then you can compute its mean to give a value for k of about 23. So we can also plot the graph of the function $23/x$ for comparison.

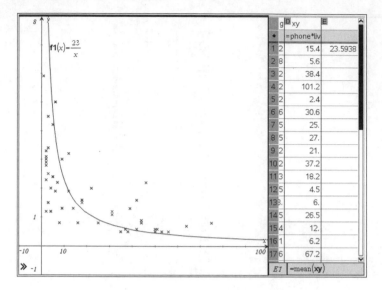

Now you can also get TIN to compute regression models for you. First a linear one, and then a power law of the form $y = ax^b$. One way to compute regression models is via the fourth icon in the 'Data and Statistics' window where you have a wide choice of regression models, including 'Linear $y = mx + b$'. This produces a slope of $m = -0.041$ and an intercept of $b = 2.756$. In the 'Lists and Spreadsheets' window we can also carry out the statistical calculation for the linear regression between phone and living to find that correlation coefficient is about $r = -0.654$.

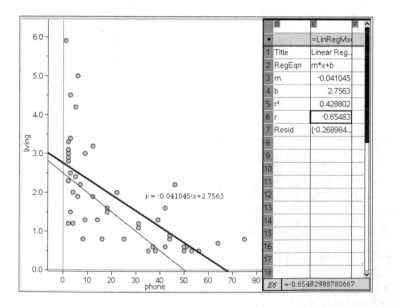

We can also try fitting a power regression model, which we'll illustrate using 'Graphs and Charts'. First we use the 'Lists and Spreadsheets' window to compute the power regression between phones and living, and to store the resulting function in f3(x).

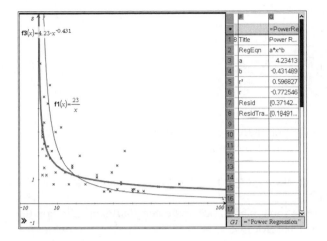

Here we see that this model is roughly $y = 4.2x^{-0.43}$ with a correlation coefficient of -0.77. You can plot this over the scatterplot. The style of the power regression function has also been changed to a thicker weight of line.

The really amazing thing is that pretty well all that we have just done in TIN can also be carried out in a graphing calculator such as a TI-83/4. We will just show a few screens corresponding to the last stages of this analysis. Of course the TI-83/4 can also exchange data with TIN. Armed with either TINs or TI-83/4s you have enormous flexibility in how to plan for work in data handling. Enhanced with data-loggers such as the Texas Instruments' CBR and CBL you also have the means of capturing real-data first hand.

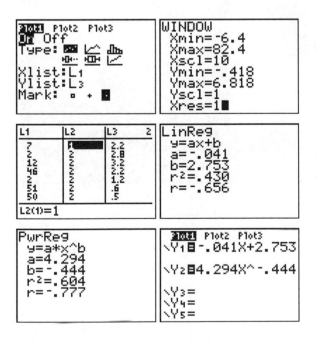

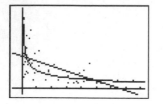

In the next section on modelling there are some other suggestions for ways of data-capture, such as taking readings from photographs.

A simple tool for providing an easy way to draw statistical charts is provided by the *Mathematical Toolkit*.

In the Chart Data area create some blank lines and enter your data. Click on the Chart Type tab and select Pie Chart for List 1.

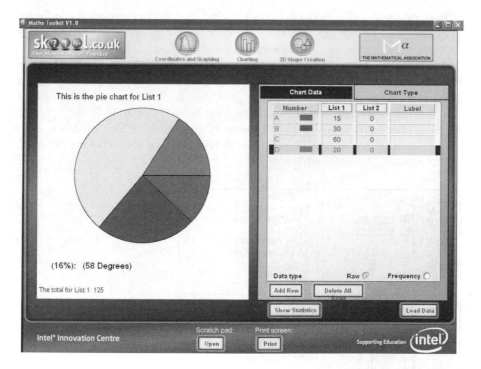

5.5(b) Simulation with random numbers

We conclude the statistics part of this section with an illustration of the use of TIN to simulate the rolls of dice using random numbers. In 'Lists and Spreadsheets' you can define a list 'die1' to hold randInt(1,6,100) – i.e. 100 simulated rolls of a dice (integers from 1 to 6 inclusive). Repeat this for list 'die2', and then make 'dicesum' the sum die1 + die2.

A die1	B die2	C dicesum	D	E	F
=randint(1,6,100)	=randint(1,6,100)	=die1+die2		=OneVar('dicesum,1): Co	
6	1	7	Title	One–Variable Statistics	
6	6	12	x̄	6.83	
1	6	7	Σx	683.	
4	2	6	Σx²	5203.	
3	5	8	sx := s_{n-1}x	2.33141	
5	2	7	σx := $σ_n$x	2.31972	
1	1	2	n	100.	
3	5	8	MinX	2.	
6	2	8	Q₁X	5.	
2	4	6	MedianX	7.	
5	5	10	Q₃X	8.	
6	6	12	MaxX	12.	
2	3	5	SSX := Σ(x−x̄)²	538.11	
3	1	4			
1	3	4			
6	4	10			
1	3	4			

A6 |=5

✎ *Can you now produce box-plots for each list?*

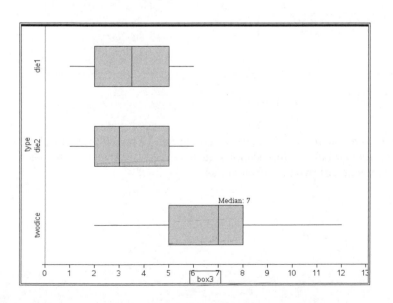

Exactly the same techniques can be used to simulate dice, to collect, display and analyse data using a graphing calculator such as the TI-83/84 Plus. There is also a useful application called ProbSim that allows you set up a wide variety of such simulations. When you have finished running this, the data can be retained in the TI-83/4 Plus List Editor for further manipulation later. Of course the data can also be transferred to a PC.

Other software packages will also support data-handling activities. For example, Autograph has a number of tools for creating, displaying and analysing data-sets, albeit not as flexibly as in TI-Nspire™. In the example below, data-sets for the two dice have been created as 100 samples from a uniform distribution of integers from 1 to 6. Each has been saved to disk as a 'comma separated variable' (CSV) file that can be read, for example, by Excel™. This has been used to add together the two data-sets and save their sum as another CSV file. Autograph can then import this file to define the third data-set 'TwoDice'. Box-plots are easily obtained for all three data-sets.

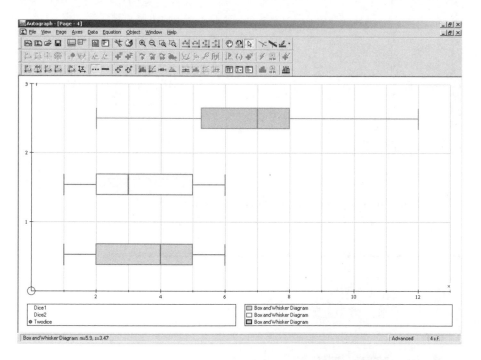

There are also some additional files, called Autograph Extras, designed to help with illustrating standard probability samples such as this. The screen on the next page shows a simulation of two dice from this set.

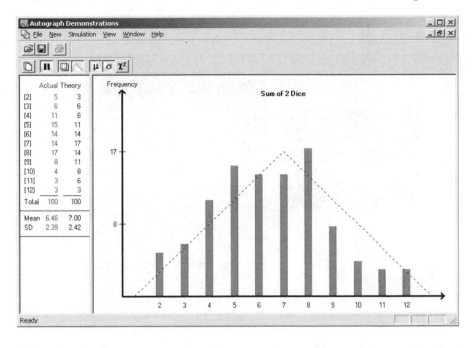

5.5(c) Modelling using captured images

Pictures, posters, photographs, etc. are all good sources of data for modelling. An excellent source is the Problem Pictures CD-ROMs from `http://www.badseypublications.co.uk/`. Digital photographs can be used together with a whole-class display as a stimulus for discussion. But now a wide variety of mathematical software also allows digital images to be imported as the background for making geometric constructions, extracting data, fitting graphs, etc. We shall give a few examples of this in practice.

The *Mathematical Toolkit* is a good starting-point – after all, it's free, and students can download it from `http://lgfl.skoool.co.uk/common.aspx?id=657`, or run it online from `http://lgfl.skoool.co.uk/common.aspx?id=901` for home use! Select the 'Coordinates and Graphing' tab, and then the 'Import media' tab. Use 'Select image', choose a picture, e.g. 'Fountain' and click 'Load'. Click 'Move media' to drag the picture so that the axes are in a suitable position, e.g. at the source of the water-spouts.

Select the 'Update/Delete Coordinates' tab, and then with the mouse over the graphing area click to add some points on a water-spout, such as those shown. Click on the 'Graphing' tab and enter a formula for the function $y1(x)$ using the pop-up calculator. If this doesn't fit as well as expected, either edit that function or enter a revised function in $f2(x)$, etc. You can also display a table for any of the currently defined functions.

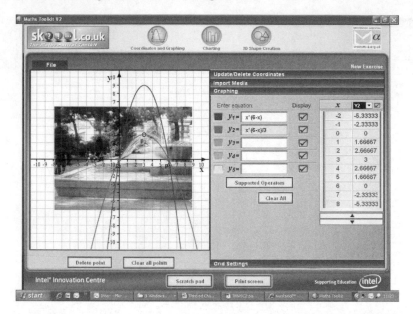

The photograph on the screen above is from the town square in Tivoli, in Italy. Currently you just have the choice to work with the six pre-stored images, but a future version will allow you to work with your own still digital images.

Our own photograph of Sydney Harbour Bridge (below) can be loaded as the background for graphing in a variety of software including Autograph. Its transparency, contrast and brightness can be adjusted to make the axes visible. The picture can be repositioned and resized. The graph's axes can be repositioned and rescaled. In a similar way to Toolkit we can enter functions via the equation editor to try to fit the upper and lower profile curves, e.g. by a quadratic and by a normal distribution function!

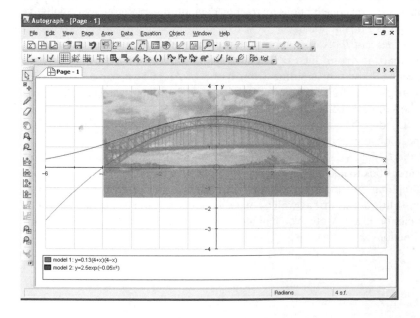

An excellent tool for reading coordinates off an image can be found at `http://maths.sci.shu.ac.uk/digitiseimage/`. The free Digitise Image program allows you to define your own origin and axis scales. A JPEG file can be imported, axes and units defined, and a set of data-points entered over the image. Their coordinates are gathered in the text window and can be exported directly into Excel™, or saved as a CSV file. Such data can then be analysed and graphed using, e.g. TI-Nspire™, Excel™ or the TI-83 Plus. Notes about the use of such software and data-files are included in the lesson-plans developed by the Mathematical Association for the Key Stage 3 Strategy.

Given the availability of digital cameras nowadays, both in schools, homes and mobile phones, there is considerable scope to bring mathematics to life by using images captured by students themselves. A very powerful tool for modelling such images is provided by dynamic geometry software such as Sketchpad or Cabri II Plus. Open the image using any imaging software such as MS Paint™ and copy it to the clipboard. Then you can paste it into an empty Sketchpad page as part of the background. Here we have an image of the Clare College bridge over the River Cam at King's College, Cambridge. This is located at longitude = 52.204°, latitude = 0.114°, and from Google Earth we can measure the width of the river at the 'Backs' as 20 m.

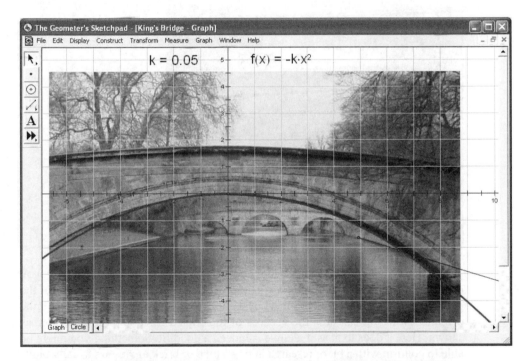

From the 'Edit' menu paste the picture as the background. Right click the picture and select 'properties' – uncheck the box marked 'arrow selectable', so that it can't be dragged about by accident. From the 'Graph' menu select 'Define coordinate system' and drag the origin to the top point of the bridge. A 'ray' has been drawn from one point on the right bank to another to mark the line of the river. Drag the unit point on the x axis until you reckon the bank will emerge 10 m to the right of the origin in the plane of the bridge. We can guess that the bridge is well fitted by a quadratic function with vertex at $(0, 0)$ but curving downwards, so it will be of the form: $y = -k\,x^2$. Using 'New parameter' from the 'Graph' menu you can define a parameter k which increases by 0.05 when high-lit and the '+' button is pressed, and similarly decrease with the '–' button. Enter 'Plot New Function' from the 'Graph' menu as $y = -k\,x^2$ and then adjust the value of the parameter k to make a good fit.

Of course we could equally well have made a geometric construction over the image. In the next example we have constructed a horizontal segment in Cabri II Plus and right clicked on it to insert a JPEG image from a file as background. This allows us to bring in our Cambridge photo as background. You can adjust the length and position of the segment to resize and reposition the image. On the blank part of the page to the right we have constructed three points A, B and C, together with segments AB, BC. By constructing their perpendicular bisectors and their intersection D we can construct the circumcircle of triangle ABC and also mark the arc CBA on it.

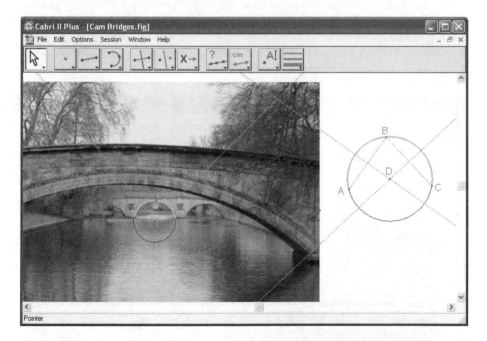

In order to move the construction to the central arch of Clare College bridge, you can either drag the points A, B and C onto the bridge's arch, or highlight all of the geometric construction on the right, copy it, paste a copy and then drag it clear of the original. Now you can drag the vertices of the copied triangle onto the bridge as shown. Here it does look as if a circle is indeed a good fit. Something you might be able to confirm with a bit of research in how stone or brick arches are usually built.

An unusual architectural example can be found in central Prague – a cubist lamp-post photographed after a conference. It is not difficult to estimate lengths and other measurements in the scene based on the height of the bystander as 1.68 m. From this we can estimate the basic building block as a frustum of a hexagonal pyramid with a base radius of 26 cm and a top-face radius of 18 cm. Armed with this information you could make a physical scale model, or create a model in 3D software such as

Cabri 3D or Yenka 3D. For further details see the article 'Cubism and Cabri' by Adrian Oldknow in the ATM's MT206 from January 2008 (`http://www.atm.org.uk/journal/archive/mt206.html`).

If you have any of the following:

- a digital camera
- a conventional camera and a computer with a scanner
- a conventional video camera and a computer with a video-card accepting video input
- a digital camcorder,

then you too can be in the image-capture business! Remember to take some good snaps back from your travels.

With a video camera (and with most still digital cameras and mobile phones) you can take a video-clip consisting of a succession of images of a moving body at a known number of frames per second (typically 25 or 30 fps). At the time of writing, a new generation of digital cameras has come on the market from Casio which are capable of recording video-clips at 210, 420 and 1,000 frames per second.

For example, instead of (or as well as) using a motion-detector to collect sensed data from a swinging pendulum, bouncing ball or spring–mass system, you could also capture images and digitize its position at known time intervals. Data can be measured and extracted from these using a variety of video-analysis software. This can be scaled to give actual measurements if the size of any part of the image is known, e.g. the diameter of the ball, or the length of the string. We will give one example here to illustrate the use of the *Mathematical Toolkit* for video analysis, and further examples will given in the section on cross-curricular work. The basic idea is very similar to that used for a still image. In this case a video-clip (of rather poor quality) is loaded showing a ball being kicked in the air. The axes can be rescaled and the image moved to get a useful origin and a realistic scale for the height of the kicker. The video can be single-stepped and positions of the ball (when visible) marked with a mouse-click. Various quadratic functions can be easily fitted to the points 'by eye'. In this example we have only recorded the x and y values, and the times at which each frame was taken. You can save your results, and, if you know what you are doing, convert your own video-files to Macromedia Flash 'swf' format and substitute them for those stored in the Toolkit's file area.

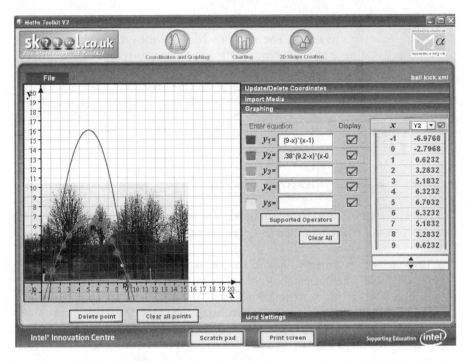

5.5(d) Modelling using practical activities and other contexts

Another good way of gathering data practically is by flexing a long plastic ruler over a large sheet of squared paper. You should be able to get a good approximation to a quadratic curve by just pulling the ends a short way towards each other. You can also make a cubic curve, with a point of inflection by pushing the ends in opposite and parallel directions. Just hold these shapes over the paper and run a felt-tip pen along them. Then you can read off coordinates afterwards from the squared paper.

Another practical approach is to use a piece of hardboard, some chain and a couple of cup-hooks. Screw the hooks into the board a metre or so apart and use them to suspend a chain some 20 per cent longer than the gap. Again you can read off coordinates from the chain. (It is easier if squared paper is placed on the hardboard beforehand.) A similar result can be obtained by suspending a length of thick rope between two points. The theoretical model is actually a curve called a 'catenary' (something we met in Chapter 1), but you should find that it is well approximated by a quadratic.

5.5(e) Bouncing and swinging

A good source of quadratic models comes from sensing motion. Anything falling under gravity, ignoring friction, etc., should have constant acceleration, and hence its velocity should be given by a linear function, and its displacement by a quadratic one. The CBR motion-detector includes a program called Ranger. One of the applications offered within the program is called Ball Bounce. In the previous chapter we give a case-study about the use of this application. Using Ball Bounce you can hold the CBR above the point of release of a ball and, with a little practice, capture data from successive rebounds. The software then uses the greatest distance value captured as its estimate of the distance to the ground, and subtracts all the distance data from it. Hence the images show heights of bounce against time.

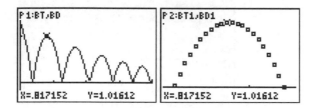

Another feature of the software's Plot Tools is the facility to extract a subset of the data. So you can select data from just one bounce in order to try to fit a quadratic model.

When you leave the program, the data is stored in lists L1 (time), L2 (displacement), L3 (velocity) and L4 (acceleration). So now you can analyse and display them just as you like. The first thing to note is that we have discrete data collected from a continuous process. The program originally sampled around 100 readings at regular intervals within a four-second span. We have extracted around 20 readings within about a one-second span. Using the Stat Plot you can display the data as a scattergram, and then do some 'by eye' fitting of quadratic functions. Of course it helps to use Trace to find an approximation to the maximum point for the graph.

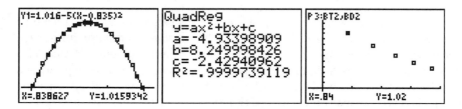

Remember that the quadratic function only models the vertical displacement y of the ball for positive values of y! Remember, too, that the graph does not show the path of the ball. It is not a trajectory in space.

Of course you can also use the built-in regression models to fit a quadratic function to the data. Also you could transfer the data to a computer and use other software for the analysis.

The correlation coefficient (0.999987) is so close to 1 as to suggest that we might have 'cooked' the data, but honestly we have not! This is just a very robust experiment.

From the theory, we know that the acceleration is given by -g, assuming no air resistance, etc. Hence the velocity is given by a linear function -$gt + b$, and displacement by a quadratic function $-\frac{1}{2}gt^2 + bt + c$. So we have also found an approximate value for g as 2(−4.934) = −9.868 ms^{-2}.

It is also interesting to study the maximum heights of the bounces and the times at which they occur. Now this time we really do have discrete data, so we must approach curve-fitting with care. What sort of function would you expect to model this data?

Here is a table of the extracted data for you to use for your own analysis.

N	x (s)	y (m)
0	0.00	1.30
1	0.84	1.02
2	1.68	0.78
3	2.45	0.60
4	3.10	0.46
5	3.69	0.37

While carrying out some work like this, some students began to get the impression that every curve might be a quadratic! So they tried fitting a quadratic function to this data. Would you expect it to be a good fit?

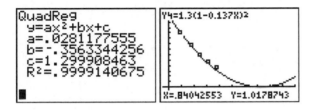

Once again the correlation coefficient is phenomenally close to 1! The corresponding second-degree equation is: $y \approx 0.028x^3 - 0.356x + 1.300 \approx 1.300 (1 - 0.137x)^2$.

Clearly we have to be cautious about not using such a function to interpolate between data-points, nor to extrapolate beyond $t \approx 1/0.137 \approx 7.3$ seconds. If you have met the 'coefficient of restitution' you might like to use the data to estimate its value, and also to see if you can confirm theoretically that the quadratic model for maximum height against time is not such a surprise.

One group of students decided to see if they could simulate a quadratic displacement curve by walking towards, and then away from, a CBR. Their results became a little confused when they got very close to the CBR, but they generated a reasonable data-set on which the class arrived at a 'by eye' fit using transformations of x^2.

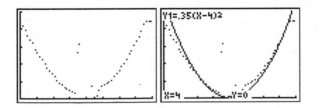

The CBR can also be set up to log data from a variety of dynamics experiments, such as with spring–mass systems and pendulums. These oscillations make a good way of introducing the trigonometric functions outside the range 0° to 90°.

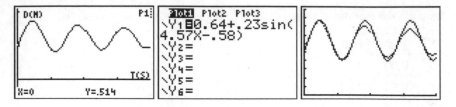

5.5(f) Swimming and running

A girl is swimming off a beach which has a straight shoreline. When she is at point G, 100 m from the nearest point N on the shore, she is stung by a jellyfish. She wants to get back to shore and pick up her towel as quickly as possible. Her towel is on the shore at a point T, 200 m from N. The fastest she can swim is 2 m/s and the fastest she can run is 5 m/s. What is the best route for her to follow from G to T, and how long will it take her?

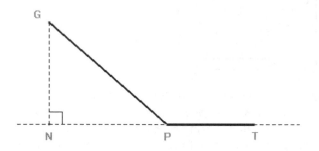

Using Pythagoras you can calculate the time taken to swim directly from G to T.

Even though this is a shorter route, it takes longer than swimming directly from G to N, and then running to T – a total of 90 seconds. Can you find some point P between N and T for which the journey $GP + PT$ takes the shortest possible time?

Clearly you will need to make one of the lengths, say NP, as the independent variable x, say, and find the other distances and times as functions of x. One way to approach this is by using the spreadsheet facility of TI-Nspire™. The screen-shot shows one possible layout. Can you see what formulas are used to generate each column? With this layout you can easily 'zoom' in on the table by changing the formula for the first column. You can easily set up a different problem by varying either the swimming speed or the running speed. You could also turn the other constants, GN and NT into parameters.

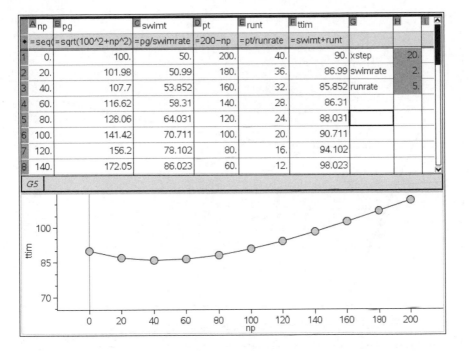

	A np	B pg	C swimt	D pt	E runt	F ttim	G		H	I
•	=seq(	=sqrt(100^2+np^2)	=pg/swimrate	=200−np	=pt/runrate	=swimt+runt				
1	0.	100.	50.	200.	40.	90.	xstep		20.	
2	20.	101.98	50.99	180.	36.	86.99	swimrate		2.	
3	40.	107.7	53.852	160.	32.	85.852	runrate		5.	
4	60.	116.62	58.31	140.	28.	86.31				
5	80.	128.06	64.031	120.	24.	88.031				
6	100.	141.42	70.711	100.	20.	90.711				
7	120.	156.2	78.102	80.	16.	94.102				
8	140.	172.05	86.023	60.	12.	98.023				

G5

The scattergram of time against the position of *P* is shown in a Data & Statistics window.

Another approach is to model the problem geometrically using a Graphs & Geometry window. The parameters 100 for *G* and 200 for *T* are entered as text and Measurement transferred to the axes. A point *P* is constructed on the segment *NP = T* and used to construct segments *GP* and *PT*, each of whose lengths is measured. The names *swimrate* and *runrate* are entered as text, as is the formula *a/b + c/d*. Using Calculate, the values of *swimrate* and *runrate* are just taken as those defining these variables on the spreadsheet, and then *a* is replaced by *GP*, *b* by *swimrate*, *c* by *PT* and *d* by *runrate* to calculate the total time. This value is transferred to the *y* axis and used to construct the point which has the same *x* coordinate as *P* and this *y* coordinate. The geometric trace of the calculated point as *P* is dragged on *NT* is the graph of the function and we can find that its minimum corresponds to a value of *NP* of about 44 m.

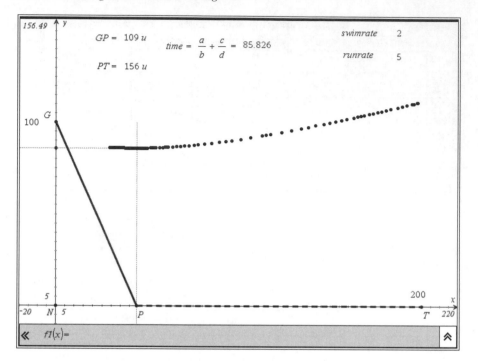

In the graph above:

$GP = 109\,u$

$time = \dfrac{a}{b} + \dfrac{c}{d} = 85.826$

$PT = 156\,u$

swimrate   2

runrate   5

$f1(x)=$

5.5(g) Problems

The 'missing' region

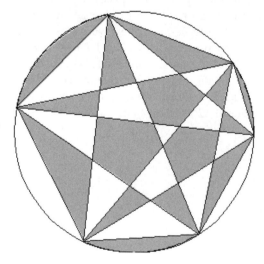

The diagram above shows six points arranged irregularly around a circle, and chords are drawn to join every pair of points. We know that there are $^6C_2 = 15$ such lines. But how many regions do they divide the circle into? By counting, it appears the answer is 31. Can you build up a table of the number of points against the number of regions and suggest what sort of function might model this (discrete!) data? Can you find a good fit (a perfect one?). Can you explain geometrically why it takes the form it does?

Here we have put the data into the lists of the TI-83/4 and formed their differences. The pattern in list L2 appeared to be doubling, until the 'missing region' disrupted things at $n = 6$. If the pattern in list L6 continued, what sort of function would you expect in L2? To relate any results to the geometry we can record the changing numbers of geometric objects. Can you find, and prove, formulas for both the number of Lines and Crossings, and hence derive the formula for the number of Regions?

Points	Lines	Crossings	Regions
2	1	0	2
3	3	0	4
4	6	1	8
5	10	5	16
6	15	15	31
7	21	35	57
8	28	70	99

The old max-box

There are a whole variety of modelling problems based upon maximizing one measurement of an object subject to constraints on other ones. A simple example is to find the rectangle of greatest area contained in a rope of length 4 m. This gives another quadratic model. Working in 3D with volumes of boxes yields cubic models.

These ideas can easily be extended to volumes of cylinders and cones. Here we take a very well-known example of the largest open tray which can be cut from a sheet of card. This time we will make use of the dynamic properties of Cabri Géomètre and the Geometer's Sketchpad. You will have to construct your own version to make it behave dynamically!

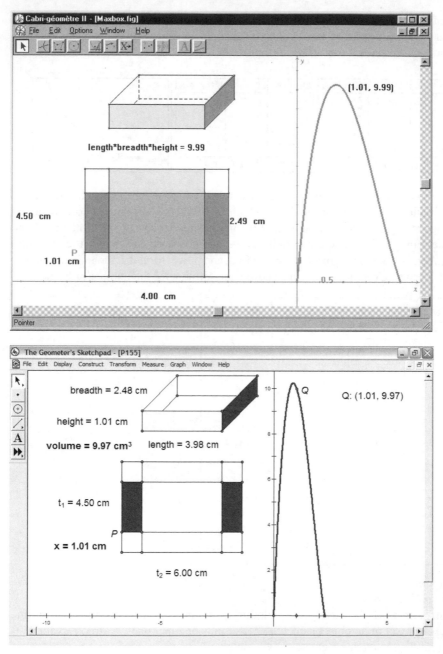

5.5(h) Measures

We conclude this section with a couple of ideas to do with 'Measures'. Using the lists of the TI-83 or TIN it is very easy indeed to change between units. For example, suppose list L1 has a series of temperatures recorded in degrees Fahrenheit and you want list L2 to hold the corresponding conversion into degrees Celsius.

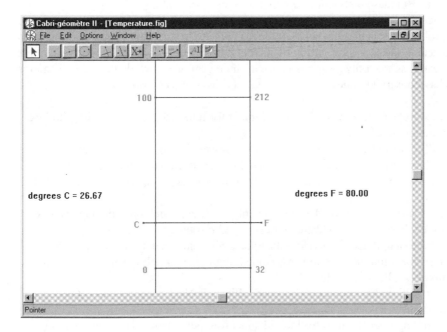

L1	▓	♦	L3	2
30	‾1.111		‾‾‾‾‾‾	
40	4.4444			
50	10			
60	15.556			
70	21.111			
80	26.667			
90	32.222			

L2 ="5(L₁−32)/9"

✎ *At what temperature are the Fahrenheit and Celsius readings identical?*

You might like to construct yourself a dynamic temperature converter using Cabri.

Can you work out how this is done?

degrees C = 26.67

degrees F = 80.00

✎ *Can you perform the construction in Sketchpad?*

5.6 LINKS WITH OTHER SUBJECTS

The current version of the National Curriculum for England goes much further than before to encourage schools to take a holistic approach to the whole curriculum and to make explicit common ground in terms of concepts, processes and a number of so-called Curriculum Dimensions, such as Healthy Lifestyles, Enterprise and Global Dimension and Sustainable Development.

We have already given an example in this chapter of an opportunity for cross-curricular work between mathematics and geography using the Cities database to focus on the Global Dimension. In the previous chapter we gave some examples of cross-curricular projects initiated by both students (bouncing-balls project) and teachers (catapults, catenaries and quadratics). Schools have developed a number of approaches to encouraging and organizing cross-subject links, often under the umbrella of Enhancement and Enrichment. The latter term, enrichment, is usually applied to off-timetable activities, such as themed days, post-examination activities, competitions and awards, science and engineering or STEM clubs, etc. – an example of this is the Nuffield Foundation's Key Stage 3 cross-curricular STEM project which requires the equivalent of around 1.5 days teaching time from science, design and technology, and mathematics. The former, enhancement, is usually applied to approaches taken within normal subject lessons to raise levels of motivation, enthusiasm, challenge, etc. by making the subject more relevant to the world outside school – an example of this is the Key Stage 3 ICT-based mathematics material from the Bowland Trust, which requires the equivalent of around a week's mathematics lessons. But these distinctions are by no means hard and fast.

There is also a misconception that cross-subject teaching is hard to deliver because of problems of scheduling, e.g. topics appearing at different times of the year in subjects A and B, or the setting of students for subject A being different to that for subject B, so that only an approach for a whole year group would be viable. Features we have observed in developing successful cross-subject work include:

- encouragement from senior management for it to take place, including finding meeting time;
- willingness of the subject teams to work towards involvement with it;
- enthusiasm from some staff members from each team to pilot the approach;
- pilot activities organized to ensure minimum pressure on staff to succeed first time;
- approaches often piloted as enrichment activities, which provide opportunities for evaluating new software, hardware and resources;
- results shared and discussed with colleagues, with invitations to participate;
- agreement that moving towards embedding the approach in subject teaching involves all;
- recognition that simultaneity across subjects is NOT required, nor often desirable;
- affording opportunities for individual staff to personalize their approaches (not one size for all);
- encouraging staff to review their own interests and expertise and to engage students with them.

So we have chosen to start with some examples of general themes in which ICT can be used as a catalyst for cross-curricular work which might engage any of a range of possible subjects depending on local interest and circumstances.

5.6(a) Modelling from real data

Data can found from many sources, especially the internet. It can be generated first-hand by recordings of experiments, use of questionnaires, etc. Some scepticism needs to be exercised when dealing with secondary sources of data: Was the data accurately recorded?, Did the way in which data was collected bias the sampling, etc.? Data can be captured from both discrete and continuous processes – so we must also exercise care in interpreting results from modelling. The processes may be deterministic, and so predictable (usually!), or random (aka stochastic) – so again we must exercise care in making predictions. The normal approach to modelling a set of (x_i, y_i) data is to try to find one function $f(x)$ from a class of functions which gives a best fit in the sense of meeting some criterion – such as minimizing the sum of squares of the errors $\Sigma(y_i - f(x_i))^2$. As the theory of least-squares is outside the 11–16 curriculum we usually start by experimenting with 'by eye' fits – so that the graph of our trial function $y = f(x)$ passes as close as possible to the scattergram of the data.

Of course very many mathematical packages will compute 'best fit' (aka regression) models for you. Once you have found a good model it can be used (with caution) for interpolation – finding approximations to values between data-points (where it makes sense to do so) – and extrapolation – predicting values beyond the range for which data was gathered. Although not often made explicit, one common aim of the algebra curriculum 11–16 in most countries is for students to become familiar with a range of important functions used for modelling: linear, quadratic, polynomial, inverse, periodic, etc. Since the great majority of data we come across is related to subjects other than mathematics, the process of modelling data using algebra and functions together with graphs and ICT is a very fundamental cross-curricular link with, e.g., science, geography, history, etc.

The first example uses the data-handling facilities of TI-Nspire™ to try to find a mathematical model for the boiling-points of hydrocarbons such as Methane CH_4, Ethane C_2H_6 and Propane C_3H_8, which have Carbon numbers 1, 2 and 3. Here is part of the table:

Carbon number	1	2	3	4	5	6	7	8	9	10	11
Boiling-point °C	−162	−89	−42	0	36	69	98	126	151	174	196

Using the Lists window we can enter data for numbers 2, 4, 6, 8 and 10. In a Graphs window we can draw the scatterplot of boiling-point bp against carbon number cn. We have made a 'by eye' linear fit $f1(x)$, but then returned to the Lists window to perform a statistical calculation: linear regression on the data, storing the resulting model in $f2(x)$, which we plot in the Graphs window.

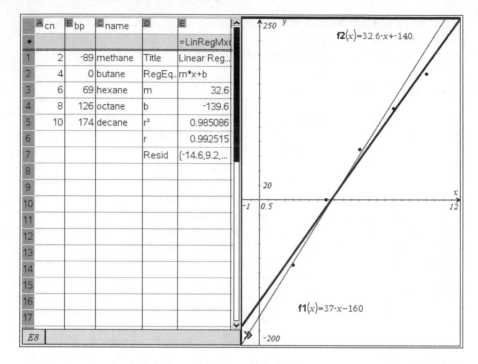

How do the values computed from 32.6 X – 139.6 compare with the boiling-points for hydrocarbons with carbon values of 3, 5, 7, 9? (This is 'interpolation'.) How about those for 1 and 11? (This is 'extrapolation'.) How well does this linear model predict the boiling-point for cn = 35, which should be 499? Try extending the Window with Xmax = 35 and Ymax = 600 say to see the graph on a different scale. What is silly about trying to predict for cn = 4.5?

This linear model is indeed one of direct proportion ('the more the Carbon number, the higher the boiling-point') but it does not model the way in which the increase in boiling-point per carbon unit appears to be slowing. So we need a function which grows less rapidly than a linear function.

One such function is a 'logarithmic' function. Can you set up a logarithmic regression and see how well it behaves on the interpolation and extrapolation tests?

It should have the desired characteristics:

- that it is always an increasing function and
- that its slope is always decreasing.

However, it probably underestimates the boiling-point for cn = 35 by quite a long way.

So we need another function which grows more slowly than a linear function and more quickly than a logarithmic function. One such function is a 'power function' of the form: $y = a x^b$ where $a>0$ and $0<b<1$. An example is $y = \sqrt{x}$ which we can also write as $y = x^{0.5}$. The problem here is that we cannot obtain negative values of y (boiling-point) corresponding to positive values of x (carbon number). However there is nothing magical about measuring boiling-points in degrees Celsius – in fact it would probably be better science to measure them in degrees Kelvin (from absolute zero) – and then all the values will be positive numbers. So we can make a new list abp to hold the results of adding 273 to the values in list bp. Now we can perform a power regression.

	A cn	B bp	C abp	D	E
			=bp+273		=PowerRe
1	2	-89	184	Title	Power R...
2	4	0	273	RegEq...	a*x^b
3	6	69	342	a	126.084
4	8	126	399	b	0.55324
5	10	174	447	r²	0.999645
6				r	0.999823
7				Resid	{-1.01217...
8				ResidT...	{-0.00548...
9					
10					35
11					901.36
12					
13					
14					
15					
16					
17					

D11 =f3(d10)

940.55 y

$f3(x)=126.\cdot x^{0.553}$

50

-2.44   38.56

f3: (35, 901)

Here we see that this model is a much better predictor for big values of C than either of the others. Here is a more complete table of data – see if you can come up with a better model still!

C	12	13	14	15	16	17	18	19	20	21	22	23
BP	216	236	253	270	287	302	316	329	343	357	369	380
C	24	25	26	27	28	29	30	31	32	33	34	35
BP	391	402	412	422	431	441	450	458	467	474	481	499

So far we have taken no account of any scientific principles which might help explain why one model is preferable to another. Suppose, for example, that we thought that there was a relationship between the boiling-point and the square-root of the carbon number, then we could make another list hold the square-roots of boiling-points and then look for a linear model connecting the boiling-points in degrees Kelvin and the square-roots of the carbon numbers. Of course it would then be quite easy to convert this into a model for the boiling-points in degrees Celsius (how?).

Can you work with colleagues, e.g. from science and geography, to set up a list of sources of data which can be used for modelling with (a) linear, e.g. y = ax + b, (b) quadratic, e.g. y = a(x + b)² + c, (c) reciprocal, e.g. y = a/x + b, (d) square-root, e.g. y = a√x + b, (e) sine, e.g. y = a sin(bx + c) + d, (f) power, e.g. y = a x^b + c, (g) exponential y = a b^x + c . . . ? Maybe you could make up a 'data-spotter's function guide' for use by the relevant departments?

A different model comes from astronomy and the discovery of Kepler's law of planetary motion.

The Italian mathematician, Galileo Galilei (1564–1642) and the English mathematician, Sir Isaac Newton (1643–1727) made significant contributions to the way we apply mathematics to physical situations. Our modern theories of planetary motion also go back a long way in history – probably starting with the Polish astronomer Nicolaus Copernicus (1473–1543) who proposed a model of the solar system in which the planets orbit the Sun, rather than having the Earth at the centre of the system. The Danish astronomer Tycho Brahe (1546–1601) made meticulous observations of planetary positions which were drawn on by the Austrian mathematician Johannes Kepler (1571–1630) in postulating his three 'laws' of planetary motion. (You can find more about these at `http://csep10.phys.utk.edu/astr161/lect/history/kepler.html`.)

The first law states that 'planets orbit the Sun in ellipses with the Sun as one focus'. The Earth's orbit is actually very close to circular. Mercury has the greatest eccentricity of the planets at just over *e* = 0.2, so we can plot the shape of its orbit to see how much it differs, say, from a circle. While the ellipse and the circle are extremely close, the Sun is quite offset from the centre of the circle, and so the planet's distance from the Sun is not nearly constant!

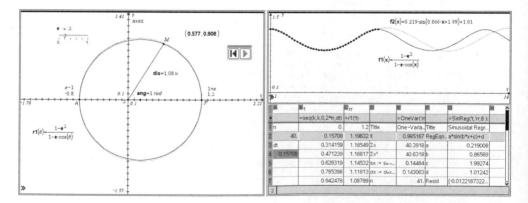

There are many ways to plot an ellipse, but in this case the polar equation is the most suitable. It has the form:

$$r = \frac{a(1 - e^2)}{1 - e\cos(\theta)}$$

where *a*>0 and 1>*e*>0. So in a graph-plotter, such as the Graph window of TI-Nspire™, we can plot the graph of the function for given values of *a* and *e*. For simplicity we take *a* = 1 and, to aid exploration, we can set the value of *e* using a slider. The origin, *S*, is the focus of the ellipse and represents the Sun. The point *M* on the ellipse represents the planet (Mercury in this case), and the points *A* and *P* represent the 'apogee' (nearest) and 'perigee' (furthest) positions from the Sun. We can even animate *M* on the ellipse to simulate the orbit. As we can see, the distance *r* of the planet from Sun varies, in this case, from a maximum of 1.2 to a minimum of 0.8 (corresponding to winter and summer). We might think that the mean distance would be 1, and that the way the distance varies with θ might be a sinusoid. We can test these hypotheses by opening a List window and defining lists *t* and *rr* to hold a set of values of θ and *r*. The scatterplot is shown of these values. We can compute the one-variable statistics for *r* to see its mean value is about 0.985 and also perform a sinusoidal regression to see how the graphed function roughly matches the plotted function. To get a better value for the mean distance you need to find the area under the graph of *y* = r(*x*) between, say, *x* = 0 and *x* = 2π and divide the result by 2π – which gives a value of *r* = 0.9798 – but in what units? Well, the mean distance of Mercury from the sun is given as about 58 million km.

✎ *What does Kepler's second law state? How might ICT be used to explore, simulate or illustrate it?*

Kepler's third law relates each planet's mean distance to the Sun with the time (period) it takes to orbit it.

	A planet	B distance	C period	D pertra	Planetary data from Solar system:
				=period^p	Distance is mean distance from the Sun in
1	Mercury	57.91	0.240931	0.11826	millions of km.
2	Venus	108.21	0.615195	0.482524	
3	Earth	149.6	1.	1.	Period is the time taken to orbit the Sun in
4	Mars	227.92	1.8809	2.57958	earth years = 365.25 days = 3.15576E7 secs
5	Jupiter	778.57	11.75	40.277	
6	Saturn	1433.53	29.5	160.226	Kepler's 3rd law relates the period to the
7	Uranus	2872.46	84.	769.873	distance – can we derive a model from this
8	Neptune	4495.06	165.	2119.46	data?
9	Pluto	5869.66	248.	3905.51	

A1 "Mercury"

$p := 1.5$

$f1(x) = 5.5\text{E-}4 \cdot x^P$

Explore ways of approaching growth and decay models suitable for 11–16 work, e.g. as simple multiplicative models in a spreadsheet where each value in a column is the previous one multiplied by 1.1, say (growth), or 0.9, say (decay). Can you develop some integrated approaches with colleagues, e.g. around cooling curves (forensics: time of death), radioactive decay (half-life and carbon dating), compound interest (loans), population models, etc.? (See examples in 3.6(d) and 3.7(a).)

5.6(b) 3D models

We are used to seeing 2D images of 3D objects every day, and we can easily tell whether or not a 2D image is a realistic portrayal of a 3D object. Whenever we view a 3D object through a lens we project a 2D image onto whatever lies behind the lens – such as on the retina of an eye, the wall of a *camera obscura* or the photosensitive film or receptor in a camera. Using photographs as the background in dynamic geometry software such as Sketchpad, we can discover for ourselves about the laws of perspective. Below is a photograph of a building in Santarém, Portugal. Basically it's a cuboid with twiddly bits. We can place a few points on the image and join them with rays to show the way in which parallel lines in the 3D object map into converging lines on the perspective image. The intersection points A,B are known as 'vanishing points' and are also sometimes called 'points at infinity', because they correspond to meeting points of parallel lines! The theory is that any line in the front wall parallel to the two rays drawn will also pass through the same vanishing point *B*, and similarly for the left-hand side wall through *A*.

Perspective forms an interesting link between Art and Design, Design and Technology, ICT and mathematics, e.g. in making accurate drawings, analysing works of art, virtual reality, CADCAM, etc. Students can make pin-hole cameras, find out about (maybe visit) *camera obscura* (e.g. in Edinburgh or Bristol), use

Sketch-Up and Google Earth to create and view 3D objects, etc. Interesting work was done by Philip Steadman, who analysed canvases from the collection of the Dutch artist Jan Vermeer (1632–75), and put forward the theory that Vermeer's studio contained a *camera obscura*. (`http://www.vermeerscamera.co.uk`).

As an example of cross-curricular work involving 3D geometry we can try to use Cabri 3D to model the molecular structure of a chemical, such as ethanol – a close relative of ethane. The chemical formula for ethanol is C_2H_6O, and its 2D-structure diagram is shown below. So to model this in Cabri 3D we just need to arrange to join nine spheres together in the correct alignment. This looks like a job for making a stick model using polyhedra, and then plonking spheres of the correct colour on each vertex!

Unfortunately Maltesers only come in one colour – milk chocolate! But here is a model using nine Maltesers held together by halved cocktail sticks.

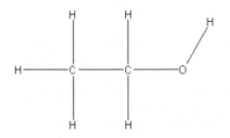

The shape rather resembles the sort of model of a dachshund which clever people can make from balloons. If we take the oxygen atom as the back of the head, and the hydrogen atom 'at the front' as its nose, then the two carbon atoms are at each end of the back. The front one of these has two hydrogen atoms below it as the front paws. However, the rear end has been rotated a bit so that one hydrogen atom looks like a paw directly on the ground, while the other two look like its (little) tail and the other paw, cocked in the air! Oh what it is to have a vivid imagination!

Visualization in 3D can be greatly improved by the careful use of colours. In the following instructions we refer to the colours of various objects, even though the illustrations are in black and white. See how well you can make a mental image of the object.

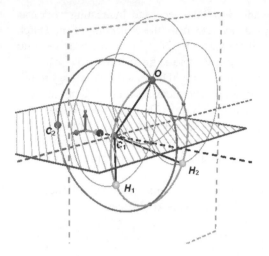

The starting-point in the Cabri 3D model is the large blue point taken as a 'slider' on the blue-dashed ray along the green base vector. The central symmetry of the origin in this point gives the large grey point marked C_1. The central symmetry of this point in the origin gives the other large grey point C_2. This establishes the positions of the two carbon atoms, and the segment joining them is 'the dog's back'. The mauve circle is constructed round the line through C_1 parallel to the red axis vector to pass through C_2 – it has centre at C_1. The large red point O is taken as a (draggable) point on the circle. The green plane shown is the perpendicular to the green base vector through O. The green circle is drawn around the green base vector passing through O. Its centre is the intersection of the blue-dashed vector with the green plane. We now need to find the positions of the two hydrogen atoms so that OH_1H_2 form an equilateral triangle – and we do this by constructing (thin green) circles in the green plane with the same radius as the green circle. These divide the green circle equally in six points, so now we can locate the required positions of two of the hydrogen atoms.

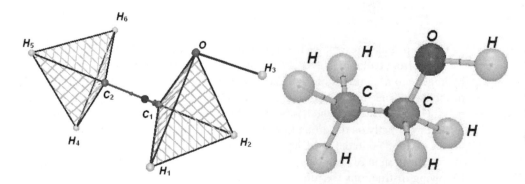

If we construct the vector 'along the dog's back' from C_2 to C_1 then we can use this to translate O to the 'nose' H_3. If we construct the 'front-end' tetrahedron $C_1OH_1H_2$ shown, then we can just use a half-turn about the origin to produce the 'rear-end' $C_2H_4H_5H_6$ tetrahedron. Then we can start to do some clearing up, and introduce coloured spheres for the atoms. Here the midpoints of each segment have been found, as have the 'quarter-points', which are used to determine the radius of each sphere.

Work with some colleagues, e.g. from mathematics, science, and design and technology, to explore 3D structures such as polyhedra, crystals (especially Fullerene aka Bucky Balls), bridges, buildings, etc. as a cross-curricular theme.

5.6(c) Animated linkages

Linkages are used in many ways to turn one form of motion into another – such as the up and down motion of a piston in an engine into the circular motion needed to turn the wheels around. Using dynamic geometry with appropriate constructions we can simulate physical linkages, drag components to explore their behaviour and use animation to set them in motion. As an example, we will model the mechanism used by an oscillating water-sprinkler – always a fascinating challenge to young people in hot weather!

Water comes into the sprinkler under pressure and turns a turbine centre A to revolve, putting the joint B into circular motion. The sprinkler bar is on the right and oscillates about centre D. The knob at the top is turned to adjust the distance from D of the joint C. C is connected to B by a fixed-length link. So if we take measurements from the sprinkler we find that AB = 1.5 cm, AD = 4.7 cm, BC = 5 cm and CD can vary between 2.5 and 5 cm. In dynamic geometry, such as Cabri II Plus, we can import the actual picture and make the construction over the image, as shown. The position of C is determined by the intersection of circles centre B, radius BC and centre D radius CD. In fact there are two intersections, but we chose the one which keeps the quadrilateral ABCD convex.

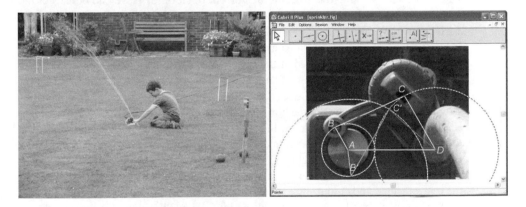

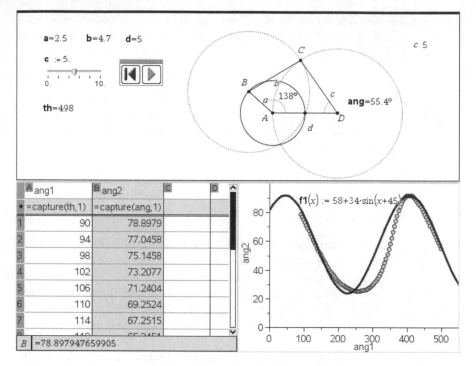

Of course the power of an animation is rather lost in a static screen-shot, but we can gather data from the simulation more easily than we can from the actual sprinkler. In the TI-Nspire™ example above, the three constant lengths have been entered as text in a Geometry screen, and each stored as a variable. The fourth length has been set up as a 'slider' so that it can easily be changed. Instead of choosing *B* as any point on the circle centre *A*, we have set up an additional variable called **th** with an initial value of 90. The point where the circle intersects *AD* is then rotated around A by this angle **th**. The reason for this is that we can animate the number **th** and so get the actual angle turned through, whereas if we measure angles geometrically they return values between 0° and 180°. Using the current position of *B* we can construct the position of *C*, and hence measure the 'sprinkle angle' *ADC*, which we store as the variable **ang**. We now want to animate the motion in which *B* rotates with constant speed around *A*, and *C* oscillates around *D* between angles **amax** and **amin**. We could also investigate the speed of the sprinkler bar.

We have added a spreadsheet and a statistics window. The spreadsheet is set up for automated data-capture of the angles **th** and **ang** in the lists ang1 and ang2. The statistics window is set up with ang1 as the horizontal and ang2 as the vertical variables. All that remains now is to set the linkage in motion. Right click on the variable **th** in the Geometry window and select Attribute. Choose animation speed, enter a value such as 4 and press Return. The Animation Controller buttons now appear. After the sprinkler has done a full sweep, pause the animation. You should see that the lists have collected the relevant input and output angle data, which are displayed as a scatter-graph. It looks as if the oscillation is between about 24° and 92° – i.e. 34° either side around 58°. So we can try fitting a trigonometric model of the form $y = 58 + 34 \sin(x + k)$. By eye we get a pretty good basic fit with $k = 45°$, but we can also see that while the data will be periodic, they differ significantly in that the motion to the left from **amax** to **amin** takes longer than the motion to the right from **amin** to **amax**. Then we can vary the value of *c* by moving the slider to investigate the other possible patterns of sprinkle coverage. At a more advanced level we could use the sine and cosine rules to express **ang** as a function of **th** for given values of *a,b,c* and *d*.

---

*Can you use simple trigonometry to calculate values for **amax** and* *amin* *in terms of* a,b,c,d*? And find the corresponding values of* **th**?*

If the water comes out of the sprinkler bar at a constant velocity in the direction of DC *can you also simulate the actual trajectory of the water-spout?*

The QCDA website has some case-study videos which include a playground project: `http://curriculum.qcda.gov.uk/key-stages-3-and-4/ case_studies/casestudieslibrary/case-studies/Swings_and_ roundabouts.aspx`. The equipment in a children's playground can include slides, swings, roundabouts, climbing frames, see-saws, rocking-horses, springs, etc. Students can visit different playgrounds, maybe in their own time, and take measurements of the apparatus as well as still and video images of them in action. If the school has appropriate portable data-logging kit, such as range-finders and accelerometer for use with notebooks, TI-Nspire™ or graphing calculators, then they can also log their own data. In design and technology they can design their own equipment using appropriate mechanisms, in mathematics they can model the static and dynamic geometry of the apparatus as well as their own motion, as a locus (c.f. the 'Tea-cup Ride'); in science they can investigate different kinds of motion. If playgrounds are considered too tame, students can provide their own records of fairground rides – at their own expense! Students can investigate the geometry of static apparatus, such as the slide – and of dynamic apparatus such as the roundabout and swing.

Work with colleagues in mathematics, science, and design and technology to develop cross-curricular approaches to modelling mechanisms, e.g. examples of four-bar linkages (nodding donkey, treadle, windscreen wipers, steering mechanisms), other linkages (e.g. piston-crank, cams and valves, pulleys), mechanisms and gearing, etc.

5.6(d) Working with real data to estimate position, speed and acceleration of moving objects

We are also used to walking, swimming, running, cycling, driving, as well as travelling by boat, train and plane. We may also have experiences of other forms of motion such as skipping, jumping, diving, trampolining, skiing, skating, horse-riding, bungee-jumping or abseiling, as well as putting objects into motion, e.g. throwing, kicking, bowling and striking.

We can capture data from objects in motion in a variety of ways, depending on the distances travelled, speeds reached, etc. Consider a long-jump for example, a video-clip should be sufficient, as if the camera is well positioned there is no need to pan or zoom. We can also easily take a measurement of the overall distance covered. What other forms of motion might that also be sufficient for?

For a journey, such as a hike, cycle or car ride, video isn't an option. Here a practical solution is to use a Global Positioning System (GPS) device to track the journey, and to download the time, latitude, longitude and altitude data afterwards.

For small trips which are not in a straight line, such as the 'Tea-cup ride', neither video nor GPS may do the trick – in which case we need some other sort of portable data-logging system such as one or more accelerometers connected to a portable device, e.g. a graphing calculator, portable data-logger or TI-Nspire™ hand-held unit. An alternative for small distances is to use wireless probes, such as the Vernier WDSS, together with a laptop with Bluetooth.

Of course some motion cannot (presently) be accurately or safely recorded by such means, e.g. a golf drive. Other forms of motion, trampolining for instance, could be captured both by video and by accelerometers.

The next few examples show different forms of data-capture and analysis from things in motion. In 3.7(b) we saw an example of the use of video-capture and analysis in Tracker 2 to estimate the launch speed of a cricket ball by a fast bowler. The screen below shows a similar approach using Vernier's Logger Pro 3.

	VideoAnalysis		
	Time (s)	X (m)	X Velocity (m/s)
1	3.772	1.901	4.316
2	3.805	2.053	4.137
3	3.838	2.161	4.295
4	3.872	2.340	4.423
5	3.905	2.477	4.009
6	3.938	2.599	3.797
7	3.972	2.724	3.753
8	4.005	2.849	3.793
9	4.038	2.972	3.958
10	4.072	3.111	4.182
11	4.105	3.259	4.192
12	4.138	3.384	4.304
13	4.172	3.549	4.344
14	4.205	3.685	4.116
15	4.238	3.810	4.203
16	4.272	3.961	4.391
17	4.305	4.112	4.491

Linear Fit for: VideoAnalysis | X
X = mt+b
m (Slope): 4.088 m/s
b (Y-Intercept): -13.51 m
Correlation: 0.9996
RMSE: 0.01788 m

The fast bowler (from Harrow School) was videoed from the boundary using a Casio Exilim EX-FH20 camera at 210 frames per second. The video player in Logger Pro recognises it as being 30 fps, and so the calculated "best fit" speed of release of 4.09 m/s corresponds to a real speed of 7x that amount i.e. 28.6 m/s, or just over 100 kph.

The video was recorded at 210 frames per second using a Casio Exilim EX-FH20 mounted on a tripod on the boundary of the field. The clip has been trimmed to just show 136 frames, and the ball has been tracked following its release. Here we have used Logger Pro 3 both to capture the data, and to calculate a best linear fit to the horizontal positions of the ball. As with high-speed TV images available now, this video is really designed to be shown in slow motion – so that you can pick up points of interest, such as whether or not the ball hit the bat or the pad. So the software 'thinks' the video should play at 30 frames per second. Applying a simple correction factor we can estimate the bowler's delivery speed as just over 100 kph.

The next example shows a similar approach being used, this time to establish whether a quadratic model gives a good fit to the trajectory of a basketball from a free throw. The video-clip can be digitized in Vidshell or Tracker, and the data exported to be pasted into a table in, e.g., Excel™, TI-Nspire™ or Fathom for analysis.

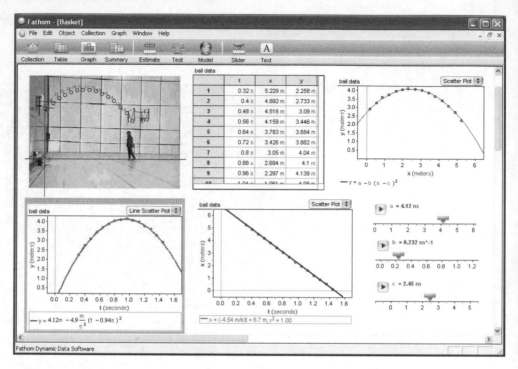

We can see from the Fathom screen-shot that the scattergraph of y against x is well fitted by a quadratic function of the type $y = a - b(x - c)^2$ where values of the parameters a,b,c can be set using sliders. By adjusting the scales for the axes we can make sure the points of the scattergraph align closely to the screen-shot of the points tracked in Tracker. Fathom will perform linear regression, and so we see that the horizontal positions x have a near perfect linear correlation with t, and so the horizontal velocity is constant at -4.54 ms^{-1}. Can you explain why it is negative? If we plot the scattergraph of y against t, we can also see that this is well fitted by a quadratic function – and this time we can use the data to estimate g, the acceleration under gravity. If the acceleration is constant, then the change in velocity in a given time is just gt, so $v = u + gt$, where u is the initial velocity. This has a straight line graph. The distance travelled in time t is just the area under this graph, which is the area of a trapezium: i.e. $y = y_0 + \frac{1}{2} t (u + u + gt) = y_0 + ut + \frac{1}{2} gt^2$ – so the coefficient of t^2 is $\frac{1}{2}g$. From the fit in the lower left part of the screen we get the coefficient as 4.9, and so we have an estimate of $g = 9.81$ ms^{-2}.

We can now see an alternative means of logging data, this time from a GPS sensor. The first screen below shows a portion of the captured data table, from which graphs of Latitude, Longitude, Altitude and Speed have been drawn – each against Time. It is quite difficult to make sense of these, but in the second screen we have some alternative representations. The graph in the upper left is of Latitude against Longitude, so it maps the actual route.

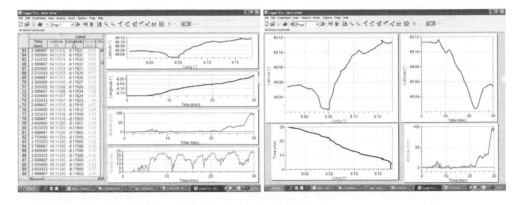

Here the Time is a parameter and from the graphs in the upper right and lower left we can see that the journey was more or less in a south-westerly direction. From the lower right we can also see that it was mostly quite low lying until the latter part when it did climb. Logger Pro 3 will export data to Google maps to show the route, which we can compare with our featureless track – and see that the route mostly followed the River Moselle south-west away from Metz, until it diverted and climbed out of the river valley. Comparing the Altitude graph with the satellite image, we can also get a topographical view of the terrain.

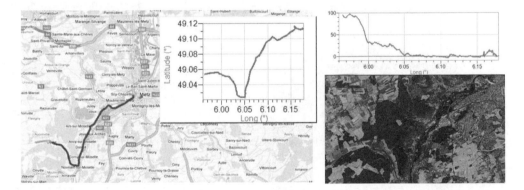

With a hand-held device such as a Garmin Etrex you can upload GPS data directly into software such as Google Earth 5 or Microsoft Autoroute to see your journey. Data can easily be exported to Excel™, TI-Nspire™ or Fathom for further analysis. GPS chips are now widely available and can be expected to be built into many future devices. Currently they open up excellent opportunities for gathering data about a location – such as the position of the school boundary – from which calculations such as perimeter and area can be made. They could be used for surveying projects to make maps of an area – where they can replace traditional implements such as tapes, chains and compasses. Quite soon they will be able to be used attached to objects – such as a javelin or model plane – to bring back data in 3D.

GPS also opens up a new approach to the collection of physical data – such as temperature, pressure, heart-rate, etc. In the past we normally associated each piece of data with the time at which it was recorded. Now we can associate it with the time and place (in 3D coordinates) at which it was measured. So, for example, if the Metz journey had been done by bicycle, we could also have logged the cyclist's heart-rate and explored how that varies with altitude.

Now we can see how all the elements can come together. A heavy wooden elephant is suspended by a strong spring from a doorframe. A metre rule is alongside to help with calibration. The computer is attached to three different pieces of equipment. Above the elephant's head is a Vernier Wireless Dynamic Sensor System (WDSS) connected to a Bluetooth receiver. Under the elephant, on the floor (out of shot) is a TI CBR2 motion-detector. Mounted on a tripod under computer control is a Logitech webcam. Vernier's Logger Pro 3 software is set up to capture data from the sensors, and also to synchronize video capture of the experiment from the webcam. The top one of the three graphs shows the Force in Newtons and vertical acceleration in ms^{-2} from the WDSS. The middle graph shows the position, velocity and acceleration recorded from the CBR2. The lower one shows position data captured from the video using the axes shown and scale taken from the ruler. The software allows for corrections to be made in the synchronization if necessary, so that as you trace along one or more graphs the data table moves to the corresponding row, and the video moves to the corresponding frame. In the screen-shot below this corresponds to the top of the elephant's bungee bounce where the velocity is zero and the displacement above the CBR2 is maximum – which we can see occurs when the force and acceleration are minimum.

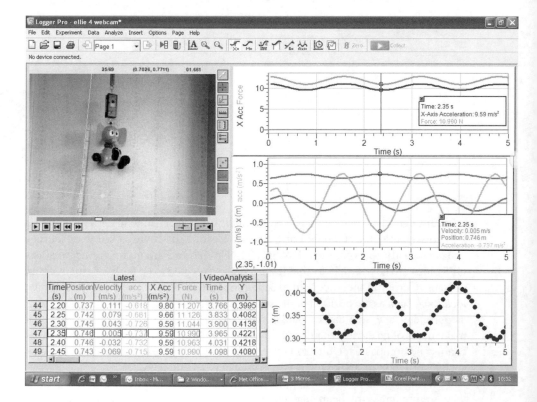

5.6(e) Connecting with the world outside the classroom – could it be rocket science?

We now live in a world full of ICT products which is creating its own digital divide. No longer is the major divide between the have and have-nots, but increasingly between the can and can-nots. The ICT skills possessed by most 11 year olds entering secondary school far exceed those of most of their teachers – and the situation will get worse! Often we take technological change for granted, without understanding the ways in which mathematics and other subjects have made that change possible. A good example is the use of sensors and simulation applied by Nintendo in their very popular Wii Sports game for the Wii video-game console. Accelerometers in the remote control unit detect the player's hand movements in virtual games of tennis, golf, baseball, bowling and boxing. The software uses mathematical algorithms on the data to control screen images of the game in action.

Students communicate with one another using mobile phones and broadband internet connections – sending messages, images and video to one another, again with little idea of what processes are going on. Clearly mathematics is fundamental to the algorithms used for compression and encryption of data. But the wireless technology depends upon a network of very powerful communication satellites in geostationary orbit. These are launched by powerful rockets, such as the European Ariane rocket. So our communications depend both upon rocket science, and also gravitational theory – so Galileo, Kepler and Newton have a lot to answer for! Our knowledge of the solar system depends upon the invention of the telescope, such as Galileo's 400 years ago, and most of these use the reflecting properties of parabolas – as does the reception of satellite television using a parabolic dish receiver. The parabolas project in Chapter 4 is an example of how some of these ideas can be integrated in a way which is both coherent from a curricular viewpoint and relevant to the world we live in.

A simple activity can be built round the cheap and safe STOMP rockets. They can be fired indoors, e.g. in a sports hall if care is taken. Students have fun stamping or jumping on a plastic box which propels air up a tube and launches a plastic rocket. The rocket is a pure projectile since, unlike chemical or water rockets, there is no power applied during the flight. Provided that there is little wind, and that the rocket is pretty streamlined, the trajectory should be well modelled by a quadratic.

Students can estimate the angle of launch elevation, the range and the flight duration, as well as measuring them with protractors, stopwatches and tape-measures (or GPS). They can also video the flight, and use data-capture and analysis. From these values they can work out the horizontal velocity (assumed constant), the vertical velocity (using trig.), the launch velocity (using Pythagoras), the maximum height reached (when vertical velocity is zero), and obtain a value for g. Using software such as TI-Nspire™, Cabri II Plus, Sketchpad or graphing calculators they can plot the trajectory as well as horizontal and vertical displacement and velocity graphs. They can even set up animations to simulate the launch, and solve problems like finding the velocity and launch angle to clear a given obstacle and land in a given place – e.g. over a tennis net to hit a target. In design and technology they can design, make and test their own rocket-launchers, as well as make more aerodynamic rockets.

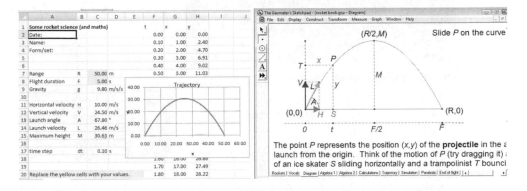

In ICT and/or design they can also design data-capture systems to be carried by the rocket to track its flight. ScienceScope produces a commercial version of an air-powered rocket (using a vertical bike pump and plastic membranes) which has a nose-cone packed with electronics (http://www.sciencescope.co.uk/rocketlogger.htm). After recapture and connection to a computer, data can be downloaded both as a CSV file suitable for opening in Excel™, and a KMV file which shows a simulated video of the trajectory in Google Earth!

The ScienceScope RocketLogger revolutionises dynamics investigations in schools. It is designed to be used in the following investigations:

- Trajectories of air launched rockets

- Drop zone investigations such as terminal velocity and air resistance
- Vehicles down a ramp
- And many more

Create a Google Earth visualisation of the rocket launch

The key features of the RocketLogger are:

- Measures acceleration in three axes simultaneously
- Measures altitude
- Logs for up to 6 minutes at over 100 samples per second

A possibly useful acronym for testing whether something would make a rich STEM activity is **AL FRESCO:** which is **A**ccessible, **L**ively, **F**un, **R**eliable, **E**asily set up, **S**afe, **C**heap, **O**pen-ended – and of course Outdoors in the fresh air!

5.7 MORE ADVANCED MATHEMATICS

In the UK, the Nuffield Foundation supported the development of a set of textbooks called *Nuffield Advanced Mathematics*, now out of print. They contain a number of useful activities which can be carried out using a variety of mathematical ICT tools and we include a few examples here. We start with some numerical approaches to the derivative of a function.

5.7(a) Differentiation and integration

The first idea is that of an Approximate Gradient Function (AGF). This uses the idea that the gradient of a function f(x) can be approximated by $(f(x + h) - f(x))/h$ for small, finite, h. We will first explore the idea with a TI-83/4 graphing calculator, but you can follow the same path using any suitable graph-plotting software. We will find approximations to the gradient of $Y1(x) = x^3 - 4x^2 + 3$ at the point where $x = 0.5$. With the function entered in the Y= editor as Y1, you can conveniently enter a value for h in Y2. The definition of the AGF in Y3 uses the values of Y1 and Y2 already defined. (These are recalled using the Vars, Y-Vars, Function menus.) The line style of Y3 has been selected as dotted. (Move the cursor over the symbol to the left of Y3 and repeatedly press ENTER to cycle through the list of possible line styles.) The graph of Y2 will not be displayed since the '=' sign has had its highlight removed.

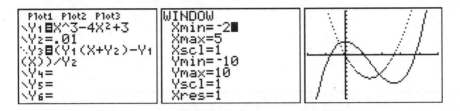

Now you can trace over the graph of Y1 describing its gradient as you go, and comparing it with the y coordinates from the Y3 graph. The TI-83/84 has a CALC menu from which you can compute the numerical derivative of a graph at a given x value. Just select 6:dy/dx and enter 0.5 for the x value. Here the TI-83's numerical algorithm gives −3.249999 as its approximation. Selecting Trace and moving to the graph of Y3 you can enter 0.5 for the x value and read off −3.2749 as the AGF value with $h = 0.01$. Try a smaller value in Y2.

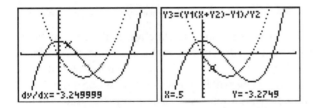

Note that the graphing window used is not square – but has been chosen to show clearly the major features of the functions. This means a tangent of slope 1 will not be at 45° to the axes. Use 'Zoom square' to correct this if you prefer.

Of course, with powerful computer software such as TI-Nspire™ we can use ready-made tools, such as sliders for parameters, to make the explorations easier to carry out. The following screen shows how we can use a slider to change the value of the step length h, and a slideable point P on the x axis to read off coordinates and slopes. The points Q and R are the intersections of the perpendicular to the x axis through P with the graphs of the functions f1(x) and f2(x).

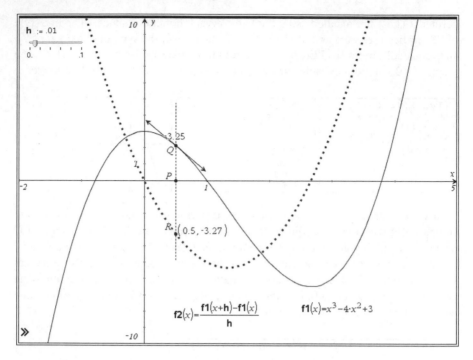

Another approach to the derivative for a smooth function is the idea of 'local straightness'. First trace Y1 and select 0.5, then use Zoom In, accepting the suggested coordinates for the centre of enlargement. Then use Zsquare to make sure that the units on both axes are the same length. This will help to ensure that a line of gradient 1 does make a 45° angle with the x axis. Now repeatedly Trace to $x = 0.5$ and Zoom In until the curve looks like a straight line. Using Trace you can explore coordinates of neighbouring points to $x = 0.5$. For example we see that the 'curve' passes through (0.5, 2.125) and (0.51, 2.092251) from which we can find another numerical approximation of −3.2749 to the gradient at 0.5.

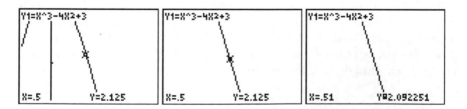

The TI-83/4 has a built-in function called 'nDeriv' which is in the MATH MATH menu.

So 'nDeriv(Y1,X,0.5)' will return the value of the numerical derivative of Y1 with X at X = 0.5. Similarly: 'Y4 = nDeriv(Y1,X,X)' will compute values of the numerical derivative at each of the values of X used for plotting a graph.

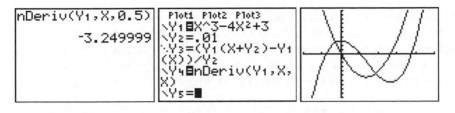

With TI-Nspire™ we can split a page into several views to compare the zoomed-in graphs.

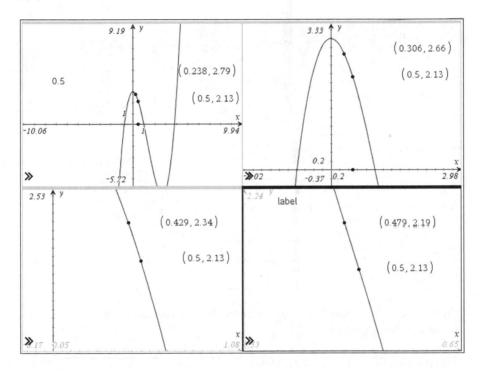

The Nuffield approach to integration is to start with the solution of differential equations as anti-derivatives. Later this is seen to be equivalent (the fundamental theorem of calculus) to finding areas under graphs. In this example the area under the function $Y1(x) = 1 + x^2$ is approximated by rectangles. Here we can use the function plotting and statistics (histogram) plotting of TIN (or the TI-83/84) to illustrate the idea.

✏️ *Try using different step lengths, different ranges and/or different functions.*

In the TIN approach first open a Graph window, and define $f1(x) = 1 + x^2$. Then open a List window and define xx as a sequence: e.g. $\text{seq}(r, r, 0, 0.9, 0.1) = 0, 0.1, 0.2 \ldots 0.9$. Define yy as $f1(xx)$ for the list of corresponding data values. We will plot the data from *xx* as a histogram, using frequencies from *yy* in a Data window together with the graph of f1(x) to show the idea of rectangles approximating the area under a graph. In the List window we have also computed the cell C2 as the sum of list *yy*, and the cell C4 as 0.1*C2, i.e. the sum of the areas of the rectangles, as an approximation to the definite integral of f1(x) from 0 to 1.

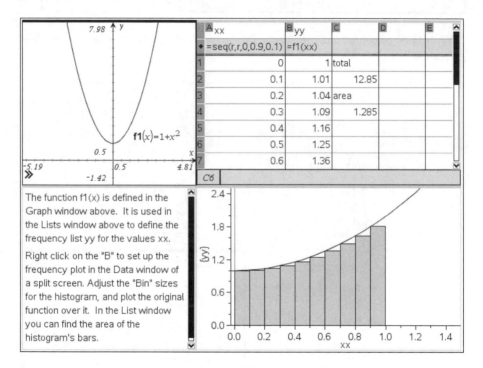

Just as there was a built-in function for numeric differentiation, so the TI-83/4 has one for numeric integration.

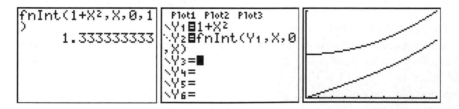

Again, we do not know the exact algorithm used by the TI-83/4, but we can easily write a little program to accumulate and plot the approximate area function for the function stored in Y1, using the values of Xmin and Xmax set in the Window. (These are found in the VARS, Window menu.)

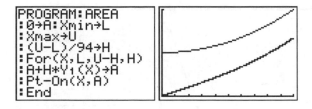

```
PROGRAM:AREA
:0→A:Xmin→L
:Xmax→U
:(U-L)/94→H
:For(X,L,U-H,H)
:A+H*Y₁(X)→A
:Pt-On(X,A)
:End
```

You could compare the output from the program with the graph generated by fnInt to check the closeness of the fit. Can you adapt the program to compute numerical approximations to definite integrals using, e.g., trapezium, midpoint and/or Simpson's rules?

5.7(b) Iterative processes

Fixed-point iteration is a common topic on many post-16 syllabuses. Here the use of a 'cobweb' or 'staircase' diagram provides a graphic illustration of whether or not the process converges. Using the 'Seq' mode on the TI-83/4 you can set up an iteration in the Y = editor and a suitable Window.

```
Plot1 Plot2 Plot3        WINDOW
 nMin=1                   nMin=1
·.u(n)◘u(n-1)²-.5         nMax=10
                          PlotStart=1
 u(nMin)◘{1}              PlotStep=1
·.v(n)=                   Xmin=-1.175
 v(nMin)=                 Xmax=1.175
·.w(n)=                  ↓Xscl=1■
```

Use '2nd' and 'WINDOW' to select 'FORMAT' and set the display to 'Web'. When you graph the function you now get both the graph of $y = x^2 - 0.5$ and that of $y = x$.

Their points of intersection are the fixed points of the iteration. Use 'TRACE' and each time you move the cursor right you will open up another line of the cobweb. Here we see that the intersection near –0.366 seems to be an attractor for the iteration, while that near 1.366 seems to be a repeller.

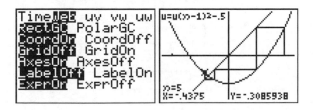

```
Time◘We◘ uv vw uw      u=u(n-1)²-.5
RectGC  PolarGC
CoordOn  CoordOff
GridOff  GridOn
AxesOn  AxesOff
LabelOff  LabelOn
ExprOn  ExprOff         n=5
                       X=-.4375    Y=-.3085938
```

Of course we can also use TI-Nspire™ to carry out the iteration and to show the 'web' diagram.

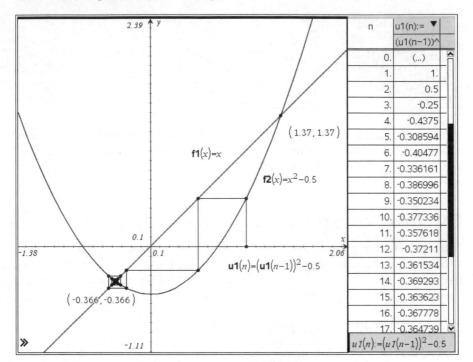

Some other graph-plotting software, such as Autograph, also has tools to help visualize iterations.

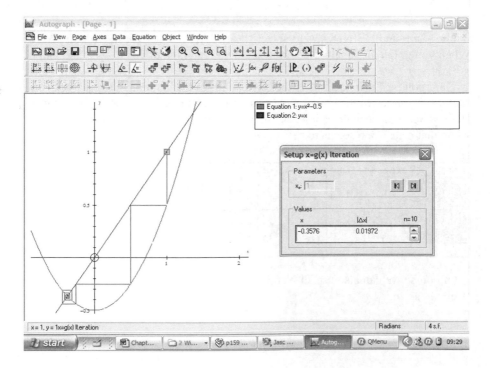

5.7(c) Complex variables

Just to show off, we can also use the TI-83/4 to explore functions of a complex variable!

One of the Nuffield books *Complex Numbers and Numerical Methods* has an investigation into the mapping of shapes such as a cardioid under a complex function such as e^{x+iy}.

First use MODE to select parametric plotting, angles measured in radians, graphs plotted simultaneously and complex numbers enabled in the form $a + bi$. The parametric equation for a small cardioid is entered in the Y = editor. The formula for its transform uses the Complex functions real and imag from the MATH menu. The line style is dotted.

With a suitable window you can see both the object and its image.

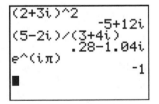

Of course now the calculator can be used for complex arithmetic as well!

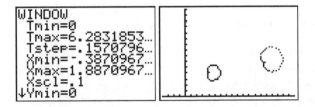

Naturally the graphic output looks better on the higher resolution TI-Nspire™ display.

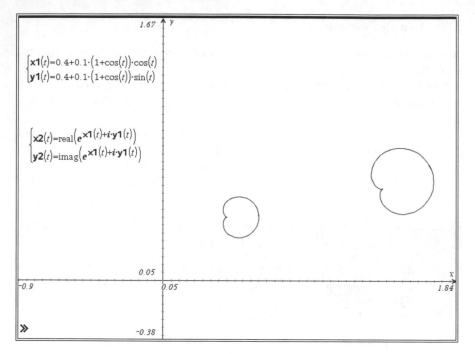

5.7(d) Coordinate geometry, conics and parametric equations

A good starting-point for work in coordinate geometry leading to conic sections and to parametric equations is afforded by the locus of a falling ladder (see the picture on the following page). *FT* is a 2 m ladder whose foot *F* can slide in contact with a slippery floor *OE*, and whose top *T* can slide in contact with a slippery wall *ON*. The starting-point is a 'thought experiment'. Concentrate on the midpoint *M* of *ON*.

✎ *What path do you think it will follow as* F *slides on* O*E?*

✎ *How about a different point of the ladder, such as* R*?*

✎ *Can you imagine either locus reflected in the axes to form a closed curve?*

✎ *Can you imagine how the locus generated by* R *will deform as* R *slides on* FT*?*

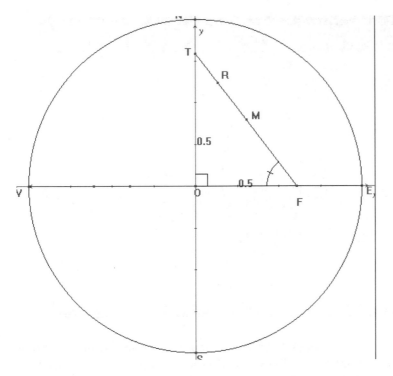

You know that $FM = MT = 1$. If P is the point on the floor directly below M, what can you say about the lengths OP and PF? Can you find the length OM? Another useful image is to imagine a point Q such that $OTQF$ is a rectangle, and to consider its diagonal OQ.

If the coordinates of M are (x,y) can you find the equation of the locus of M? If the angle OFT is given by the parameter t, can you find x and y as functions of t? Try checking this out using the parametric plotting mode of a graphing calculator, such as the TI-83, or graphing software such as TIN.

✎ *What does the locus look like if* t *can take all values between 0° and 360°?*

✎ *Could you make a Cabri or Sketchpad construction which models this?*

✎ *Could you use angle* FTO *instead?*

✎ *Suppose the distance* FR *is given by another parameter* p, *can you find both the Cartesian and parametric equations of the locus of* R?

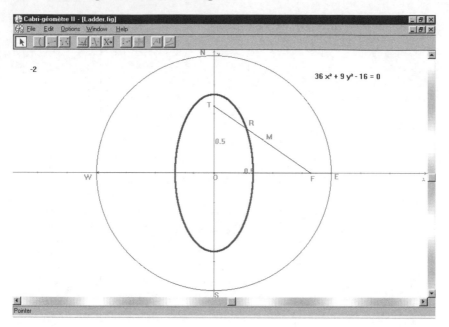

In addition to circles and arcs, Cabri has the ability to construct conics. This tool is based upon a construction by Blaise Pascal (1623–62), and needs five points to define the conic. Reflecting *R* in the axes provides four of them and just choosing any other point of locus does the trick. Using the Equation and Coordinates tools from the measurement menu you can now check out the Cartesian equation of the locus of *R* and see how it varies as you slide *R* on *FT*.

The curve that many people see in their mind's eye when trying the thought experiment is not the locus of *M*, but the curve which has *FT* as its tangent. If you reflect *FT* in the axes and construct the four loci of these segments with *F* you will not actually see a curve, but your eye will detect a smooth edge hinted at by the boundary of this bunch of segments. To show this curve you need to work with lines rather than segments. In the Preferences window from the Option menu you can select whether the locus of lines will be shown as the Envelope, or not. So the next image shows the curve enveloped by the bundle of tangent lines like *FT*. This curve is called an 'astroid' and its parametric equations are:

$$x = 2 \cos^3 t$$
$$y = 2 \sin^3 t.$$

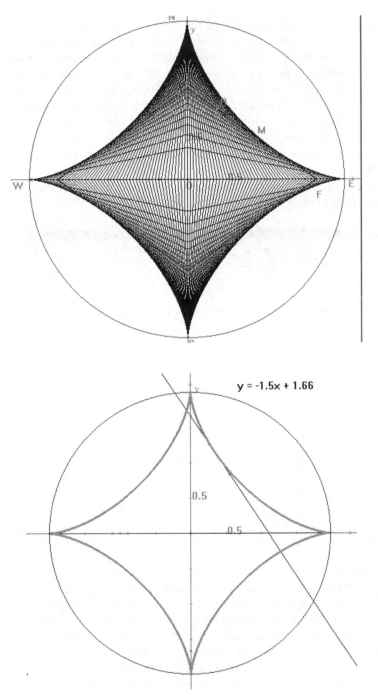

$$y = -1.5x + 1.66$$

An excellent source of ideas for constructions and curves is E. H. Lockwood's *A Book of Curves* (Cambridge University Press, 1967). The other 'classic' is H. M. Cundy and A. P. Rollett's *Mathematical Models* (Tarquin, 1987).

We conclude this section on coordinate geometry with another example of the power of dynamic geometry, this time to illustrate the focus–directrix definition of the conics. We have used Numerical Edit to enter values for the parameters a and e (the eccentricity). Using the Calculator tool we have computed the coordinates of the focus F $(ae,0)$ and the point D on the directrix $(-a/e,0)$. A segment XX' has been constructed along the x-axis as the domain for the independent variable P. Distance PD has been measured and we now seek if there are points Q such that $FQ = e.PD$, i.e. such that e is the ratio between the distances from Q to the focus and from Q to the directrix. Using the calculator we can compute $e.PD$ and transfer this measurement to a vector from F. The circle through that last point is the locus of all points distance $e.PD$ from F. If this intersects the perpendicular to the x axis through P at points Q and Q' then these points belong to the locus.

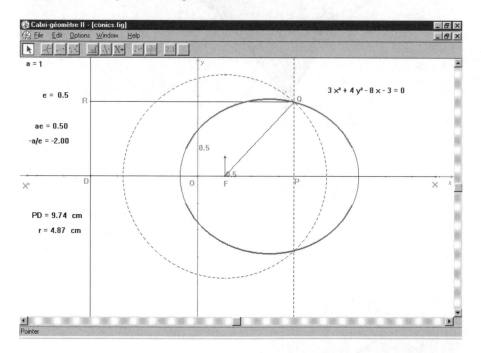

Using Q, Q' and three other points on the locus we can define a five-point conic and read off its equation. Now, if you double-click on the value for e you can increase and decrease this to see what happens as e first reaches 1 and then gets bigger.

In Sketchpad you can use the New Parameter option from the Graph menu to enter values, such as a and e, together with units, if needed. The distance DP will have units in cm, and so will the multiple $e.DP$ – so selecting this and the focus F you can use the Circle by Centre + Radius command from the Construction menu. The loci of the intersection points Q,Q' with P make up (most of) the conic. Unlike Cabri, Sketchpad doesn't have a built-in function for conics.

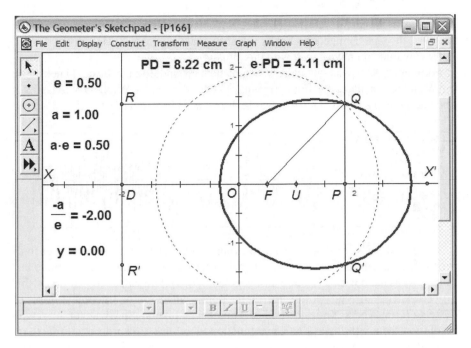

5.7(e) Trigonometric functions and relationships

The next example is from trigonometry, and has a sting in its tail! The idea is to use a graphical approach to 'discovering' trigonometric identities, such as $\sin 2x = 2\sin x \cos x$.

On the TI-83/4 we have plotted the graphs of $\sin x$ and $\cos x$ in degrees in $[-360, 360]$ and superimposed the graph of their product. Clearly the zeros of this function are the unions of the zeros of both sine and cosine, and so it looks like a sine wave but with twice the frequency. However, its amplitude is smaller than those of either sine or cosine. One of its maxima is at $x = 45°$, so the amplitude is $\sin 45° \cos 45° = (1/\sqrt{2}).(1/\sqrt{2}) = \frac{1}{2}$. This suggests the identity: $\sin x \cos x = \frac{1}{2} \sin 2x$, which you can check by graphing 'both sides of the equation' to see if they appear identical.

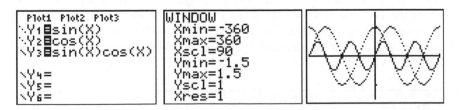

The following is a true story! Kate, a newly qualified teacher, had used this approach with a class of 16–17 year olds and was very pleased with the results. But there had been an absentee. When Sam, returned, the teacher explained the task and left Sam to get on by herself. After a short while Sam showed Kate her results. She had discovered that $\sin 45x$ has the same zeros as $\sin x \cos x$, double the amplitude, and with the sign changed. So Sam's 'identity' was: $\sin 45x = -2 \sin x \cos x$.

How would you have coped with this situation?

Fortunately Kate was sure of her mathematical ground, even if she could not figure out what the calculator had done 'wrong'. So she changed the WINDOW to [-90,90] and was able to show that $\sin 45x$ was really very wiggly indeed!

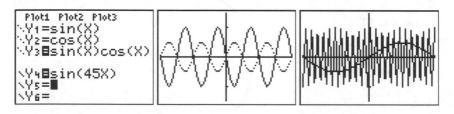

The calculator's 'mistake' is easy to explain. It evaluates the function at each of the 94 or so pixels across the screen. Provided this is not too far away from the last point it joins them with a 'blobby' line segment. For certain values of k in $\sin kx$, this will be exactly 'in sync' with $-\sin 2x$ at the points where x is an integral multiple of 720/94 (720 is Xmax-Xmin and 94 is the number of pixels). So whatever the screen resolution there will always be some function which has this property. In fact you may know how to expand $\sin 45x + \sin 2x$ as $2 \sin 47/2x \cos 43/2x$.

✎ *Can you calculate the value of* k *if, say, there were 100 pixels across the screen?*

Another useful example in trigonometry concerns motivating the use of radians. If you use nDeriv to explore the derivative of the sine function when x is measured in degrees in [−360,360] the result is very unexciting! Tracing the nDeriv function reveals that it is virtually indistinguishable from the x axis, with a maximum value of only 0.01745329. Of course this is not particularly surprising since the line joining $(0, 0)$ to the first maximum $(90,1)$ has a gradient of 1/90, so the gradient of $\sin x$ at $x = 0$ is not going to be much larger. In fact the reciprocal of 0.01745329 is 57.29579, so the slope is about 1 in 60. We can easily change the unit from degrees, say, to right-angles. This just means we divide the Window's Xmin and Xmax by 90 to get the interval [−4, 4] and graph the function given by $y = \sin 90\ x$. Here we see that the graph of nDeriv now looks like a cosine function, but with an amplitude greater than 1 (actually 1.5707957).

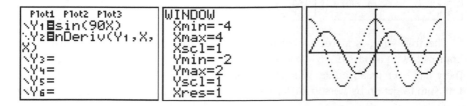

🖎 *Try re-graphing in multiples of 60°.*

🖎 *What is the significance of 57.2979?*

🖎 *What familiar number appears if you double 1.570957?*

5.7(f) An historical problem

We conclude this section on ICT use to explore more advanced mathematics with an interesting historical problem. As you may know, Isaac Newton (1642–1727) and Gottfried Leibniz (1646–1716) are both credited with the invention of differential and integral calculus independently at about the same time. On the Continent, it was the Swiss brothers Jean (1667–1748) and Jacques (1654–1705) Bernoulli who did most to publicize Leibniz's work. Jean was engaged as tutor by the Marquis Guillaume François Antoine l'Hôpital (1661–1708) in Paris in 1692. In return for a regular salary, Jean agreed to keep l'Hôpital informed of his mathematical discoveries and to let him do as he liked with them. L'Hôpital published the first textbook on differential calculus *Analyse des Infiniements Petits*, published in 1696. This includes what we now call 'l'Hôpital's rule', which had actually been discovered by Jean Bernoulli! As one of his examples to illustrate the power of differential calculus l'Hôpital solved the following problem in mechanics.

Here a rope of length *a* is attached at *A*, and its free end *C* carries a small pulley. Another rope of length *b* is attached at *B*, on the same level as *A* and 1 m away. This rope passes over the pulley at *C* and carries a mass at its free end *D*. L'Hôpital used differential calculus to determine the minimum value of the *y* coordinate of *D*, i.e. the point of equilibrium of the system. Can you do this? (Maybe the symbolic manipulation such as in TI-Nspire CAS™ would help?) L'Hôpital used values of *a* = 0.4 m and *b* = 1 m. You could use the angle *BAC* = *t* as parameter to find the parametric equation of the locus of *D*. Actually we are seeing an arc of a closed curve. If *b* is greater than 1 + *a* then the locus is the whole curve, but the part above the horizontal axis only makes sense if *AC* is a stiff rod, rather than a piece of rope. Do you think this curve is an ellipse?

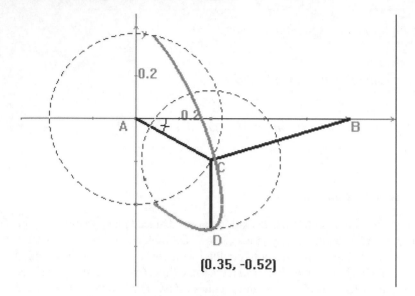

[0.35, -0.52]

We would be very surprised if Newton was impressed by this analytic technique. He would have known that the tensions in the parts of the rope *CB* and *CD* would have to be equal, and that, in equilibrium, their components along the tangent to the circle at *A* would have to be equal. Hence *AC* produced must be the angle bisector of∠*DCB*. So that gives a means of constructing the solution geometrically.

✎ *Can you construct the solution geometrically?*

Chapter 6

Why integrate ICT into mathematics teaching and learning?

This chapter looks at what others have said, done and researched about the links between mathematics, ICT, IT and education. It is intended to help you answer for yourself the question: 'Why should we aim to integrate ICT into mathematics teaching?' The range of references at the end of this chapter should be particularly helpful if you intend to undertake any further academic work, such as an MA module, as part of your own professional development.

6.1 THREE POSSIBLE REASONS

We are in an era of increased educational accountability, and one in which a certain scepticism has grown about accepting the judgement of professionals. In many aspects schools are being asked to produce policies and development plans 'in the light of research and inspection evidence'. We have recently seen a huge change in the organization and methodology of the teaching of mathematics in primary schools in England through the National Numeracy Strategy. This strategy claims to be based on just such research and inspection evidence. However, in her plenary address to the British Congress on Mathematics Education in Northampton, July 1999, Professor Margaret Brown analysed these claims, point by point, to show that in each case there is conflicting research evidence. In essence, then, it is rare in education that one can point to genuinely persuasive evidence that treatment X will have a beneficial effect in terms of characteristic Y. Because of the rapid pace of change of technology, and the political issues surrounding mathematics education, it is hardly surprising, then, that we cannot identify overwhelming research evidence to support the claim that using ICT in teaching mathematics significantly improves students' learning of mathematics. In fact we should probably be rather sceptical of any research which made such a claim. This is not to deny that some important and interesting research has been conducted, nor to deny that the converse case has been demonstrated! In this chapter we will point to some interesting pieces of research, to surveys of research and calls for research. We will also look at some official reports that have impacted on ICT and mathematics in the last 20 years, as well as pointing to some work suggesting future directions in mathematics education.

In addressing the title of this chapter we can identify at least three reasons for promoting the integration of ICT in mathematics teaching in schools:

1. desirability
2. inevitability
3. public policy.

Desirability

In order to show that ICT use is desirable we need to say in which ways it is desirable.

There may be many of these. In terms of students, the use of ICT may:

- engage their attention and motivate them;
- stimulate their curiosity;
- encourage them to develop their problem-solving strategies;
- provide models and images which aid them in concept formation;
- improve their test and examination results, etc.

In terms of teachers, the use of ICT may:

- improve their efficiency;
- reduce their administrative burden;
- release more time to address students' needs individually;
- provide better records of students' progress;
- be a stimulus to re-thinking their approach to mathematics teaching;
- be a stimulus to re-thinking their understanding of mathematics;
- be a means to communicate with other teachers sharing common problems, etc.

In terms of schools, the ICT may:

- improve efficiency and reduce teaching costs;
- improve examination results and the school's position in 'league tables';
- improve educational inclusion, reduce truancy, social disruption, etc.;
- improve provision for students who are not learning in their native tongue, etc.

For example, international comparisons between educational results in subjects such as mathematics tend to receive a lot of media attention, such as the Trends in International Mathematics and Science Study (TIMSS) and the Pisa Study. So it might be thought nationally desirable for a country, such as England, to take steps to improve its performance. However, there are inevitable questions about comparing like with like. For example, in some countries the teaching of the use of electronic calculators is a compulsory part of the curriculum, whereas in others it is not. So it is not surprising, then, that when questions are chosen for such international comparisons they are taken as far as possible from the intersection of the various countries' curricula. However, a particular skill, such as the addition of fractions, may represent a considerably larger proportion of one country's curriculum than another's. So imbalances are inevitably built into the system. It may also appear that a number of countries that discouraged the use of calculators, such as in South East Asia, performed better in TIMSS tests than those in Europe and America, say, which encouraged their use. But is it calculator use that is the critical factor, or would these countries achieve even better results if at the time they had also promoted calculator use?

So establishing a case for desirability is still a question of values and judgement. It is also, inevitably, a political one, especially in regard to the funding of educational research, and to the credentials of the researchers, their brief and their methodology. The issue is clouded further by the involvement of commercial interests. In Europe we are seeing an increasing amount of so-called public–private partnerships between government and major companies. The amount of public money available to support educational research has been eroded, and increasingly researchers seek sponsorship from private firms. Not surprisingly, many such companies express preferences towards lines of enquiry more directly related to their own priorities. So it may well be that important, feasible research remains unconducted for want of essential support.

Inevitability

Technology becomes inevitable where the conventional alternatives no longer exist, become prohibitively expensive, or impose such obvious restrictions that their use cannot be rationally supported. For example, many fields of publishing have moved from print to electronic form. This applies to conference proceedings, to reference works such as encyclopaedias, to small-circulation textbooks, to specialist journals, etc. So we can safely claim that it is technologically inevitable that a school reference library should provide access to materials on CD-ROM and the internet. Can we make a similar claim for the provision of ICT tools in mathematics? Well, certainly in England it used to be common practice to teach the use of tables of logarithms and, in some cases, slide rules in secondary schools as aids to computation. So the move to making the teaching of calculator use compulsory for students aged 9–11 could be seen as acceptance of such a technological inevitability, especially as calculators are more powerful, more convenient, easier to use and cheaper than the alternatives.

The year 2000 was UNESCO's international year of mathematics, and in the UK it was promoted by the Department for Education and Employment (DfEE) as 'Maths Year 2000'. Interestingly one official aspect of that programme was a celebration of the power and use of the calculator. A far cry from the official line even two years' previously. In February 2000 we wrote: 'The jury is still out on, for example, the educational inevitably of the use of graphing, statistical, geometric and algebraic ICT tools in addition to the numerical computational tool – the calculator. However, their mathematical inevitability is beyond doubt.'

Since then we have seen considerable changes at the Department for Education and Skills (DfES, now DCSF) resulting in the current drive to make ICT use embedded in the teaching and learning of subjects such as mathematics. One strong economic rationale behind such educational policies is the need for a technologically innovative industrial and commercial sector for the UK to sustain its world position economically.

In short we do not have the raw materials or cheap labour to compete, so we must do it by being smarter. Similar analyses are affecting policy in other countries such as France. In particular the French government has encouraged the introduction of ICT tools in mathematics as a way of reducing the time (and resources) available for mathematics teaching! So whether something becomes educationally inevitable depends upon the socioeconomic evolution of the purposes of education.

Public policy

To date, this policy has mainly concentrated on equipping and training teachers to use ICT. However we are now facing the most exciting prospect of a world in which all learners could have access to personal powerful ICT and portable ICT. In the UK the government has been cooperating with a charity called the E-Learning Foundation to recycle computers for family use (`http://www.e-learningfoundation. com/`) as well as to provide broadband access as a step to ending the so-called 'digital divide'.

For sometime now, organizations in many countries have been evaluating the personal use of technology in education. The visionary Professor Negroponte from the Massachusetts Institute of Technology (MIT) established the One Laptop Per Child (OLPC: `http://laptop.org/en/`) project, with the aim of getting powerful low-cost computing into learners' hands worldwide at a target cost of $100 per laptop. While this has led to some infighting within multinational IT companies, the development of the so-called 'net-book', such as the Asus Eee-PC has brought the possibility of worldwide computer ownership much closer, although maybe at a starting price of nearer $200. The development of new ranges of smaller, faster, more efficient processors, such as Intel's Atom processor, coupled with Microsoft's decision to make a basic version of Windows XP widely available at very low cost, have opened the doors to education-specific ICT such as Intel's Classmate PC (`http://www.intel. com/intel/learningseries.htm`), recently adopted by the Portuguese government. Its Magellan project will equip 500,000 Portuguese primary school students with their own laptop (`http://en.wikibooks.org/wiki/One-to-One_Laptop_Schools/Portugal`). New models of net-books will have wireless communication, built-in cameras, sensors such as GPS and accelerometers.

As far as public policy in the UK is concerned there has been a remarkably consistent acceptance of the educational benefits of ICT over the past 20 years, irrespective of which political party has been in power nationally or locally. Within the UK, education is a matter for regional decision-making, and so there are separate departments for England, Scotland, Wales and Northern Ireland. Within England, the government has, for the first time, split off Higher Education and further education from schools. The latter falls under the Department of Children, Schools and Families (DCSF) and the former under the Department of Innovation, Universities and Skills (DIUS) – recently combined with the Department for Business, Enterprise and Regulatory Reform (BERR) to form the Department for Business, Innovation and Skills (BIS). Within the DCSF the key strategy is known as 'Every Child Matters', which includes 'Personalized Education' (`http://www.dcsf.gov.uk/ everychildmatters/`). Within BIS lies the Science and Society strategy, and also 'Digital Britain' (`http://interactive.dius.gov.uk/science andsociety/site/`).

At the moment government strategy is usually turned into action through its agencies, which, for education include:

a. the Qualifications and Curriculum Development Agency (QCDA: `http://www.qcda.gov.uk/`),
b. the Training and Development Agency for Schools (TDA: `http://www.tda.gov.uk/`) and
c. the British Educational Communications and Technology Agency (Becta: `http://www.becta.org.uk/`).

Each of the agencies is currently involved in supporting aspects of ICT in education. The year 2009 saw the introduction by QCDA of a new secondary school National Curriculum for England with a much greater emphasis on personal learning skills, and all schools have been involved in reviewing their curriculum. It has also seen the announcement by the TDA of a new ICT training programme for all teachers involving the Open University and e-Skills UK. For several years now Becta has been working with teachers' professional Subject Associations, such as the Association of Teachers of Mathematics (ATM) and the Mathematical Association (MA) to promote the embedding of ICT in teaching and learning core subjects. This has included working with Teachers TV on 'Hard to Teach Maths' (`http://www.teachers.tv/video/29853`), revising the Student's Entitlement document and developing a grid for ICT use at GCSE maths.

Ofsted's 2009 mathematics report 'Understanding the Score' provides a helpful review of the success and, otherwise, of public policies (`http://www.ofsted.gov.uk/content/download/7137/73098/file/Mathematics%20-%20understanding%20the%20score.pdf`).

The National Centre of Excellence for the Teaching of Mathematics (NCETM: `http://www.ncetm.org.uk/`) has been prioritizing work in ICT both through its sponsorship of school-based projects and through a major conference held in March 2008. The website provides an excellent means for communities of teachers to keep in touch and to exchange ideas, resources and information. It also coordinates regional professional development support through its network of regional coordinators. The National STEM centre at York University also has a remit to gather together resources to support teachers of all the STEM subjects including mathematics (`http://www.nationalstemcentre.org.uk/`).

6.2 REFERENCES TO RESEARCH FROM HOME AND ABROAD

Against that background, we now provide a selective set of references to the extensive literature about ICT tools and the mathematics curriculum.

6.2(a) Calculators

Fey, J. and Hirsch, C. (1992) *Calculators in Mathematics Education*. Reston, VA: National Council of Teachers of Mathematics.

Foxman, D. (1996) *A Comparative Review of Research on Calculator Availability and Use, Ages 5–14*. London: SCAA.

Jones, K. (2003) 'Research Bibliography: four-function calculators', *MicroMath*, **19** (1), 33–4.

Jones, S. and Tanner, H. (1997) 'Do calculators count?', *Micromath*, **13** (3), 31–6 (`http://www.swan.ac.uk/education/research/smeg/calc/html`).

Ruthven, K. (1997) *The Use of Calculators at Key Stages 1–3*. London: SCAA

SCAA (1997) *The Use of Calculators at Key Stages 1–3*. Discussion Paper No. 9, March. London: SCAA.

Shuard, H., Walsh A., Goodwin, J. and Worcester, V. (1991) *Calculators, Students and Mathematics*. London: Simon & Schuster.

6.2(b) Graphing calculators and other personal, portable technology

Ainley, J. and Pratt, D. (1995) 'Planning for portability', in L. Burton and B. Jaworski (eds), *Technology in Mathematics Teaching*. Lund, Sweden: Chartwell-Bratt, 435–48.

Becta (2003) *What the Research Says about Portable ICT Devices in Teaching and Learning* (`http://www.becta.org.uk/research/reports/docs/wtrs_porticts.pdf`).

Bowell, B., France, S. and Redfern, S. (1994) *Portable Computers in Action*. Coventry: NCET.

Dunham, P. H. and Dick, T. P. (1994) 'Research on graphing calculators', *The Mathematics Teacher*, **87** (6), 440–5.

Hennessy, S. (1997) *Portable Technologies and Graphing Investigations: review of the literature*. CITE technical report No. 175. *Buckingham:* Open University, Institute of Educational Technology.

Hennessy, S. (1999) 'The potential of portable technologies for supporting graphing investigations', *British Journal of Educational Technology*, **30** (1), 57–60 (summary: full version of review article available at `http://edu.leeds.ac.uk/research/groups/cssme/graphCalc.html`).

Hennessy, S., Fung, P. and Scanlon, E. (1999) *Portable Information Technologies for Supporting Graphical Mathematics Investigations: findings of the PIGMI Project*. CITE technical report No. 187. Buckingham: Open University, Institute of Educational Technology.

Hennessy, S., Fung, P. and Scanlon, E. (2001) 'The role of the graphic calculator in mediating graphing activity', *International Journal of Mathematical Education in Science and Technology*, **32** (2), 267–90.

Jones, K. (2005) 'Graphing calculators in the teaching and learning of mathematics: a research bibliography', *MicroMath*, **21** (2), 31–3.

Oldknow, A. (1995) 'Personal technology and new horizons', in L. Burton and B. Jaworski (eds), *Technology in Mathematics Teaching*. Lund, Sweden: Chartwell-Bratt, 97–108.

Oldknow, A. (1998) 'Personal computing technology: use and possibilities', in D. Tinsley and D. Johnson (eds), *Information and Communication Technologies in School Mathematics*. London: Chapman & Hall.

Penglase, M. and Arnold, S. (1996) 'The graphics calculator in mathematics education: a critical review of recent research', *Mathematics Education Research Journal*, **8** (1), 58–90.

Ruthven, K. (1990) 'The influence of graphic calculator use on translation from graphic to symbolic forms', *Educational Studies in Mathematics*, **21** (5), 431–50.

Smart, T. (1995) 'Visualisation, confidence and magic', in L. Burton and B. Jaworski (eds), *Technology in Mathematics Teaching*. Lund, Sweden: Chartwell-Bratt, 195–212.

Stradling R., Sims, D. and Jamison, J. (1994) *Portable Computers Pilot Evaluation Report*. Coventry: NCET.

Waits, B. K. and Demana, F. (2000) 'Calculators in mathematics teaching and learning: past, present, and future', in M. J. Burke and F. R. Curcio (eds), *Learning Mathematics for a New Century: NCTM 2000 Yearbook*. Reston, VA: National Council of Teachers of Mathematics, 51–66.

6.2(e) Geometry and visualization

Christou, C. *et al*. (2007) *Developing an Active Learning Environment for the Learning of Stereometry*, ICTMT, Hradec Králové, Czech Republic.

Christou, C. *et al*. (2007) 'Developing student spatial ability with 3D software applications', paper presented at the 5th Congress of the European Society for Research in Mathematics Education (CERME), Larnaca (22–26 February 2007).

Coxeter, H. (1969) *Introduction to Geometry*. London: Wiley.

Goldstein, R. *et al*. (eds) (1996) *Dynamic Geometry*. Coventry: NCET.

Hoyles, C. (1998) 'A culture of proving in school mathematics?', in D. Tinsley and D. Johnson (eds), *Information and Communication Technologies in School Mathematics*. London: Chapman & Hall.

Hoyles, C. and Healey, L. (1997) 'Unfolding meanings for reflective symmetry', *International Journal of Computers for Mathematical Learning*, **2**, 27–59.

Jones, K. (2002) 'Research bibliography: dynamic geometry software', *MicroMath*, **18** (3), 44–5.

Lu Yu-Wen, A. (2009) 'Linking Geometry and Algebra: English and Taiwanese upper secondary approaches to the use of GeoGebra', in M. Joubert, (ed.) *Proceedings of the British Society for Research into Learning Mathematics*, **29** (1).

Nemirovsky, R. and Noble, T. (1997) 'On mathematical visualization and the place where we live', *Educational Studies in Mathematics*, **33**, 99–131.

Royal Society (2001) *Teaching and Learning Geometry 11–19* (report of a working group chaired by Professor A. Oldknow). London: Royal Society/JMC.

Ruthven, K., Hennessy, S. and Deaney, R. (2007) 'Constructions of dynamic geometry: a study of the interpretative flexibility of educational software in classroom practice', *Computers and Education*, **51** (1), 297–317 (available online at `http://dx.doi.org/10.1016/j.compedu.2007.05.013`).

Ruthven, K., Hennessy, S. and Deaney, R. (2007) 'Incorporating dynamic geometry systems into secondary mathematics education: didactical perspectives and practices of teachers', (draft paper available online at `http://BERA04_DGS.doc`).

Schumann, H. and Green, D. (1994) *Discovering Geometry with a Computer: using Cabri Géomètre*. Lund, Sweden: Chartwell-Bratt.

Wells, D. (1991) *The Penguin Dictionary of Curious and Interesting Geometry*. London: Penguin.

Yu-Wen, A. L. 'Linking Geometry and Algebra: English and Taiwanese Upper Secondary Teachers' Approaches to the use of GeoGebra', *Proceedings of the British Society for Research into Learning Mathematics*, **29** (1), 61-6.

6.2(d) Algebra and computer algebra systems

Barzel, B. *et al*. (1999) *New Technologies – New Means of Mathematics Teaching*. Holabrunn: Pedagogical Institute of Lower Austria.

Cuoco, A. *et al.* (eds) (2003) *Computer Algebra Systems in Secondary School Mathematics Education: NCTM 2003 Yearbook.* Reston, VA: National Council of Teachers of Mathematics.

Goldstein, R. *et al.* (1995) *Algebra at A-level: how the curriculum might change with computer algebra.* Derby: ATM.

Hunter, M. *et al.* (1995) 'Using a computer algebra system with 14–15 year old students', in L. Burton and B. Jaworski (eds), *Technology in Mathematics Teaching.* Lund, Sweden: Chartwell-Bratt, 307–24.

Oldknow, A. and Flower, J. (eds) (1996) *Symbolic Manipulation by Computers and Calculators.* Leicester: Mathematical Association.

Royal Society (1996) *Teaching and Learning Algebra Pre-19* (report of a working group chaired by Professor R. Sutherland). London: Royal Society/JMC.

Sutherland, R. (1995) 'Algebraic thinking: the role of the computer', in L. Burton and B. Jaworski (eds), *Technology in Mathematics Teaching.* Lund, Sweden: Chartwell-Bratt, 275–880.

Taylor, M. (1995) 'Calculators and computer algebra systems – their use in mathematics education', *The Mathematical Gazette,* **79** (484), 68–83.

6.2(e) Computers and the mathematics classroom/curriculum

Ball, D. *et al.* (eds) (1987) *Will Mathematics Count?* Hatfield: AUCBE.

Bennett, P. (1991) 'Effectiveness of the computer in the teaching of secondary school mathematics: 15 years of reviews of research', *Educational Technology,* **31**, 44–8.

Bloomfield, A. and Harries, A. (eds) (1996) *Teaching, Learning and Mathematics with IT.* Derby: ATM.

Clark-Wilson, A. (2009) *Approaches to In-Service Teacher Development in England and Wales Concerning the Use of ICT in Secondary Mathematics.* ICTMT 9 Proceedings, France: University of Metz.

Clark-Wilson, A. (2009) *Evaluating TI-Nspire™ in Secondary Mathematics Classrooms* (available online at `http://www.chiuni.ac.uk/teachered/documents/Clark-Wilson2008TI-NspireFinalReportv5.pdf`).

Clark-Wilson, A. and Oldknow, A. (2009) *Inspiring Maths in the Classroom* (available online at `http://education.ti.com/sites/UK/downloads/pdf/Inspiring_Maths_in_the_classroom.pdf`).

Committee of Enquiry into the Teaching of Mathematics in Schools (chair Dr W. H. Cockcroft) (1982) *Mathematics Counts.* London: HMSO.

DfES (2001) *ImpacT2 Report.* London: DfES (available online at `http://www.becta.org.uk/impact2`).

Fletcher, T. (1983) *Microcomputers and Mathematics in Schools.* London: DES.

Goldstein, R. (1997) 'Integrating computers', *Micromath,* **13** (1), 25–7.

Green, D. and Oldknow, A. (1996) *Developing IT across the Mathematics Department.* Coventry: NCET.

Hoyles, C. (ed.) *Girls and Computers* (Bedford Way Paper 34). London: Institute of Education.

Hyde, R. (2004) 'What do mathematics teachers say about the impact of ICT on pupils learning mathematics?', *Micromath,* **20** (2), 11–13.

Johnson, D. (1995) 'Information technology – the virtual reality of the school mathematics classroom', *Proceedings of the First Asian Technology Conference in Mathematics.* Singapore.

Jones, K. (2004) 'Celebrating 20 years of computers in mathematics education: a research bibliography', *Micromath*, **20** (1), 29–30.

Jones, K. (2004) 'Using interactive whiteboards in the teaching and learning of mathematics: a research bibliography', *Micromath*, **20** (2), 5–6.

Jones, K. (2005) 'Using Logo in the teaching and learning of mathematics: a research bibliography', *Micromath*, **21** (3), 34–6.

Jones, K. (2005) 'Using spreadsheets in the teaching and learning of mathematics: a research bibliography', *Micromath*, **21** (1), 30–1.

Joubert, M. (2009) *Using Graphing Software in the Classroom: understanding the role of the computer*, ICTMT 9 Proceedings, Metz: University of Metz.

Kaput, J. (1992) 'Technology and mathematics education', in D. Grouws (ed.), *Handbook of Research on Mathematics Teaching and Learning*. New York: Macmillan, 515–56.

Kaput, J. (1998) *Technology as a Transformative Force in Math Education: Transforming Notations, Curriculum Structures, Content and Technologies*. NCTM Standards 2000 Technology Meeting.

Kennewell, S., Tanner, H. and Parkinson, J. (1999) 'A model for the study and design of teaching situations with ICT', in D. Watson and T. Downes (eds), *Learning in a Networked Society*. Dordrecht: Kluwer, 129–38.

Kieren, T. (1998) 'Towards an embodied view of the mathematics curriculum in a world of technology', in D. Tinsley and D. Johnson (eds), *Information and Communication Technologies in School Mathematics*. London: Chapman & Hall.

Knights, C. (2009) *The Perceived Impact of ICT on Mathematical Learning by Mathematics Teachers in the UK*, ICTMT 9 Proceedings, Metz: University of Metz.

NCET (1995) *The IT Maths Pack*, Derby: ATM; Leicester: MA.

NCET (1995) *Mathematics and IT: a pupil's entitlement*. Coventry: NCET.

Noss, R. and Hoyles, C. (1996) *Windows on Mathematical Meaning*. Dordrecht: Kluwer.

Office for Standards in Education (2004) *ICT in Schools – the impact of government initiatives: secondary mathematics*. London: Ofsted.

Ofsted (2002) *ICT in Schools: effect of government initiatives*, HMI 423. London: Ofsted.

Ofsted (2008) *Mathematics: understanding the score*. London: Ofsted.

Oldknow, A. (1985) 'Mathematics and microcomputers: a Pendley Manor report', *Mathematics in Schools*, **14** (2), 26–8.

Oldknow, A. (ed.) (1995) *Mathematics and IT at Work*. Coventry: NCET.

Oldknow, A. and Taylor, R. (1999) *Engaging Mathematics*. London: Technology Colleges' Trust.

Sutherland, R. (1998) 'Teachers and technology: the case of mathematical learning', in D. Tinsley and D. Johnson (eds), *Information and Communication Technologies in School Mathematics*. London: Chapman & Hall.

Sutherland, R. and Mason, J. (eds) (1993) *Exploiting Mental Imagery with Computers in Mathematics Education*, NATO ASI Series F, Vol. 138. Berlin: Springer.

Tanner, H. and Jones, S. (2002) 'Using ICT to support interactive teaching and learning on a secondary mathematics PGCE course', *Journal of Information Technology in Teacher Education*, **11** (1), 77–91.

Watson, D. (ed.) (1993). *The Impact report: an evaluation of the impact of information technology on children's achievements in primary and secondary schools*. London: King's College.

6.2(f) The mathematics of change

Kaput, J. (2000) 'Technology as a transformation in math education', in E. Galinde (ed.), *Technology and the NCTM Standards 2000*. Reston, VA: NCTM.

McFarlane, A. *et al.* (1995) 'Developing an understanding of the meaning of line graphs in primary science investigations using portable computers and data logging software', *Journal of Computers in Mathematics and Science Education*, **14** (4), 461–80.

Oldknow, A. and Taylor, R. (1998) *Datacapture and Modelling in Mathematics and Science*. Coventry: Becta.

Oldknow, A. and Taylor, R. (2007) 'Mathematics, science and technology teachers working collaboratively with ICT', *International Conference on Technology in Mathematics Teaching 8*. Hradec Králové, Czech Republic.

Chapter 7

Where is it all going?

In this chapter we attempt to take a peek into the future, and to look at how ICT, mathematics and mathematical pedagogy may develop in the next generation. At least this should raise the question: 'Where is it going?', even if does not actually provide any very reliable answers! Even trying to foresee the future a year ahead is a very dangerous pastime. But we thought we would have a go at trying to look at some of the pointers from the past to suggest some possible educational futures for maybe 15–20 years from now.

Education has become far more reactive as politicians, commercial interests and pressure groups have targeted its process and content, not just its organizational structure. The culture of 'leave it to the professionals, they know best' has long since been left behind! But those of us working in education do have a duty to stand up for things we hold to be important. So, for the future health of mathematics education, we need to be aware of ways in which our tenets may be threatened, and perhaps start to organize ourselves in ways which can help protect our integrity. On a lighter note, this kind of speculation can also be a fun activity for discussion with a group of students on a Friday afternoon!

Again we need to consider past developments, and future scenarios, for all three players in our little drama: ICT, mathematics and education.

ICT has, arguably, the shortest past, at least if we take the silicon chip as being its starting-point. However, mass communication, particularly in the form of radio, television and the press, has had a major impact on national and international politics this century. Totalitarian regimes have increasingly found it difficult to hide facts from their populace when radio and TV sets in homes can receive uncensored reports and images from other countries. Clearly, too, information and communication have been major factors in military intelligence (and espionage), and maybe in averting many major international conflicts since the 1950s – although sadly not those in the Middle East.

In the late 1970s, as silicon-chip technology was getting established, and its range of applications beginning to take shape, BBC TV showed a series of futuristic programmes called *The Mighty Micro*. These were written and presented by the late Chris Evans, who worked at the National Physical Laboratories. It is salutary now to return to Evans' book, also called *The Mighty Micro*, to see just how many of its apparently wild prophecies are now realized, such as home shopping, the cashless society, online newspapers, etc. In the first edition (February 2000) we wrote:

> For example, this week one of us has bought an airline ticket from Gatwick to Glasgow on the internet, exchanged drafts of a conference report with an editor in Australia by e-mail (including digital photographs of participants) and transferred funds from a savings account to a current account through online banking. So many aspects of the 'cashless' (and 'armchair') society are already established.

Since then we have seen a revolution in terms of domestic use of digital cameras, camcorders, webcams, mobile phones, photo-quality printing, broadband access, internet shopping, e-mail, downloading of media such as films to DVDs, music to CDs and MP3 players, etc. In its turn we have also seen a downside through the rise of piracy, pornography, spam e-mail, viruses, etc.

7.1 ICT, SOCIETY AND THE WORLD OF WORK

One major social change that ICT has already brought is the destruction of many, many jobs in what we may call 'processing' industries. For example, as recently as the 1970s, many companies had large spaces, known as 'drawing offices', where highly skilled and respected employees, called 'draughtsmen', worked at drawing-boards to produce accurate and detailed drawings. These were the means of taking ideas from designers and putting them in a conventional form from which others could make objects. Now designers can use commercial CAD packages on computers directly to produce such drawings without need for the human go-between. Similarly, in the 1960s all commercial aircraft carried a 'navigator' as a member of the flight crew. These have all been made redundant by various refinements in electronic (now satellite-controlled) navigational aids. Increasingly those who originate ideas, designs, strategies, etc. can document and disseminate them directly using ICT tools without need for the large force of employees who previously were the human-information processors. Furthermore, the manufacturing process has also become far more highly automated. Our (first) industrial revolution can be seen as really just replacing farm work with labour-intensive machine-minding. Not until the introduction of full-scale robotics in the last twenty years or so have we really seen automation of the manufacturing process, with its consequent loss of jobs.

So, according to many economists, the future employment needs of industry are at the extreme ends of the intellectual and social scale. To maintain competitiveness there is a strong need for creative, versatile and highly skilled designers. There will always be a range of more physical, mundane tasks where human musculature is better adapted (and more cost-effective) than a robotic solution. But the job-displacing effects of ICT do not end in industry. We have already seen a large shift in employment from production to the so-called 'service industries'. We have also seen the loss of many 'processing' jobs in commercial firms such as banks and other financial institutions.

These trends mean that we will continue to see large changes in the world of employment opportunities for our students in the years to come. They also mean that society needs to be re-evaluating the purpose of education. But as teachers we cannot afford to be complacent. If teaching is seen just to be about spreading knowledge, filling empty vessels, training people to do new tricks, etc., then surely ICT can do those jobs more effectively and economically? New multinational conglomerates have been formed from mergers between conventional publishers (including those of educational books) and so-called 'media moguls' (with interests in broadcasting and/or newspapers), often also involving collaboration with computer (software, hardware and internet) companies. The thesis is that we now have the ICT means to provide mass-access to information, and that the current commercial task is to ensure that sufficient 'content' for each school subject becomes available. So, if we are willing to take a 'Gradgrind' view of education, at least in the so-called 'academic' subjects, then we are indeed on the road to redundancy. (Thomas Gradgrind was the mill-owner in Charles Dickens' *Hard Times* who, according to *Collins' Dictionary* 'regulated all human things by rule and compass and the mechanical application of statistics, allowing nothing for sentiment, emotion and individuality'. In an oft-quoted example he teaches his own children that 'a cow is a quadruped ruminant' – as if we would ever do anything like that in mathematics!)

So far, then, we have pointed, perhaps rather gloomily, to the past, and potential future, impact of ICT on employment. More optimistically, we can expect advances in ICT to mean continual increases in processing speed, transfer rates, storage capacity, picture definition, etc. at decreasing prices. Current developments in technologies, such as for display and interconnections, mean that schools should not have to adapt to the physical constraints imposed by current technology such as the shape of desk-top computers, monitors and other external displays, or the position of power-points, network cabling, etc. We should be able to expect to select and position the ICT tool to suit both the educational context and the physical characteristics of its built environment. Of course this applies equally well outside the school – in homes, libraries, museums, cafés, etc. The current government's Building Schools for the Future programme places great emphasis on flexibility in the use of both spaces and resources – as well as the flexible deployment of ICT, which accounts for 10 per cent of the budget. Improved communication also enables students to share experiences with their contemporaries in other parts of the country, or abroad. In particular it can support 'virtual classrooms', via video-conferencing, where otherwise communities would be too far apart to make educational provision viable.

7.2 IMPLICATIONS FOR EDUCATION AND THE CURRICULUM

In thinking about future directions in education we need to be prepared to challenge some of our long-held conventions. In doing so we are not subscribing to any particular point of view, but we feel that it would be unhelpful, maybe catastrophic, to adopt an ostrich-like position towards the potential for change. By considering carefully such issues, which you may at first find rather depressing, we hope that you will be in a stronger position to justify the retention and enhancement of those aspects you feel are the most important and fundamental to the process of education.

There is nothing really magic about choosing a number like 30 for a reasonable class size. This is about the number of young people who can fill a standard-size classroom without excessive discomfort. In some educational circumstances this can be far too many, in others we see duplication with parallel classes being taught in the same way. We already accept divergence in several situations, for example with respect to specially equipped rooms for science or technology. In mathematics many schools choose to set, or band, students by ability, and usually prefer to accept larger group sizes for the upper bands to allow more personal attention in the lower ones. In nineteenth-century England a typical Victorian elementary school might have, say, a hundred students under the direction of a single schoolmaster or mistress. He or she was the manager of the learning, and was supported by a group of helpers who might be senior students ('prefects' or 'monitors') or apprentice-teachers. This is a model still to be found in many universities, where the professor gives a lecture to a large class, who then attend workshops (or 'labs') in smaller groups under the supervision of a graduate student. The main difference is that the university students are learning voluntarily (at least in theory), so that the monitor does not need to resort to physical violence to keep them on task!

So here are a few interesting questions for the future of schools and teachers. How can we organize schools in particular (and learning, more generally) in flexible ways which use ICT to best advantage in catering for the needs of our students? Of course, wrapped up in that is the question: 'How do we need to (re-)define the needs of our students, in terms of the knowledge, skills, understanding, social interactions, moral education, etc., for them to take a full part in society?' Of course this implies that teachers will be able to take full advantage of the available ICT, and that has implications for their (i.e. your) continuing professional development. But another, very live, issue is one that affects other professions, such as medicine, too. Do (or should) all teachers need to be equal, or would it be more effective to have some 'super-teachers' who give inspirational lead 'lectures', and are the real 'subject experts', who are supported by groups of, perhaps less well-qualified (and paid) support teachers? Given the current problems in many countries of recruiting sufficient new mathematics teachers with good subject qualifications it would not be surprising if politicians were seeking to apply ICT in this way to alleviate such problems. We need to be able to distinguish between policies based on sound educational arguments and those addressing issues pragmatically, such as supply and demand of teachers, financial restraints on the global salary bill, etc. Is subject expertise all that matters, or is education a qualitatively different process from, e.g., medicine? Do teachers possess and practise important skills other than just subject knowledge? If so, can these be effectively articulated and valued (or have they already been sufficiently defined), or is the throwing away of baby-rich bathwater inevitable?

When considering such questions in the context of a particular subject on the (current) school curriculum we again need to be prepared to reassess the arguments for the inclusion of the subject, especially in the case of mathematics where it is a compulsory subject of study for all students. In England the majority of secondary schools have been designated as 'specialist schools', which have been given extra funding to develop subject specialisms and whose aims include strengthening the educational applications of ICT. These are organized through a body formerly called the Technology Colleges Trust (TCT) – now the Specialist Schools and Academies Trust (SSAT). In the report *Engaging Mathematics* for the TCT (Oldknow and Taylor, 1999), we did some research on why employers take on those with mathematical qualifications (particularly graduates), and what skills they were particularly looking for. The clear and consistent finding was that they sought mathematical processing skills (such as making hypotheses, gathering data, testing and validating models, communicating using symbols, diagrams, etc.), rather than any particular content knowledge. Coupled with this, they also sought what they called the 'soft skills' (and what we now call the 'core skills') of problem-solving, working in groups, communicating with others, competence with ICT, etc. While there must be more to mathematics education than just meeting employers' needs we would be very perverse (and suicidal?) if we did not ensure that we can accommodate them as far as possible. This was one major reason for the Treasury-inspired *Inquiry into Mathematics 14–19* undertaken for the government by Professor Adrian Smith and its 2004 report *Making Mathematics Count*.

As an extreme example let us consider the place of calculus. In England and Wales the tradition has been that this is a subject to be taught to students in the 16–19 age range within an examination subject called 'Pure Mathematics'. It involves learning a set of basic techniques in differentiation (e.g. chain rule) and integration (e.g. integration by parts). The techniques are usually practised by working through a set of textbook examples without any context, and then by working at past examination questions. Some formalized 'applications' are usually introduced, such as using differentiation to find the maximum of a function which, for instance, models the volume of a box, or by using integration to find the volume of a container by rotating the area under a curve. Now this takes no account of the historical context of the development of calculus by Leibniz and Newton, who were trying to solve the differential equations resulting from predictive models in physical science. It certainly isn't approached at this stage as a rigorous branch of 'pure mathematics' in the current usage of that term. computer algebra systems (CASs), such as Mathematica, Maple and TI-Nspire™ CAS™, are designed to perform such 'processing tasks' as symbolic differentiation and integration, and are extensively used in industry, commerce and research, where such techniques need to be accurately and quickly applied. So, when designing mathematics curricula for the future, at any level, we must be much more explicit about the rationale for inclusion of aspects of content in terms of the needs its study will fulfil.

We also need to be more prepared to examine the rationale for teaching subjects in isolation. This varies between countries, but the UK position in schools is beginning to move forwards from an era of greater curricular isolation. Students currently go to lessons in a range of subjects, many of which have features in common, such as their use of data. In a time of concentration on 'joined-up' politics it would seem only natural to expect a more 'joined-up' approach to education. The current revision of the English 11–19 curriculum is stimulating such an approach, as is the Science, Technology, Engineering and Mathematics (STEM) agenda following the Roberts report, *SET for Success*, for HM Treasury. The use of ICT can be a catalyst in this process. For some time we have been working with a group of teachers in mathematics, science, geography, design technology and physical education looking into the use of ICT, particularly hand-held devices such as graphing calculators, data-loggers and OHP displays used with computers, across subjects. More recently this has involved cross-curricular STEM work in schools via the Nuffield KS3 STEM project, and also rich mathematical tasks through the QCA Engaging Mathematics for all Learners project.

7.3 MATHEMATICS AND TECHNOLOGICAL DEVELOPMENT

So we have considered some possible developments in both ICT and education. But what of mathematics itself? There are some now well-established links between mathematics and aspects of computing such as networks, digital logic, coding, etc. Similarly, a variety of mathematics courses have been established, with titles such as 'Discrete Mathematics' or 'Decision Mathematics', specifically to complement studies in information technology or the like. Yet it is often the unexpected applications of the less obviously applicable branches of mathematics which are the most exciting. For example, geometry is a subject which is rapidly disappearing from the curriculum both in schools and in universities in the UK. Clearly computational geometry (the design of efficient algorithms for graphical displays) is very important for a whole range of computer graphics. However, it is in this field that an unlikely application for fractal geometry has emerged. The English-born mathematician Michael Barnsley has pioneered the use of Iterated Function Systems (IFS) as a means of efficiently transmitting high-resolution images for digital television. See the Wikipedia article at `http://en.wikipedia.org/wiki/Iterated_ function_system` for an example of how to generate a fern leaf.

Number theory has seemed to be one of the least applicable aspects of mathematics, but now it underpins the data-encryption algorithms essential for the secure transmission of information of all sorts, from bank transfers to calls on mobile phones. So 'blue sky' research in pure mathematics still has a strong claim for public support, even if there are no immediate prospects of applications. However, it is also clear that the number of users of ICT tools far exceeds the number of researchers needed to develop new tools.

Mathematical modelling is an important approach to the application of mathematics, particularly in the sciences, which receives very little explicit attention at school level but which is fundamental in very many important aspects of our lives. The enormous strides in the speed and power of computing devices now mean that many of the world's problems such as pandemics and extreme weather conditions should be predictable, and hence enable us to take precautionary measures beforehand. The 2020 Science Group is an international group of leading research scientists, and mathematical modellers, which met in 2005 to produce the *Towards 2020 Science* report, encouraging governments to invest more in computationally based research methods (`http://research.microsoft.com/en-us/um/ cambridge/projects/towards2020science/`).

So again we have another example where hard decisions may need to be made about the balance of resources to be devoted to training new researchers as opposed to the more general education required to support the needs of industry and commerce.

It is clear that change is here to stay! It is also clear that mathematics will continue to play a vital part both in the development of ICT and its effective application in the world outside education. What is less clear is the ability of the mathematics education community, at all levels, to articulate just how vital mathematical skills are, and how their nurture and development in new generations of students is a creative and expert task quite distinct from training. If we can achieve this we can truly claim to be integrating ICT into teaching and learning, rather than preparing the ground for our replacement by it!

We very much hope you have enjoyed reading this book, and that it has given you the stimulus both to integrate ICT into your own teaching, and to face the challenges which the future will inevitably bring.

Further reading

Emmott, S. (ed.) (2006) *Towards 2020 Science*. Cambridge: Microsoft Research.

Oldknow, A. and Taylor, R. (2000) *Engaging Mathematics*. London: SSAT.

Oldknow, A. and Taylor, R. (2008) 'Mathematics, science and technology teachers working collaboratively with ICT.' *e-Journal of Mathematics and Technology*, **2** (1).

QCDA (2009) *Engaging Mathematics for all Learners*. London: QCDA.

Roberts, G. (2001) *SET for Success*. London: HM Treasury.

Smith, A. (2004) *Making Mathematics Count*. London: DCSF.

Appendix

Previous editions of this book have been accompanied by a CD containing trial versions of software and a variety of useful files. However, the information on CDs can quickly go out of date and up-to-date trial versions of software can generally now be downloaded from the internet. For this reason this third edition of the book is supported by a section of the Continuum website devoted to it. This means that at regular intervals the authors will be able to update materials.

The materials on the website will include

- useful documents giving information for teachers such as 'The pupil's entitlement to ICT in mathematics' ;
- information on websites with links to these;
- exemplar files in the various types of software described in the book such as Autograph, Cabri, Excel™, Logo™, Geometer's Sketchpad and TiNspire™;
- further information on some of the activities mentioned in the book.

Index